security profession. Every page resonates with real-world wisdom, hard earned experience, and a deep understanding of what it truly means to lead under pressure. He focuses on the reality, focusing on human behavior, stakeholder engagement, community spirit, and cultural understanding, which all speak to my love languages in my own chosen path. As you flick through every page you can feel and see his energy, and personality shine through. This isn't just a book, it's a legacy! I'm proud to know Michael, honored to call him a friend, and even prouder to learn from him through this incredible work."

Lee Oughton, *Security Author, Speaker, and Kindness Crusader, Mexico*

"This book is a refreshing and vital contribution to the evolving landscape of security and risk leadership. Michael Gips masterfully weaves personal experience, practical insights, and stories from the front lines into a compelling guide that bridges the gap between theory and real-world application. His emphasis on whole-of-person leadership, emotional intelligence, and risk-informed decision-making aligns closely with the principles of Presilience and the dynamic demands of our time. It's an essential read for any security professional looking to lead with authenticity, agility, and purpose."

Dr. Gavriel Schneider, *RPP, CPP, CCRO, Award winning Security and Risk Expert and Author of Presilience: How to Navigate Risk, Embrace Opportunity, and Build Resilience, Australia*

"Michael Gips has crafted a thoughtful and engaging book that brings leadership to life through both timeless wisdom and practical insight. Drawing on his extensive experience and the perspectives of leading security and risk professionals worldwide, he offers guidance that is both grounded and inspiring. It challenges the reader to reflect on what kind of leader they aspire to be and the leadership styles that align with their values. One of the book's greatest strengths is that it offers real-world leadership examples, volunteer opportunities, and networking advice you can apply right away to enhance your career journey. Whether you're an experienced executive or just starting your career, you'll find valuable tools and fresh perspectives to help you lead with clarity, confidence, and purpose."

Lisa Oliveri, *CPP, PCI, Senior Security Executive, International NGO, USA*

"*It's Not in the Manual: Real-World Leadership for Security and Risk Professionals* by Michael Gips is an insightful yet fun tour of leadership development. Based on Mike's decades of experience, he provides numerous examples of how readers can develop their own leadership skills. Full of wisdom and wit, the book is a great research-backed examination of leadership principles and frameworks. These are amplified with anecdotes from his own experiences and those of his vast network of friends and colleagues. Yet, Mike keeps it entertaining, sprinkled with humor and pop culture references such as movies, streaming series, advertising campaigns, and more. In sum, Mike provides a great mix of leadership theory, humor, and actionable insights that will help current and aspiring leaders grow their skills. It is a must-read for leaders of any level."

Christopher Stitt, *Supervisory Special Agent (ret.) EMBA, CPP, CEM, Crisis Management Expert, Adjunct Faculty Member, Author, and Speaker, USA*

"This is excellent read from an outstanding business mentor who has devoted years to developing the next generation of leaders. *It's Not in the Manual: Real-World Leadership for Security and Risk Professionals* not only provides practical resources to help advance leadership skills, but it's also entertaining, enriched by Michael Gips's unique storytelling style and powerful insights gained from his decades of experience. His sensible guidance will challenge leaders to reflect on their style while giving them the tools they need to be successful—in the security industry and beyond. Gips has given us an honest guide for real-world leaders with real-world problems. This must-read book accurately reflects the leadership style of its author, a seasoned mentor who's always looking for ways to help others grow and discover new opportunities."

Solveiga Jaskunas, *"The Immigrant Voice in HR," Consultant, Mentor, Speaker, USA/Lithuania*

"Michael Gips is one of the few truly globally renowned experts in the field of holistic risk/security and leadership. He did not follow any of the traditional routes into the industry, which gave him a unique perspective. In his book *It's Not in the Manual: Real-World Leadership for Security and Risk Professionals*, Mike shares his exceptionally broad knowledge in ten chapters to stimulate security risk leaders. Peppered with real life examples and humor, it is an informative and enjoyable read, and I would recommend it to everyone in the security and risk profession."

Godfried Hendriks, *Past President, ASIS International, Netherlands*

It's Not in the Manual

What makes a great leader in security and risk? It's not in the manual.

It's Not in the Manual shatters the illusion that effective leadership in security, risk, and resilience is all about titles, certifications, or rigid frameworks. In a world where cyber threats, insider risk, reputational landmines, and geopolitical chaos overlap, this book delivers something far more valuable: hard-earned wisdom, human vulnerability—and a wry sense of humor.

Written with both erudition and pop culture sensibility, the book blends field-tested insights with sharp wit, drawing from sources as varied as Socrates and Snoopy, Bill Gates and Bill Bryson, quantum physics and playground fistfights. If you're looking for a dry leadership tome, keep looking. This is leadership with levity, candor, and conscience.

Whether you're navigating a crisis, building a converged risk function, mentoring the next generation, or just trying to get your team to stop using "password123," the lessons here are real-world, actionable, and often unexpected.

Drawing on hundreds of conversations with practitioners, thought leaders, and executive coaches—from museum security directors to startup founders to crisis-tested veterans—the book moves fluently between the tactical and the philosophical. You'll find leadership lessons in Texas Hold 'Em and trauma, case law and commercials, streaming series and streaming data.

From managing complexity and polycrisis to fostering wellness and adaptive thinking, It's Not in the Manual goes where conventional guides don't. It doesn't just teach you how to lead. It shows you why it matters, when it falters, and what it takes to lead through uncertainty with integrity.

If you've ever felt unprepared to lead in the face of chaos, contradiction, or moral ambiguity, this book is for you.

Witty yet grounded, insightful yet practical, It's Not in the Manual is the leadership companion every security and risk professional didn't know they needed—until now.

Michael Gips is a highly regarded executive and thought leader in security and risk management, as well as an attorney, writer, journalist, researcher, and business professional. He is Managing Director in the ESRM practice at Kroll, where he consults for clients including multinational corporations, the AmLaw 100, critical infrastructure, higher education, family offices, real estate companies, cultural institutions, and other organizations. For six years prior he served as principal of his own firm, Global Insights in Professional Security.

Previously Mike served as the Chief Global Knowledge and Learning Officer for ASIS International, where he oversaw Learning, Content, Certification, Standards & Guidelines, Production, Enterprise Security Risk Management, and other departments. Mike was also responsible for ASIS's corporate security function. In addition, he developed the CSO Roundtable (now the CSO Center for Leadership and Development), an organization that includes hundreds of the most senior security executives at the biggest corporations around the world. He also served as editor and publisher of Security Management, where he authored hundreds of articles. Mike also was a major contributor to ASIS's standards and guidelines on ESRM and Senior Security Executive.

Mike has received many commendations, including Top 40 Global Thought Leader (Life Safety Alliance, 2024, 2025), top 20 most influential security leaders in the Americas (Security Journal Americas, 2023, 2024), #1 most influential global security thought leader in security (IFSEC, 2022), top twenty most influential global security leaders (International Security Journal, 2022), Outstanding U.S. Security Consultant (OSPAs, 2021), #6 most influential global thought leader in security (IFSEC, 2021), and one of the most influential people in security (Security Magazine, 2019). He has received almost 20 awards for his writing, including some of the writings that have been adapted for this book.

On the volunteer side, Mike is president of the Life Safety Alliance, an officer for the Global Consortium of Law Enforcement Training Executives, and head of the security committee for a large house of worship near Washington, DC.

Among his many research publications are papers, reports, and chapters on ESRM, the size and scope of the security sector, convergence, blockchain, business continuity and Covid, security professionalization, the use of drones by law enforcement, and security as a business enabler.

Mike frequently presents on security, risk, leadership, and legal topics at conferences and webinars, on issues such as disinformation, insider risk, liability, trends in access control, and security skill sets.

Mike's security-related certifications included Certified Protection Professional, Chartered Security Professional, Certified in Security Risk Management Body of Knowledge, Certified Insider Risk Programme Manager, and Registered Presilience Professional.

A graduate of Tufts University (Phi Beta Kappa, summa cum laude) and Harvard Law School, Mike also has obtained security certificates from R.L. Oatman & Associates (2006), the Wharton School (2015), Tel Aviv University International (2016), IE Business School Madrid (2017), Signpost Six (2021), and Risk 2 Resilience (2024).

Security, Audit and Leadership Series

Series Editor: Dan Swanson
Dan Swanson and Associates, Ltd., Winnipeg, Manitoba, Canada

The scope and mandate for internal audit continues to evolve each year, as does the complexity of the business environment and speed of the changing risk landscape in which it must operate. The fundamental goal of this exciting series is to produce leading-edge books on critical subjects facing security and audit executives and practitioners. Key topics addressed include Leadership, Cybersecurity, Security Leadership, Privacy, Strategic Risk Management, Auditing IT, Audit Management and Leadership, and Operational Auditing.

Analysis of Threat Perceptions: NATO and Türkiye's Cyber Terrorism Policies
By Mehmet Emin Erendor

Members, Methods, and Measures: Unlocking the Secrets of IT Leadership
By Thomas E. Armstrong

Philosophy.exe: The Techno-Philosophical Toolkit for Modern Minds
By Matthias Muhlert

Guardians of the Digital Age: Securing the Future
By Elçin Biren

Ironwill 360° Leadership: A Blueprint for Level 5 Unicorn Leadership
By Douglas P. Pflug

Behavioral Insights in Cybersecurity: A Guide to Digital Human Factors
By Dustin S. Sachs

Integrated Assurance: Unified Risk Strategy
By Patrick Hayes

Preparing for Sustainability Audits: A Practical Guide for IT Sector
By Mahsa Fidanboy

Scaling Pyramids: Leadership Lessons from a Mid-Level Bureaucrat
By Christopher Stitt

Program Architecture: Fight the Good Fight
By Gideon T. Rasmussen

Operation Carder Kaos: How One Agent Penetrated the Underground Community
By Richard K. LaTulip

Digitalization and Women's Rights Women and Sustainability: Volume 2
By Muharrem Kılıç and Sezer Bozkus Kahyaoglu

Governance, Risk and Compliance: Demystifying the Risk and Data Privacy Landscape
By Dr Michael Brass

It's Not in the Manual: Real-World Leadership for Security and Risk Professionals
By Michael Gips

It's Not in the Manual
Real-World Leadership for Security and Risk Professionals

Michael Gips

CRC Press
Taylor & Francis Group
Boca Raton London New York

CRC Press is an imprint of the
Taylor & Francis Group, an **informa** business

Designed cover image: Shutterstock ID: 150831014

First edition published 2026
by CRC Press
2385 NW Executive Center Drive, Suite 320, Boca Raton FL 33431

and by CRC Press
4 Park Square, Milton Park, Abingdon, Oxon, OX14 4RN

CRC Press is an imprint of Taylor & Francis Group, LLC

ISBN: 978-1-041-07752-7 (hbk)
ISBN: 978-1-041-08673-4 (pbk)
ISBN: 978-1-003-64648-8 (ebk)

DOI: 10.1201/9781003646488

Typeset in Caslon
by KnowledgeWorks Global Ltd.

Contents

Acknowledgments

This work is the result of life full of observing, exploring, honing, contextualizing, and exercising leadership. I treated it as a real-life discipline rather than an academic one, though I know the literature is replete with worthy studies. Except for the few occasions when I took formal leadership courses—at the ASIS International programs in Wharton and IE Business School, for example—all my leadership reading has been for personal enjoyment and edification.

That said, there is a world of people to acknowledge—family, friends, work colleagues, associates, neighbors, social media connections, and so on—who have contributed to my leadership journey. Many modeled exemplary leadership attributes, some less so. A few I will tacitly acknowledge for showing me what I didn't want to be. But most were shining lights.

More than 35 years in the working world has introduced me to probably tens of thousands of people from all over the world in the security risk world alone, more if you look at risk more generally, such as lawyers, auditors, financial officers, and so on. Thank you. You've influenced me more than you know.

The dozens of professionals interviewed for or mentioned in this book also have my profound appreciation. It is your stories that are the heart of this work.

For everyone who made it into print, dozens of others have been unfairly excluded by timing and circumstance. Your stories are no less worthy.

Special thanks to the people and organizations who have given me permission to adapt work for this book that I originally created for them. At the top of the list is BNP Publishing's Security magazine, which enlisted me as its Leadership & Management columnist in 2020. For this book, I've relied heavily on many of the more than 60 columns I've written since that time. Thanks to the warm and wise editors I've worked with over that period: Diane Ritchey (who personally brought me on), Maggie Shein, Madeline Lauver, and Rachelle Blair-Frasier.

I've pulled from other magazines as well: Security Management, where I worked for years; Security Technology Executive; International Security Journal, and Security Journal Americas. I'm particularly grateful to my former colleagues at ASIS (especially Teresa Anderson, Peter Piazza, Marta Lawrence, Megan Gates, Nello Caramat, Andy Cutler, and Sue Carioti) as well as to Steve Lasky at STE, to Victoria Hanscomb at SJA, James Thorpe at ISJ, Saurabh Bajaj at access control company Swiftlane, and to Nancy Perry at Police1.

Many thanks to the pre-readers who volunteered to critique early drafts of this manuscript: Chris Stitt, Lisa Oliveri, Mike Brzozowski, Dr. Gavriel Schneider, Godfried Hendriks, Lee Oughton, Lisa Gans, and Solveiga Jaskunas. Your observations and suggestions improved this work tremendously. Also much appreciation goes to Brian Harrell, who wrote the engaging foreword.

I also treasure the support of Gabriella Williams at Routledge and Nancy Rebecca at KnowledgeWorks Global, as well as constant encouragement from Dan Swanson, who inveigled me into this enterprise through pure charm and persistence.

My workout and ice hockey buddies have encouraged me along the way, including Steve Giuli, Giuseppe Randazzo, Jason Nehmer, and the rest of the Admirals, Aeros, and Mutineers. Lifelong friends have been profound influences: Erik Kahn, Brice Kirkendall, Pete Silverstein, Steve Venable, Paul Robinson, Ben Witherell. I wouldn't be who I am without them. Nor would I be without my parents, Philip and Barbara Gips, brothers Steve,

Dave/Archie, and James, sister Dana, in-laws, cousins, nephews and nieces, etc.

Lou Mizell, the most interesting and courageous man in the world, has challenged me at every turn: Semper Fi, if I'm allowed to say that as a non-Marine.

My dog Murphy has literally been at my feet for every word I've typed. And, of course, most love and affection go to my daughters, Lauren and Ellie (who helped me create the index), and my wife, Michelle. They were able to take my mind completely off the book when I needed a break. It also helps that they are not 100 percent clear on what I do for a living.

Note About Names, Job Titles, and Employers

This book incorporates interviews and experiences with hundreds of security and risk professionals. I include many, many names and am acutely aware of the potential perception of name dropping. but I've striven not to include a single gratuitous name. People are specifically identified only when it adds important context, credibility, insight, or value for the reader. In many cases, it would dishonor them not to identify them specifically and give them their due.

As for their professional titles and employers, in many cases I have provided their title and employer as of the final edit of this manuscript prior to publication, but it is inevitable that some of this information will change before publication and shortly afterwards. People switch jobs and retire, so employment situations will eventually be out of date. In other cases, I have intentionally identified the professional with a prior title and/or employer when it more fittingly captured the context of their comments and experiences. I've also eliminated company associations in a few cases on request.

Foreword

BY BRIAN HARRELL

From global conflicts and cybersecurity threats to domestic risks and emerging technologies, the challenges facing the security profession are more dynamic than ever. For security professionals, staying ahead in this rapidly changing landscape requires more than just technical knowledge—it demands adaptability, strategic thinking, and a deep understanding of the forces shaping our future. The threat landscape has changed and these threats are becoming more complex, thanks in part to emerging technologies like artificial intelligence. Cyber threats are not just increasing; they're getting smarter and more diverse. We're seeing more advanced ransomware tactics and state-sponsored espionage heavily influenced by geopolitical tensions. Security managers and executives must stay informed on international affairs and understand how policy decisions at home and abroad shape security strategies. Security threats don't exist in a vacuum. Adversarial countries and criminals continue to conduct cyber campaigns targeting the United States, with the People's Republic of China presenting the most active and persistent cyber threat to the United States Government, private sector, and critical infrastructure networks. Political shifts, diplomatic relations, and economic stability all impact the landscape.

The modern Chief Security Officer (CSO), or senior security executive, is business savvy and fully understands the impact that security has with respect to "keeping the lights on," business resilience, reputational risk, and regulatory compliance. Today's security pro must be an educator rather than an enforcer as he or she must be able to re-frame the security conversation away from mere loss avoidance and towards competitive advantage, efficiency, and risk reduction. They must be technically adept, with an intuitive understanding of a company's assets, how attackers might penetrate them, and how to defend against intrusions. And because no company, no matter how invested it is in security, is fully immune from physical and cyber threats, the security pro must also understand how to deter, detect, and mitigate the attacks that do occur.

The esteemed and well-respected author of this book, Michael Gips, understands this backdrop well. In this erudite but accessible book, Mike helps both experienced and novice leaders navigate this complex landscape with authority, humility, and grace. The useful lessons come a mile a minute, but Mike tries to not take himself too seriously. He instead articulates the "bigger picture" with ample entertaining yet instructive vignettes and personal experiences. After all, this career field can drive you mad if you let it.

Perspective matters, and while we can't respond to every threat as quickly and as efficiently as we would like, we do need to "rack and stack" based on risk. Risk to our "crown jewels," risk to our people, and risk to our data. Mike discusses how to focus the conversation on what matters most and how to effectively talk to your board, external stakeholders, or even your employees.

Sometimes, CSO actually means "Chief Storytelling Officer," and this book tells some good ones. While tactical "boots on the ground" knowledge is necessary, the modern security manager must think macro, not micro. He or she must balance security needs with the organization's strategic business plan, identify risk factors, and determine solutions to both. The security professional acts as the organization's representative with respect to inquiries from customers, partners, and the general public regarding the organization's security strategy.

Recent ransomware, denial of service, phishing, and other malware attacks are calling for board members to ask the difficult questions about their company's risk. What is the company's risk appetite? Have threat and vulnerability assessments been conducted to evaluate company risk? Does the organization have the expertise and resources needed to reduce risk? Have mitigations (controls) and countermeasures been adequately deployed? What risk has the organization mitigated, removed, transferred, or accepted? Every business has risk. Whether you are generating electricity for the power grid or operating a neighborhood lemonade stand, calculating and mitigating risk is a key factor to an organization's success and survival.

As strategic leaders of the company, if you can promote a culture of security, it becomes an integral part of the way the organization functions. This is one of the best and most important protections that any organization can have. Security executives should push employees to understand that when they engage the board on topics of customer data, infrastructure upgrades and business impacts, security should be discussed in detail.

This is the new normal as we embrace "secure by design." After all, benign neglect, indifference, or ignorance will not end well and could result in irreparable reputation and product damage.

This sort of wisdom is baked into this book in every chapter.

The biggest mistake that security pros make is when they become complacent and think they've solved all the problems they are facing. In this business, you never really solve the risk problem—you manage it. Great security managers are always scanning the horizon: They use the "A" word constantly, and that word is "anticipate." What is the enemy avenue of approach, adversary tactics, or new threat that we're not prepared for? So, the modern CSO must be a prognosticator, crisis manager, and adept at handling events that spills onto the front pages of the newspaper while solving the problem, projecting calm, and keeping stakeholders informed. Easy task, right? Easier once you've read this book.

Brian Harrell served as the 6th Assistant Secretary for Infrastructure Protection at the U.S. Department of Homeland Security under President Donald J. Trump (45) and has led large organizations as a Chief Security Officer.

Preface

I have been managing risk my whole life without even thinking about it. So have you. So has everybody. It's the risk that attaches to every decision we make, from what route to drive to work to where we decide to dine.

While this book does dip into some issues of personal risk management, its primary purpose is to document what I've learned about risk leadership during my 30+-year professional journey. Along the way, I've figuratively worn many risk "hats: barrister's wig (as an attorney), press hat (as a journalist and as a media trainer), fedora (as a corporate executive), beret (as a security professional), yarmulke (as the head of security at a Jewish institution), and mortarboard (as an academic).

Though I address each of these experiences and disciplines in this book, I focus on security risk leadership. And since I've been publishing articles on that topic since 1993, I've been able to draw on some of those writings for this book. I use these articles as jumping-off points for updated analysis and elaboration and have added substantial amounts of content published for the first time.

My goal is to stimulate your thinking and practice of security risk leadership and to make this book a brisk and enjoyable read. I do, however, bring the breadth of my experience to these pages, so you will read examples derived from family life, law, journalism, sports, media training, association leadership, and more, wherever the stories are pertinent, interesting, and helpful.

The book starts with a brief overview of risk, leadership, and their nexus, including how to identify your leadership qualities. I urge you to do the work of figuring out how to tap into those qualities, and I give you some tools for doing so. Chapter 2 plunges further into risk and leadership, with a bit of history, trends, risk psychology, cognitive biases, and the whole of person model. The chapter sets the stage for the process for becoming a security risk leader. Chapter 3 explores popular types of leadership with ample examples and analysis, to include servant leadership, crisis leadership, visionary leadership, and a couple of my own. This chapter demonstrates how you can harness elements of each.

Chapters 4–6 comprise the heart of the book, enumerating the qualities of great leaders, among them humility, cultural sensitivity, communication, inspiration, mentoring, curiosity, empathy, ethics, and many more. To me, this cluster of chapters is the meat and potatoes of leadership. You probably won't shine in every attribute, but as long as you have a variety on your plate you will have the tools to succeed.

Thought leadership takes the stage in Chapter 7, including the value of thought leadership and how to become a thought leader. Where do you start? How do you gain credibility? Is thought leadership even worth it?

Chapter 8 focuses on leading during transitions, adversity, or in situations often excluded from leadership work, including when joining a new employer, when dealing with traumatized people, when you don't have a team, or when looking for a new job. This is where I draw some of the most interesting examples and delve into the least-explored aspects of leadership.

As any leader knows, landmines proliferate just under the surface of the path to effective leadership. These include excessive ego, complacency, and others, which are addressed in Chapter 9. Chapter 9 shows you how avoid, escape, and recover from these setbacks.

Finally, Chapter 10 projects security risk leadership for tomorrow by exploring future-forward topics. It is meant to challenge your view of risk leadership as you progress in your career.

To guide your journey and to recognize my passion for ice hockey, I have inserted "breakaways" between chapters that look at security risk leadership through a pop culture lens. What do movies, streaming series, TV ads, and comics have to do with such a serious mission? Find out along the way. That's in addition to leadership lessons from such sources as NFL football, beer league hockey, and other fields not typically associated with security risk leadership.

As a nod to my legal training, I have distributed "sidebars" through the text that serve as way stations. Sidebars (which, in legal parlance, are attorney-judge discussions out of earshot of the jury) are a bit too tangential or esoteric to be part of the main text, but too germane, instructive, or amusing (to me, anyway) to be relegated to a footnote. Some of the sidebars contain brief interviews, satirical asides, recommendations, explanations, or capsule summaries. Since you are privy to the sidebars, consider yourself the judge, not the jury.

Finally, to heighten the shenanigans even more, I close out every chapter with a quote that captures the essence of the preceding material, which I call "From the Lips of Gips."

Note to the Reader

The idea for this book came about naturally. For several years, I have served as the "Leadership & Management" columnist for *Security* magazine. Over time, I realized that many of the themes I explored in those columns (such as risk, humility, communication, and humor) deserved more breathing room. So I decided to expand them into a longer and more comprehensive work.

This book draws extensively from those original columns, which I have updated, expanded, contextualized, and otherwise integrated here. The leadership of *Security* magazine has generously granted permission for me to adapt those pieces. *Security*-drawn and -inspired content appears in the following sections:

Volunteerism as a Leadership Accelerator
A Brief History of Risk and an Opportunity for Leadership
Security Risk Leadership Lessons from Movies
History of Leadership Thought
Values-Based Leadership
Crisis Leadership
Communication
Humor in Leadership? Funny You Should Ask
Leading Without Leading: A Modestly Disruptive Proposal
Developing Others
Recognizing Others
Knowing Your Limits

Inspiration: Speeches, Messaging, and Momentum
Kindness/Empathy
Learning from Failure
Rules, Lists, and Leadership Lore: Use with Caution
Risk Leadership Lessons in Television Ads
Security and Leadership Podcasts Worth Your Time
The Publishing Landscape
Mastering Social Media
How Relevant Is Thought Leadership, Anyway?
Leadership for Nonleaders
Leading through Career Transitions
Taking the Helm: Leadership with a New Employer
Job Hunting and Ghosts: Leadership in the Search Process
Startups: Leading at the Edge of Innovation
Orchestrating Turnarounds
Working Alone: Leading Without a Team
Stepping Down from Leadership
Leadership for Less-than-Stellar Practitioners: Can Charisma Beat Competence?
The Ego Trap
Monitoring Trends and Developments
This Leadership Theory, Too, Shall Pass

Likewise, I've adapted a few articles originally published elsewhere. Each outlet has kindly granted permission for me to reuse and rework that content:

Police1:
Wellness and the Will to Lead
Security Journal Americas:
Leverage Risk Psychology for Organizational Leadership
Recognizing Our Biases
Security Management:
Practical Lessons from Gettysburg
Humility
Security Technology Executive:
Influence
Swiftlane:
Kindling the Security Spark in Students

This content has been reimagined with fresh insight, integrated into broader themes, and incorporated into newly developed chapters.

Introduction

"All I know is that I know nothing." That's Plato, quoting Socrates. Don't panic. Although Plato comes up later in this book, you don't need to be steeped in philosophy to read further. The quote suggests that relative to the universe of things we can possibly know, our actual knowledge is infinitesimal. I certainly feel that way.

Although I have been a risk professional, in varying disciplines, for decades, much of what I understand about leadership, and how I practice it, comes from my experience with other people. I have not originated a new leadership theory. I haven't bootstrapped my way to running a billion-dollar startup. I haven't contributed much to academic leadership literature. I've never taken a ragtag pro sports team to the championship, negotiated a peace treaty, or pioneered any field.

Instead, I've witnessed, gathered, assessed, applied, adjusted, emulated, and evaluated leadership skills, principles, traits, and examples modeled by others. Some of these people would be recognized as notable leaders. Many more are unknown but excel in the field of risk. Some have been outstanding situational leaders. A few have done the right thing at a critical time, while otherwise keeping a low profile. Many wouldn't consider themselves leaders at all: security guards, HR staff, secretaries, paralegals, control-room operators, coders, auditors, investigators, installers, researchers, risk analysts, business continuity planners, compliance specialists, journalists, trainers, industrial hygienists, salespeople, and crisis consultants. You get the idea.

Let me revise the above quote attributed to Socrates. I know a second thing: There's no person from whom I can't learn something. Everyone knows something I don't, has insights I lack, has experienced things I haven't, has influenced other people or initiatives in ways that I couldn't, and has added value to the world in a unique way.

That's why this book is less about what I think than it is the revelations and practices I've witnessed, adopted, tried out, or just admired. Over these pages you will live the stories of and learn from the wisdom of a diverse range of professionals from throughout the wide

DOI: 10.1201/9781003646488-1

world of security and risk. Their stories, of course, are filtered through my admittedly somewhat quirky lens.

My inspirations, and your guides, range from high school students to those reflecting on long careers. They inhabit the worlds of IT, IP, and IDs. They are solo practitioners or work for multibillion-dollar enterprises. Collectively, they help organizations thrive in uncertainty and they take care of people.

In every case, leadership wasn't forged in professional environments alone. Every example of leadership in this book, every bit of guidance, derives from a holistic approach to leadership, what is often called the whole-of-person model.

We don't cordon off aspects of our lives like they do in the streaming series *Severance.* In that show, a company implants a chip in the brains of its workers that "severs" their work and home identities. So-called "innies" (office personas) and "outies" (home-life personas) have separate memories, experiences, relationships and, to some extent, personalities.

The titular leader of the innies is only the façade of a boss, lacking experience, depth, awareness, and nuance. His outside world doppelganger is no better. By contrast, today's most well-rounded leaders blend their various lives. Overworking employees or discouraging personal growth outside the workplace—or, as in *Severance*, eliminating nonoffice life entirely—can lead to burnout, dissatisfaction, and diminished performance. The series is a tocsin of the dangers of personal segmentation.

We don't sequester our leadership experiences into separate buckets of volunteering, academics, family, pastimes, and work/profession. At the very least, they bleed into one another. When we are most effective, we freely transfer and apply skills, traits, strategies, tactics, and experiences among these spheres. Raising a family can contribute to the leadership required to lead a task force in the office. Volunteering as a parent chaperoning a class trip can help you manage personalities in your C-suite. Running a book club can boost your ability to be a lead a corporate task force.

Whole-of-person leadership has other benefits as well. It not only prioritizes professional development and hard work, but it also promotes self-care, a salubrious family and social life, and mental and physical well-being. Work and personal growth are complementary.

Staff who feel supported become more loyal, productive, creative, and resilient.

When I was growing up, one of five children, my mother ran the house. She seemed to make every major decision, be it about home repairs, vacations, education, whatever (though my father may have had input on buying cars). Dad played with us children and was a good father, but he was passive, letting my mother make most of the decisions.

In other words, he was a typical suburban father in the 1970s, who commuted to work and missed most of the chaos at home during the week.

My father died several years ago (and my mother passed shortly before publication of this book), and I hesitate to say this, but he came across as follower, not a leader. Don't get me wrong; he wasn't a milquetoast by any means. He didn't back down from challenges. He had a fiery temper when pushed too far.

One day as a teenager I visited my father's Manhattan office to see what he did as a graphic designer and a partner at his small firm. He transmogrified as he crossed the doorstep. From a quiet observer he sprang into action. He commandeered every office, looking over the work of designers and suggesting modifications or encouraging them to consider different concepts. Staff lined up for his opinion. Everybody sought his approval. He was no martinet; he was superb at what he did, graphic design, and had strong opinions, but he was fair. He was passionate about art and design, the spark that turned him into a leader. His partner dealt with business operations.

My father's home/work dichotomy exemplifies the often-fluid nature of leadership, its ebb and flow, surging when we are passionate and engaged, receding either when we are uninterested or willing to defer to another authority, as my father did with my mother at home.

Leadership can spark in any part of our lives, including work, school, recreation, volunteering, and family. You can leverage leadership skills and experience in one area to improve another. You may not think you are a leader. Maybe you are a cybersecurity engineer, mid-level intelligence analyst, security supervisor, or store-level loss prevention manager. You may manage tasks or projects, but not people. But no doubt you lead elsewhere in life. Your church turns to you to run the clothing drive. You're the captain of your company softball team. You are the young professional liaison for the local chapter of your professional association.

This book is not a work of scholarship or textbook. While it references research and leadership authorities, it makes no claims to academic rigor. I encourage you to review the works I cite or acknowledge, but I'm not going to bury you in models and frameworks, though I do mention a few germane examples.

My goal isn't to bore you with theory or cant, but to engage you with storytelling and insight. As such, this book compiles and crystallizes insights from a 35-year career as a professional working with risk, primarily as a security professional, but also as an attorney, VP of a business unit, and journalist. By featuring the stories of dozens of professionals in security and risk management, this book will help you discover your own skills, identify leadership situations you may encounter, and understand how fellow professionals lead.

1

Understanding the Risk-Leadership Nexus

Chapter Objectives

- Understand the concept of whole-of-person leadership and how personal and professional roles reinforce each other.
- Identify your individual leadership traits and how to leverage them for risk leadership using personality and strengths assessments.
- Explore environments—professional, personal, and volunteer—that cultivate and reward risk leadership traits.

Your Unique Leadership Qualities

Do a self-assessment of your leadership and personality. Plenty of books and guides are available to assist you. It's a good practice to ask colleagues and friends to identify your leadership traits.

Formal assessments of leadership traits and styles populate the Internet. Five of the best-known tools are DISC, the Myers-Briggs Type Indicator (MBTI), Gallup's StrengthsFinder, the Saville Assessment, and 360 Degree Feedback. I've only used MBTI and Gallup, and the former was three decades ago, so my judgment of that assessment is outdated.

I took the Gallup assessment seven years ago, and I still derive value from it. A significant element of the value of any of these tools is your ability to understand, contextualize, and implement the findings. An executive coach can help, especially if your employer is willing to provide one. My executive coach, Jeff Snyder, facilitated aspects of my self-discovery by squiring me through the assessment and helping me to apply the findings.

Jeff did so as he was facing a terminal diagnosis of ALS. He was so committed to his clients and "unlocking their excellence" that he

DOI: 10.1201/9781003646488-2

continued coaching, in a wheelchair with his head steadied in a cradle, until a few days before he died. His wife would sit next to him, holding a water bottle with a straw to his lips so his mouth wouldn't run dry. It was an almost unimaginable commitment to his clients.

The version of the Gallup test I took, CliftonStrengths 34, ranked 34 of my attributes from strongest to weakest. These 34 traits are divided into one of four different themes: executing (getting things done), influencing, building relationships, and thinking strategically. Strategic thinking emerged as my dominant theme.

So how did my 34 fall? My top five were Input (consuming information), Ideation (conceiving ideas), Achiever (accomplishing goals), Learner (storing and processing information), and Intellection (thinking and exercising the brain). None of them involved relationship building, perhaps the most vital theme of leadership.

But Jeff pointed out that Positivity came in at number 7, and he encouraged me to lead with that characteristic as often as I could. I demurred, fearing I would seem like a Pollyanna, but he assured me that was unlikely to happen given my personality and my perception among friends, family, colleagues, and the professional community.

He was right. Critical analysis and data ingestion alone don't make a good leader. They are useful building blocks, but they lack the human element. I realized that I used Positivity in other aspects of my life—encouraging teammates as the captain of a recreational ice hockey team, for example. To me, Positivity isn't a foolish or naïve optimism. In fact, other traits in my top ten include responsibility, maximizer, and self-assurance. Leveraging these traits, I routinely demonstrate that whatever team I'm leading can accomplish things with work and a good attitude, and that I will lead by example.

By the way, among my weakest attributes are Woo (getting strangers to like you), Harmony (always seeking areas of agreement), and Restorative (adept at problem solving). This doesn't necessarily mean that I am bad at these things, just that they aren't my strongest attributes, and I'd be more effective leading with traits that come more naturally. (Incidentally, Jeff encouraged my wife Michelle to take the Gallup assessment, and Woo topped her list. She is a great salesperson.)

I am in no way associated with Gallup or CliftonStrengths, nor do I claim to speak on their behalf. The above analysis represents my understanding of and experience with the tool. If you are interested in learning about the assessment, I encourage you to check out the website. Look at other assessment tools as well, such as the ones listed previously, to determine if one suits you better, or if any suit you at all.

Here's an example of how to draw upon your natural strengths and avoid others you are less adept with. I was contracted to perform an in-depth SWOT analysis for a large security company that dominated its market. It was exploring opportunities to offer new products and services, and it wanted to know what the market "was thinking." The client initially hesitated when I suggested interviewing their current customers. I wanted to persuade them that the best gauge for determining whether they could credibly enter that market was by talking to current clients. After all, they know how you operate, have an existing relationship with you, and would simply require an upsell, not a new sale. I sensed the company felt that current customers associated them with their traditional products and services, which fell in the guns, guards, and gates school. Could long-term clients switch their perception of them from staid to innovative?

It appeared that the company didn't want to disturb what had been working for years. Why would you provoke the client by soliciting candid feedback on the company? It might trigger a reevaluation of the company, putting the annually auto-renewing contract in jeopardy. That's a very reactive and risk-averse mindset, of course.

Facing resistance, I intentionally led my discussions with the firm with Positivity. My Woo was woeful, comparatively, so I wouldn't be able to charm them. My premiere strengths, mostly involving strategic thinking, might not connect with company executives on a personal level.

I painted a promising picture of strengthened relationships with clients, new product and service opportunities, an enhanced brand image, and many potential new customers. But my portrait couldn't be Panglossian. Extending this artistic metaphor, I needed a detailed sketch, maybe an underpainting, to support the portrait I was developing. In this case, the sketch was based on my other top attributes: Input (affinity for consuming and processing massive amounts of information), Ideation (fascination with concepts and connecting disparate phenomena), Learner (keen interest in improving understanding), and Intellection (producing well thought out ideas). My Achiever trait, at number 3, would ensure I produced a compelling report.

The company signed off, but because they were so risk averse, I hedged my bet on Positivity by assuring them that I would talk to only a few of their clients. The results were fascinating—and invaluable. Clients offered ideas for products and services that the company hadn't conceived of. They suggested ways to improve current offerings, at little or no cost. They essentially filled in the SWOT analysis with considered insights.

But mostly, they were just happy I called.

Clients confided that they heard from the company only when their contract was up for renewal. The company performed well, so clients almost always reupped. But they were missing a relationship, and my conversations opened the door to a connection.

And talking about potential for a stronger connection and an increase in products and services, I led those talks with Positivity, certainly not Woo, especially since I was a hired consultant, not a sales or marketing person. Two customers told me that this was the most positive and energized they felt about the company in years. They told me that this initial outreach should become regular. Just touching base reinvigorated stale relationships.

Mapping Your Leadership Zone

After you have assessed your traits, preferences, passions, experiences, and motivations—perhaps using a diagnostic tool—how do you select environments in which you can lead or grow to lead? Or does the opportunity choose you? While you should be intentional about your goals and trajectory, sometimes the mission chooses the missionary, so to speak. One of the most trodden paths to and within leadership is via volunteering.

Part of being a risk leader is creating an environment that encourages leadership. But how do developing risk leaders identify those environments when they have limited job opportunities? Getting into the security industry is easy; opportunities become scarcer as you ascend the ladder, especially since many professionals change jobs every few years to move up. It's not unusual for a LinkedIn post advertising a mid-level corporate security manager position to draw several hundred applicants.

Look for key indicators when you are job hunting. Does the organization/department/boss promote continuous learning? Will they pay for courses, certifications, and supporting materials? Do they offer formal leadership training? Mentorship programs? Do their vision and mission statements include development or growth?

On platforms such as Glassdoor, current and ex-employees offer blunt commentary on their organization, department, and leaders. They frequently discuss the atmosphere for professional development, feedback, and leadership growth.

These reviews may not always be accurate. Some come from spite. In other cases, after a negative review is posted, a spate of positive reviews appears, perhaps the result of management calling out the troops to counter the damaging post.

You're likely to get more honest reviews by searching on LinkedIn for former employees of the company, department, or leader where you are considering working. Current employees may be suspicious or guarded. And while ex-staff may be bitter or jaded toward their former role, they still included the position and company on their LinkedIn profile, meaning they are not trying to scrub them from their history. If you contact them, be candid and appreciative, but remember that everyone has their own perspective, and there is a unique backstory or set of circumstances that colored their experiences.

LinkedIn is also a good place to track career progression. Jonathan Perillo is a friend and professional colleague who is a senior corporate security manager at a major insurance company. He also runs a safety training startup. Simply by looking at LinkedIn, I can track leadership. I can see that he started his career as a security officer (foundational security experience), joined the Marine Corps and became an aircraft mechanic (military training), left the military and became a guard supervisor (hands-on management), started a bail bond agency (entrepreneurship), and led security for a Class A property (career growth). He then joined Hartford Steam Boiler as a security and life safety supervisor before being promoted to manager (broadening of duties, internal advancement) before taking on his current role. You can almost visualize his development along the way of his fascinating journey with his LinkedIn snapshot, which seems like a solid leadership-growth trajectory. Of course, if you know Jonathan and can ask him yourself. But the timeline is a quick, effective snapshot.

Paul Moxness might just have the ultimate leadership progression at a single employer. He started as a security officer at the SAS

Scandinavia hotel, became a special projects coordinator for Radisson SAS Hotels and Resorts, rose to corporate security advisor, got promoted to director of corporate security, and ultimately became VP of Corporate Safety and Security at the Radisson Hotel Group.

Volunteerism as a Leadership Accelerator

I often hear from security professionals who want to flex into volunteer leadership opportunities but don't know where to start. What roles align with their experience and skills? How much day-to-day responsibility is required? How do you discover these positions? How heavy is the workload?

Having served in many such roles, I present this summary of volunteer leadership roles that answers those questions. Most of these are unpaid, though some may come with honoraria and/or reimbursement for travel and other expenses. Before engaging in any of these opportunities, especially ones in which you represent an organization, get written clarification of duties and responsibilities, determine your exposure to liability, and ascertain whether insurance is needed and available.

The list is organized by experience level/skill set required, from least to most. I also rank factors such as lift/workload and activity type (operational, tactical, and/or strategic).

Mentor

Example: Formal and informal mentorship programs dot the security and risk universe, with the more rigorous ones establishing expectations and documenting activities and achievements. They also may be segmented by role, experience, gender, objective (for example, to help someone prepare for a certification exam), or other factor. Many experienced professionals find equal reward as mentors or protégés.

Experience Level: Any.

Activity Type: Strategic and tactical.

Lift: Medium.

Source for Article, Report, or Survey

Example: Authors need experts to share their experiences, insights, and opinions.

Experience Level: Any.
Activity Type: Operational and tactical.
Lift: Light. To maximize your opportunities, register as an expert commentator on sites such as HARO (Help A Reporter Out) and reach out to relevant trade publications.

Association Ambassador

Example: The Latin American Security Association (ALAS) selects individuals such as Alfredo Yuncoza of Venezuela and Marcos Sousa from Brazil to promote the ALAS brand, stimulate greater participation in association activities that help professionals develop and grow, and attract new members.
Experience Level: Depending on the association, entry-level to senior.
Activity Type: Strategic, tactical, and operational.
Lift: Light to medium, heavy if you are called upon to host or support a conference.

Internal Organizational Team Member/Leader

Example: Many organizations assemble groups that cross departments, such as risk committees or wellness councils.
Experience Level: Any.
Activity Type: Strategic, tactical, and operational.
Lift: Varies by organization.

Security Advisor

Example: Many houses of worship, community groups, clubs, etc. with limited budgets need security counsel or full-fledged security committees.
Experience Level: Any.
Activity Type: Strategic, tactical, and operational.
Lift: Varies.

Blogger/Poster/Podcaster or Podcast Guest

Example: You can host your own blog, podcast, etc. on your own site, LinkedIn or elsewhere, or contribute to security outlets that solicit outside material, such as *Security* magazine. If that's too much, many risk-related podcasts seek experts with interesting experiences or perspectives. Consider going beyond risk-focused programs as well, especially to risk-adjacent podcasts for which you can offer singular observations.

Experience Level: Any.

Activity Type: Strategic, tactical, and operational.

Lift: Varies by activity and frequency.

Higher Education Ambassador

Example: The California Cybersecurity Institute assigns professionals to assist students who are seeking to enter the cybersecurity field.

Experience Level: Any.

Activity Type: Strategic and tactical.

Lift: Commensurate with activity.

Author/Contributor

Example: The many security publications that serve the security risk industry and profession continually seek new voices, stories, and experiences. Start with a topic you know well and with which you are comfortable. You want to begin at a position of credibility and develop your skills and reputation from there. Fortunately, editors will be able to vet your content, offer guidance, and enhance the end product.

Experience Level: Any, but content should match experience and expertise.

Activity Type: Operational.

Lift: Heavy during research, writing, and editing.

Chapter Leader/Community Leader/Regional Leader

Example: Among ASIS's leadership opportunities are subject-area community chairs, as well as steering committee representatives for Women in Security and Next Generation Professionals. Myriad other security and risk organizations (e.g. RIMS, International NGO Safety and Security Association, Cloud Security Alliance) offer a wide variety of chapter, community, subject-matter, and regional leadership opportunities.

Experience Level: Mid-level.
Activity Type: Strategic, tactical, and operational.
Lift: Medium.

Presenter/Panelist

Example: Hundreds of speaking opportunities are available every year at the likes of the Security 500, ISJ Leaders in Security, ASIS's various conferences (GSX, ASIS Europe, ASIS LatAm), ISC West, IFSEC International, ESX, International Security Expo, the National Sports Safety and Security Conference, as well as dozens of smaller live and virtual events. Many of these require formal submissions that undergo a rigorous review against many competing proposals. (More about breaking into this opportunity in Chapter 7.)

As a mentor, I encourage you to promote new voices by inviting colleagues with less speaking experience to present. For instance, my colleague Christopher Stitt has been working the circuit to build up his speaking repertoire. Gavriel Schneider, an accomplished risk scholar and practitioner, and I invited him to join us in presenting on Maximizing Cultural Intelligence for a Global Workforce at the 2024 GSX conference. He presented lessons from his vast international experience as a Diplomatic Security agent, logging time at posts in Baghdad, Ouagadougou (Burkina Faso), San Salvador (El Salvador), and Panama City. Stitt returned the favor to me by having me join him for a session on creating a high-performing risk management culture for a RIMS Enterprise Risk Management conference.

As a mentee, I encourage you to seek seasoned speakers to copresent with. These experienced professionals often want to give back to their profession, and this is a tangible way to do so. They can also buttress your confidence. My colleague Hari Pratap Shekhawat reached out to me in late 2021 looking to jumpstart his security speaking career. I had recently been asked to speak to the Greater Atlanta Chapter of ASIS, so I paired with Hari to virtually present to the chapter on the topic of overlooked insider threats. He has since amassed an impressive array of speaking engagements.

For newer speakers, a good steppingstone—gigs that are far easier to obtain—is presenting at the chapter level for large organizations, for smaller groups, or for nonsecurity organizations seeking an expert speaker. Seek out guest speaking spots at colleges and universities. R.C. Miles, who has had a rich career as a security executive, started out working with security canines, and his first presentations focused on that topic as a guest speaker in a criminal justice course at Texas State University.

For Lisa Oliveri, who has served as head of security for multiple international nongovernmental organizations (NGOs), speaking opportunities developed naturally as she built her reputation as a source of expert resources for the NGO community. She is a vocal advocate for the varied benefits of volunteering and, early in her speaking career, gained recognition for presenting a practical resource she co-authored that clarified insurance coverage complexities for security professionals.

Virtual engagements, such as podcasts and webinars, abound. Stitt has presented virtually on cybersecurity awareness for employees and family members of the Chesterfield County, Virginia, government and has become a frequent podcast guest on a variety of topics including leadership, risk, resilience, and emergency and crisis management. He also sharpens his skills through speaking at meetings of smaller local civic organizations such as Rotary Club.

Experience Level: All, but primarily mid- to senior-level professionals.

Activity Type: Tactical.

Lift: Heavy during preparation and presentation.

Association/Interest Group Founder

Example: It sounds forbidding, but security and risk professionals can create their own interest groups, whole associations or organizations, and everything in between. Elisa Mula, for instance, founded Moms in Security, where she says she advocates "for increased legislation supporting community safety, addressing critical issues like child trafficking." Among his many efforts to advance the security and risk fields, Grant Lecky has been developing the

United Associations Initiative, "a global security network comprised of associations and related entities across all security disciplines that have chosen to participate to collaboratively examine the current and potential future states of the security profession." In just a few months, more than 100 groups from around the world had come on board. Finally, Essam Choudhary and Mike Saltijeral formed the Security Innovation Hub to drive advancements in safety and security.

Experience Level: Varies, but primarily mid-level to senior.

Activity Type: Strategic, tactical, and operational.

Lift: Heavy

Committee/Council Leader

Example: The International Association for Healthcare Security and Safety (IAHSS) has committee and council membership opportunities for its Affiliation Council, Data Warehouse Committee, Education Council and so on. OSAC, formerly known as the U.S. State Department's Overseas Security Advisory Council, has regional and subject-matter committees such as Aviation and Energy. Many of these organizations are almost begging to fill these roles. If you step up and perform, you can ascend quickly. A case in point is uber-volunteer Matthew Porcelli, who has become an industry leader largely through volunteer engagement, as well as via mentorship, speaking gigs, and article authorship.

Experience Level: Mid-level to senior.

Activity Type: Strategic, tactical, and operational.

Lift: Medium.

Standards Developer

Example: Several security, risk, and risk-adjacent associations, such as ASIS, Security Industry Association (SIA), RIMS, the Information Systems Audit and Control Association (ISACA), the Building Industry Consulting Service International (BICSI), the National Fire Protection Association (NFPA), the British Standards Institution, and the Institute of Electrical and Electronics Engineers, have bodies that develop standards and guidelines. I've contributed to ASIS standards and guidelines on ESRM, the senior security executive role, and workplace violence.

Experience Level: Mid-level to senior. Standards-making bodies seek out recognized authorities for these roles.

Activity Type: Strategic and operational.

Lift: Light to medium for oversight, heavy for standards creation, drafting, and revision.

Corporate Advisory Board Member

Example: Small security startups often pull together advisory boards for business advice, strategic direction, and corporate oversight. While some pay, others are not compensated but can be sources of business referrals. Larger security companies frequently have advisory boards as well, and they typically compensate members for time, counsel, and travel.

Experience Level: Predominantly senior level.

Activity Type: Strategic.

Lift: Light to medium.

Contest/Awards Judge

Example: Award schemes proliferate. The OSPAs (Outstanding Security Performance Awards) recognize excellence in various categories, including best consultant, in-house security director, team, and new product. The International Security Journal Leaders in Security Awards assembles judges who vote on nominees for commendations such as solution innovation, operational excellence, cybersecurity leadership, and mentorship. *Campus Safety*'s BEST Awards honor the top safety and security solutions at schools and healthcare centers.

Experience: Senior.

Activity Type: Operational.

Lift: Light to medium, with intense flurries of activity.

Editorial Board Member

Example: Some industry publications have editorial boards that help set direction, review specialized content, and provide gravitas.

Experience Level: Senior.

Activity Type: Strategic.

Lift: Light.

Regional or Global Association Board Member

Example: I serve as president of the Life Safety Alliance, and many security foundations and organizations, such as the International Security Management Association (ISMA), ASIS's CSO Center for Leadership and Development, OSAC, and AIPSA (Associazione Italiana Professionisti Security Aziendale), have boards composed of the most senior security executives at major organizations.

Experience: Senior.

Activity Type: Strategic.

Lift: Medium to heavy.

Volunteering for Fun and (Non)Profit

Volunteering is a great way to develop and manifest leadership skills, but volunteering solely for leadership's sake is a hollow endeavor. Make sure that the cause inspires you and the activities you will carry out fulfill you.

Three essential elements of volunteerism are intellectual inquisitiveness, passion, and initiative.

"The number one thing that gets me going is curiosity," says Becky Lane, a former executive at The Monitoring Association and the Acting CEO of the Life Safety Alliance, a volunteer role. "I'm always curious to see and learn how other people operate."

Some of the best volunteer leaders have an insatiable appetite for knowledge and understanding.

Second, if you are passionate enough about something, you will do what you need to make it happen. Say you are avid about securing the metaverse. Post about it on LinkedIn, publish your own blog and discuss the issue with colleagues. Once you do so with authority, organizations and colleagues will seek you out to participate in panels, write an article, work on a paper, or start an organization or working group.

"Volunteering is not for everyone," says Kevin Palacios, who runs an Ecuador-based security/executive protection firm called HELPS Latam. "You need to be the kind of person who believes in giving without expecting anything in return and actually commits to give until it hurts."

Those are strong words, and selflessness is indeed a powerful force. But volunteers don't need to plunge into major commitment right away. In fact, it would be foolish to do so before determining whether you are comfortable in the role, the fit is right, the time obligation is doable, and you are providing value.

For some, volunteer leadership comes naturally. They join a group and become president or chair in a few months. Many others, however, are not as extroverted or driven.

Chances are, however, no one is going to ask you to volunteer if you don't have a history of volunteering or involvement, especially in a large organization where you might not know many members.

That's where the third critical component, initiative, comes into play.

Put yourself out there. Networking at events or online is a good option, but not the only one.

You might join a mentoring program as a protégé. Doing so will create a connection with a colleague who may be a prolific volunteer. That colleague can explain the steps they took toward volunteer leadership, model positive behaviors, make introductions, and recommend specific positions, such as speaker/presenter, committee member, volunteer risk advisor, or other role as listed earlier in this chapter. In many cases, the mentor-mentee relationship is reciprocal: each learns as much as they teach.

The easiest entry point into volunteering, besides being recruited by someone, is to focus on areas of need. Serial volunteer Matthew Porcelli, a security manager at Harvard Protection Services, devotes time on behalf of ASIS, the Institute of Strategic Risk Management, the Life Safety Alliance, and the Security Institute. Porcelli says that his "activity and outreach was and is based in what areas were in need the most of assistance."

"I made a point to integrate myself into the volunteer fabric of those organizations, see where I could help the most, such as with young security and risk professionals, and do the best I can to promote confidence and awareness to the global membership," Porcelli adds.

Once you have shown proficiency and commitment, don't be surprised to move up the ladder quickly. As Lane puts it, "When you volunteer, you are THE volunteer. Slots open up and someone needs to step up and fill them."

While curiosity, passion, initiative, dedication, and hard work suffice for many volunteer leadership roles, some areas require extra skills. For example, writing, hosting a podcast, and presenting at conferences demand at least basic competency in communicating. To excel requires more.

"You first need to be an avid reader and lifelong learner to start producing content and creating," contends Palacios. "Meeting your hero authors is a great starting point if you want to contribute."

Alfredo Yuncoza, who has held senior leadership positions with the International Foundation of Protection Officers, ASIS, CAPSI, and other organizations, agrees. He hosts a streaming radio show out of Caracas called Con Seguridad Radio.

"I initially developed leadership skills at Junior Chamber International," he relates, including communication. He put those skills into practice and matured them in other organizations.

Porcelli says he has presented with some of the industry's most respected professionals, but he had growing pains just like everyone else. And he's still learning. That's the sign of an excellent volunteer leader. To break in as a presenter, he pitched ideas to trusted colleagues and pulled together speakers, oversaw the development of proposals, and coordinated presentations. He has chaired the committee that selected the proposals that would be accepted for GSX, one of the security world's most prestigious events.

It's often said that to develop yourself as a leader, you should surround yourself with people smarter than you are. That applies equally in volunteer roles. But I'd take that a step further.

As I mentioned in the Introduction, it helps to have the attitude that everyone is "smarter" than you in some way; in other words, they have something valuable to add. Especially in a professional environment, colleagues will have different skills, knowledge, capabilities, and strengths that you can benefit from or leverage.

While this book presents a map of volunteer leadership channels, the pathways are infinite. Find your own route. Or make your own.

Chapter Takeaways

- Leadership extends beyond job titles and appears across life domains, from family to recreation to volunteering.
- Tools like Gallup CliftonStrengths can help you uncover hidden leadership traits and unlock authentic influence.
- Volunteer roles and informal leadership opportunities can serve as springboards for more visible leadership roles.

From the Lips of Gips: "Gips puts the 'i' in GPS. That's my way of saying, quit waiting for someone else to navigate."

2

A Deeper Dive into Risk and Leadership

Chapter Objectives

- Gain a historical perspective on risk and learn how risk concepts and models can elevate leadership.
- Examine how psychological biases and heuristics influence risk decision-making and organizational leadership.

A Brief History of Risk and an Opportunity for Leadership

It's amazing to think that the Greeks, prodigious contributors to math, science, logic, law, architecture, rhetoric, philosophy—you name it—didn't know much about risk. Sure, Greek mythology begins with Zeus, Poseidon, and Hades divvying up the universe in a game of dice. But they never employed risk management as a methodology to take the future into their own hands.

As Peter Bernstein wrote in his 1996 bestseller *Against the Gods: The Remarkable Story of Risk*, "Despite the emphasis that the Greeks placed on theory, they had little interest in applying it to any kind of technology that would have changed their views of the manageability of the future." They left the future to the winds.

It took until the Renaissance and Protestant Reformation, argues Bernstein, before people thought of the future as more than a mere matter of luck or predetermination. Today's understanding of risk management emerged from the work on probability theory of three 17th-century Frenchmen: Blaise Pascal, Pierre de Fermat, and the Chevalier de Mere. Then two Brits, John Graunt and Edmund Halley, developed the first actuarial tables, and a legitimate domain of study was born.

Risk management as a corporate discipline emerged after the Second World War, about the same time that corporations began to add a discrete security function. Over the years, risk management has grown

DOI: 10.1201/9781003646488-3

into a strategic business imperative, as witnessed by the prominence of such organizations as the World Economic Forum (which releases an annual risk report) and the broad adoption of enterprise risk management frameworks, such as COSO's enterprise risk management framework and ISO 31000 (the standard for risk management).

Security doesn't always fare as well. Most risk leadership comes from others who identify as risk management professionals: auditors, actuaries, attorneys, compliance managers, financial officers, IT executives, marketing directors, and so on.

But how many have truly mastered risk and can readily apply its principles in their environment?

How many understand the business as well as the senior security executives?

It's time for security professionals to redefine themselves as risk management professionals and take their place among risk leaders.

There's no shortage of material or demand in a VUCA(D) (Volatile, Uncertain, Complex, Ambiguous; some authorities include Digital) world. Widespread disinformation, much of it by nation states. An increasingly polarized society. Razor-thin supply chains. Extreme weather. Changing climate patterns. Water scarcity. Rampant cyberattacks. Geopolitical uncertainty. Institutionalized economic espionage. New and evolving extremist groups. The list of chronic and acute risk elements goes on and on.

But how can security professionals best develop a risk mindset based on probability and rigor rather than intuition and emotion?

Texas Hold 'Em players may be the best models. As professional poker player and corporate consultant Annie Duke writes in "Thinking in Bets: Making Smarter Decisions When You Don't Have All the Facts," "Poker players have to make multiple decisions with significant financial consequences in a compressed time frame and do it in a way that lassoes their reflexive minds to align with their long-term goals." She encourages readers to think of all decisions as bets, with something at stake. She might have security professionals ask: What are the consequences of deploying an officer patrol versus maintaining stationary posts? Is the protection provided by multifactor access control authentication worth the staff inconvenience? What does a trendy blockchain solution offer that a vanilla distributed database doesn't?

Long-held beliefs often dictate how we make decisions (video surveillance deters crime, so let's install an enterprise-wide system, or does it?), and we usually don't vet those beliefs. Duke suggests "taking an inventory of the evidence that informed us," by asking questions such as: Where did I get this information? What is the quality of my sources? Is the information up-to-date? And what are plausible alternatives to my conclusions? Moreover, instead of thinking about the future from the present, effective risk managers look back from a successful future and figure out how they got there, a process known as backcasting.

You've probably committed to learning how your employer's business operates and how you can support it, and you may well be burnishing your communication and emotional intelligence skills. Understanding and dealing with risk is yet another critical component of security leadership, a step that will enshrine you as an organizational risk leader. And while you don't have to learn ancient Greek to get there, a little poker know-how doesn't hurt.

Evolution of Risk Leadership

Although I've been in the risk world for decades, have more than my share of academic degrees, graduate certificates, licenses, certifications, and published research, I have not developed my own research-backed model of risk. Others have, however, and their work has built a good foundation for managing risk (actually, thriving in risk) in a VUCA(D) world.

Once technical and compliance-focused, risk scholarship in the past 20 years or so has become a more holistic and strategic field, emphasizing leadership, resilience, and adaptability. Frameworks such as ISO 31000 remain valuable tools, though they are making room for more dynamic and proactive models that integrate human factors, complex systems thinking, and emerging threats like cybersecurity and geopolitical instability.

Scholars and practitioners (or the combination of the two, often called "pracademics") today emphasize risk leadership, which entails a proactive and strategic approach to risk, rather than a reactive one. Today's leaders must now foster a risk-aware culture, make decisions in uncertainty, and build resilience at all organizational levels.

While risk is still siloed ("Enterprise Risk Management" means something different to CFOs than it does to CSOs), it is incorporating disciplines that previously didn't rise to the board level outside of specific industries or environments. The ubiquity of cyber incidents, as well as the disruption caused by the COVID-19 pandemic, has helped open the door to more comprehensive views of risk. Research has shown that functions such as physical security, cybersecurity, business continuity, and life safety are at least slowly converging and increasingly finding a home in the risk family, sometimes under a chief risk officer.

Several key thinkers are driving this evolving approach to risk and risk leadership. Dr. Gavriel Schneider, a friend and colleague, has developed a model called "Presilience" that fuses proactive resilience and risk leadership. (I once asked him if Presilience was a model, framework, philosophy, approach, or toolkit, and he said, "All of the above.") Presilience is based on solid research into often-ignored factors including the whole-of-person model, decision-making (covering critical thinking, meaning-making, heuristics, cognitive biases, fast and slow thinking, etc.), emotional intelligence, group dynamics, business processes, high-reliability organizations, and "stactical" behavior (strategic and tactical), all of which are underpinned by what Schneider calls "risk intelligence."

Equally influential has been David Rubens, a specialist in risk and crisis leadership, focusing on low-probability, high-impact issues. His leadership of the Institute of Strategic Risk Management highlights the importance of leadership skills in crisis response in a world featuring the quicksilver transformation of risk. Others whose contributions have redefined risk leadership include Ortwin Renn, whose work on risk governance has influenced how organizations navigate large-scale interconnected risk, and Ulrich Beck, who wrote about the "Risk Society."

The modern approach to risk recognizes that checklists and compliance still have an important place, but dynamic organizations focus on strategic thinking, operational and strategic resilience, and cultural alignment.

Leadership-driven risk management favors proactivity over reactivity, agility over hierarchy, interdisciplinary thinking over siloed thinking, and decision-making with incomplete information over paralysis or abeyance. Risk is not an abstract concept or afterthought; it is embedded in corporate strategy and culture.

Current and Future Trends in Risk Leadership

Emerging Trends

- AI and Digital Risk Leadership—As AI and automation reshape industries, risk leaders are now focusing on digital ethics, cybersecurity, and algorithmic risks.
- Psychological Aspects of Risk—Behavioral economics and neuroscience are being integrated into risk theories, examining how individuals and organizations perceive and respond to threats.
- Climate and ESG Risks—Environmental, Social, and Governance (ESG) concerns are now central to risk strategy, with growing emphasis on sustainability and regulatory compliance.

Future Directions

- AI-Driven Risk Intelligence—Leaders are increasingly using AI and big data to enhance predictive risk analysis. However, ethical AI governance has become a new risk area requiring leadership oversight.
- Decentralized Risk Decision-Making—Organizations are shifting from hierarchical risk models to more decentralized approaches, where employees and frontline managers play a greater role in real-time risk management.
- Resilience Engineering—Borrowing from engineering principles, risk leadership now incorporates resilience engineering, ensuring systems can adapt and recover quickly from disruptions.
- Ethical and Sustainable Risk Leadership—With growing ESG pressures, risk leaders must now address social responsibility, climate risks, and long-term sustainability in decision-making.

Leverage Risk Psychology for Organizational Leadership

Good risk managers assess their organization's risk profile and apply appropriate strategies and measures commensurate with their appetite and tolerance.

Very good risk managers adapt their risk management approach to be flexible in a fast-moving world, heightening organizational resilience and ability to recover from a crisis.

Excellent risk managers combine strategic and tactical thinking. They adopt a future focus and an opportunistic mindset that enable their organization to anticipate crises and leverage opportunities that arise from them, leaving them stronger afterwards.

The best risk managers and risk leaders also incorporate an extra element: they understand the psychology of risk. They are students and shapers of the organization's psychological approach to risk, as well as of the risk psychology of leadership, asset managers, rank and file employees, and other stakeholders. They also understand their personal psychological approach to risk—a whole-of-person approach—which they apply to staff throughout the organization.

After all, people are the most important component of effective risk management: knowing individuals' risk appetite and tolerance, understanding their motivations and biases, and comprehending how organizational culture and structure influence decision-making and judgment.

Often unrecognized, misunderstood, or ignored, personal risk psychology is a crucial underpinning to risk management.

What is risk psychology? Understanding and leveraging psychology enables you to understand why people—most importantly, yourself—think, feel, and act the way they do, especially in trying or stressful situations. That's critical for the following reasons:

- It Predicts Reactions: Risk isn't just about things that might go wrong; it's also about how people respond to these situations. Knowing psychology can help you predict what people might do in different scenarios.
- It Leads to Smarter Choices: Biases and mental shortcuts can twist thinking. By understanding these biases, we make better, clearer decisions.
- It Enhances Communication: Whether it's giving instructions or sharing information, knowing how people think and what motivates them can make communication more effective.
- It Teaches Mental Toughness: Psychology teaches us how to be mentally and emotionally tough, so we can recover quickly from difficult situations.
- It Encourages Healthy Practices: Understanding psychology helps in getting people to take action before problems happen, like following safety rules or looking after their mental health.

- It Motivates Staff: Good leaders need to know how to motivate and guide their teams, especially when things get stressful. Psychology can offer tips on how to do this well.
- It Helps Handle Crises: In a crisis, knowing about psychology can help manage stress and fear, both for yourself and others. It's about keeping a cool head and helping others do the same.

Recognizing Our Biases

In a famous ongoing experiment, subjects are asked to watch a short video featuring three people in white t-shirts and three people in black t-shirts passing basketballs. (Warning: if you are unfamiliar with the experiment, mark this page now and shut the book without reading further. Watch the experiment online here: https://www.youtube.com/watch?v=vJG698U2Mvo. I'll wait.)

Subjects are asked to silently count the number of passes made by the people in white shirts. The six players move around, change positions, fake tosses, and otherwise make it difficult to track the pass count.

During the video, a woman dressed in a gorilla suit walks among the players, turns to the camera, thumps her chest, and walks out of the picture. Half of the viewers concentrate so fully on counting the passes that they never see the gorilla. (I missed it too.) When you watch the video without fixating on the passes, it is shocking to realize that you could have possibly missed the great ape.

According to Daniel Kahneman in his 2011 bestseller *Thinking, Fast and Slow*, the study reveals two important things: "We can be blind to the obvious, and we are also blind to our blindness."

That's a particularly bad place to be as a security professional.

Yet we often get stuck in ruts and enslaved by our own biases. We may unconsciously give in to the anchoring effect, whereby, for example, reading about a specific risk probability in a magazine case study embeds that number into the assessment of risk in our own security environment, despite the situation having no correlation with the case study.

Or we may succumb to the availability heuristic, in which while determining the likelihood of an event, we give undue weight to immediate examples that come to mind. For example, a security practitioner for a retailer may instantly recall the heavy media coverage of shoplifters cleaning out stores with impunity and tailor the retailer's security approach accordingly, even if a risk assessment would have dictated otherwise.

The list of cognitive biases is long. I asked industry experts how to avoid these traps, to see the gorillas while counting basketball passes. Adriaan Bosch, a senior security consultant at Buro Happold in London, England, notes that part of the problem is our obsession with metrics. "The nature of our profession is to create structures that can be measured and quantified, and thus there are so many standards and guidelines," Bosch says. "The problem is that the threat is often dynamic, and adversaries are able to develop strategies to counter the well-intended structures and standards." Getting past that mindset is difficult, he continues. "I have often hit a wall where I would suggest a new mitigation method and the response would be: 'Where has this been tested,' or 'To what standard is this aligned?'"

Susana Marquez Pedrouso, a Spain-based security and loss prevention professional, points out that a prominent example of focusing on the wrong things is the COVID-19 pandemic. Relatively few companies had detailed business continuity plans for a virus; fewer still were prepared for years-long disruption.

"That's why I believe the obsession to structure risk and crisis management to the limit is creating a very slow capacity to react in many organizations," she says. "There has to be room to be creative, to innovate, to understand threats and consequences which might never have nailed down."

Pedrouso echoes Bosch's comments about the predominance of metrics. "I'm finding more and more security departments drowning in KPIs and protocols, reducing the capacity to perceive new issues and anticipate from a fresh perspective," she says.

The upshot is that we must continually keep an open mind when thinking about threats, risks, and vulnerabilities. Risk is truly dynamic, and assessments should be frequent, considering such factors as political, economic, and social developments, trends in specific industries, new technology, cultural shifts in the workforce, and so on.

Doing so continuously is a monumental task, perhaps impossible. But doing so regularly and often is realistic.

It's when we work with blinders on that the gorilla of unforeseen threats strolls into our midst. And we all know what an 800-pound gorilla does when it shows up: anything it wants.

The problem is that we are all biased, in the sense that we tend to respond in a certain way due to flaws or distortions in our decision-making without realizing it. Cognitive biases and heuristics are mental shortcuts that our brains use to simplify decision-making in everyday life. While they can be helpful in quickly processing information and making decisions, they can also lead to errors in judgment. Identifying, acknowledging, and overcoming biases is critical in assessing risk.

Cognitive biases are patterns of thinking that can lead to irrational or inaccurate decisions. They're often affected by our experiences, emotions, or social influences. For example, "confirmation bias" leads us to favor information that validates our existing beliefs and ignore information that contradicts them. If you believe an alarm provider is the best, you might only notice positive reviews about it and ignore the negative ones.

Heuristics are simple, efficient rules (either learned or hardwired into our brains) that help us make quick decisions. One common heuristic is the "availability heuristic," where we judge the likelihood of an event based on how easily examples come to mind. If you've recently read about attacks in hospital emergency rooms, you might overestimate the danger of entering a hospital, even though it's statistically very safe.

Another important heuristic in risk management is the affect heuristic. This refers to the process of relying on emotions to make a quick decision. In crisis scenarios, this can have tragic consequences. Consider an active shooter situation in a building that houses a daycare center. An employee in the building gets word of an assailant in the building and, overriding the organization's clear policies and procedures and the employee's own scenario training, ignores their own safety to get to their child.

Mental shortcuts can be both beneficial and problematic. On the plus side, they speed decision-making and help us ignore extraneous information in a complex world. For instance, if you always drive the same route home because you are familiar with the traffic patterns, you're using a heuristic to make a quick and effortless decision for your commute.

On the other hand, biases and heuristics can lead to flawed decisions. For example, taking the same route home every day may make you an easy target for kidnappers or armed robbers.

Understanding cognitive biases and heuristics helps us recognize when our decision-making might be going astray. By being aware of these mental shortcuts, we can make more reasoned and objective decisions.

Cognitive Dissonance

Cognitive dissonance describes the discomfort that results when a person holds two or more contradictory beliefs, values, or ideas simultaneously, or when these beliefs are challenged by new information or new interpretations. This state of tension drives individuals to reduce the dissonance, either by changing their beliefs or rationalizing the contradictions.

In the context of risk intelligence, understanding and managing cognitive dissonance is crucial for several reasons, including improved decision-making, adaptability and learning, enhanced risk evaluation, and innovation and creativity.

Strategies to handle cognitive dissonance effectively include:

1. Recognize and acknowledge cognitive dissonance. Understanding that it's a common psychological response can make it easier to address.
2. Increase your knowledge on the subject causing dissonance. Educating yourself might help reconcile conflicting beliefs or justify a change in attitude.
3. Be flexible and open to change, which can help you adapt based on new information or understanding, reducing the psychological discomfort associated with dissonance.
4. When you notice conflicting beliefs, consider which belief aligns more closely with your values and overall goals, and adjust accordingly.
5. Engage in critical thinking to evaluate the validity and reliability of the information that is contributing to the dissonance. This can help prioritize which beliefs might need reassessment.
6. Seek advice. Discuss your thoughts and feelings with others. Sometimes, external perspectives can provide clarity or alternative ways of thinking about the issue.
7. Make small gradual changes instead of drastic ones. Gradually adjusting your beliefs can reduce the impact of dissonance.

8. Reflect on why you hold your current beliefs and how they align with your actions. Reflection can lead to deeper understanding and easier reconciliation of conflicting thoughts.

By actively managing cognitive dissonance, you enhance your ability to make decisions that are more aligned with your true self and values, which is essential for developing risk intelligence and fostering resilience in various aspects of life.

Whole of Person Model

A recurring theme in this book is that no one can completely cordon off aspects of their lives. Work life, social life, family life, and virtual life all spill over into each other. Consequently, understanding anyone's risk psychology requires understanding of how they perceive risk within these separate spheres and holistically, what is referred to as the Whole of Person Model. This approach ensures a comprehensive, adaptive, and proactive management of risk, enhancing overall performance and resilience in a complex and interconnected environment.

Organizations can take on the collective risk psychology of their personnel or populations. In fact, risk psychology—and, accordingly, risk tolerance and appetite—can differ by team, floor, department, facility, campus, or geography. It's critical to recognize that these risk profiles can be at odds with each other.

For example, software companies are under constant pressure to get new products, versions, and updates into the hands of consumers, making tough decisions along the way on dealing with software vulnerabilities, privacy issues, and other potential risks of moving quickly. Sales and marketing teams tend to be risk-tolerant, while departments such as compliance and legal are risk-averse. But even within the software development team there may well exist substantive differences in risk psychology. While it may not be feasible for a risk manager to calculate a risk psychology profile for every staff member, risk managers from various departments, facilities, geographies, etc. can collectively create risk profiles of key staff and determine the risk profiles of everything from small teams to the entire enterprise.

Simply by becoming aware of the importance of personal perceptions of risk, including the biases and heuristics that undergird those perceptions, constitutes a key step in building an organization that is adaptive, resilient, and empathetic.

SIDEBAR: COGNITIVE BIASES AND HEURISTICS IN SECURITY

Countless cognitive biases and heuristics exist. The following appear frequently, or have significant consequences, in the world of risk management. Others are personal favorites.

Automation Bias. The tendency to defer to information produced by automation or technology when making a decision. The authors frequently see this occurring with generative AI, when individuals rely on false information generated by that technology.

Confirmation Bias. Looking for the answer that supports your hypothesis, ignoring conflicting information. For example, if I believe women are inherently more trustworthy than men, I might discount female staff as internal fraud suspects.

Decision Fatigue. People will often ignore alarms, security warnings, and other alerts if they are bombarded by them. This is problematic when it afflicts patrol staff and SOC personnel, among others.

Dunning-Kruger Effect. Overestimating one's own knowledge, ability, competence, or judgment. "No corporate spy on LinkedIn will be able to coax any valuable information from me."

I once hosted two prominent global security professionals in my house, and I insisted they stay the night instead of booking a hotel. At 5 am, the carbon monoxide detector alarm started blaring. It had never made a peep in the 25 years I had lived in my home. Three experienced security executives convened around the detector, inspecting it as it blasted away, until my daughter Lauren, who was in town visiting from New York, emerged into the hallway. Lauren, who knows nothing about security but plenty about common sense, said, "Why are you all just standing here? Let's get outside." That's Dunning-Kruger, as well as herd mentality, below.

Herd Mentality. Going along with the crowd: "No one else is leaving the building during this fire alarm, so I won't either." Worse than the author and colleagues gaping bleary-eyed at a carbon monoxide detector are people who hide in their office during an alarm, assuming it will be a false alarm.

Hindsight Bias. The mistaken assumption that we understand the past and will be able to apply it to future scenarios. Much was learned from the 2020 Covid pandemic and ensuing shutdown, but the next global crisis will reveal lessons that weren't learned from 2020 as well as a host of new issues.

Hostile Attribution Bias. Assuming that someone's actions derive from hostile or negative intent, rather than benevolent or neutral intent. An example is a physical security executive concluding that a cybersecurity executive's overture to work together means that the latter wants to take over the physical security function.

Not-Invented-Here Syndrome. Scorn for or resistance to ideas, knowledge, skills, approaches, etc. that are not homegrown. For example, an organization that builds its own cybersecurity tools may reject cloud-based solutions that have superior threat-intelligence capabilities.

Outcome Bias. Judging a decision based on the result rather than the quality of the decision-making. This is a common trap for security professionals. For example, a security manager might install a comprehensive security system in a facility that is routinely bypassed by staff who bring outsiders into the building without incident. Outcome bias suggests that the process of developing and installing a new system was sufficient even without policies restricting guest access afterhours.

Pareidolia. Finding meaning or patterns that don't exist from random data. Discovering correlations that aren't there can derail investigations, for example. In the short run, artificial intelligence might exacerbate that tendency, as well, especially if queried about possible links among disparate data.

Plan-Continuation Bias. Failure to recognize that a given plan, such as a business continuity plan, doesn't apply or no longer applies. Many companies failed to realize that, a mere few weeks into the Covid-19 pandemic, their business continuity plans had reached the end of their useful lives.

Sunk Cost Fallacy. Continuing to invest resources in a losing cause, even when it's clear you would be better off cutting ties, simply because you have already invested significant resources. Consider security managers who have devoted time, manpower and money in initiatives and equipment, and continue to do so even when they don't get the results they desire.

Chapter Takeaways

- A strong grasp of historical and evolving risk frameworks strengthens your credibility as a security or risk leader.
- Understanding cognitive biases and heuristics improves risk-based decisions and builds organizational resilience.

From the Lips of Gips: "Risk history is just two loud voices: one swearing it'll happen tomorrow, the other insisting it never will."

BREAKAWAY I
SECURITY RISK LEADERSHIP LESSONS FROM MOVIES

Welcome to the first breakaway. Consider these to be stretch breaks in which I invoke pop culture references to explore security and risk leadership in a more casual way.

We will start with leadership lessons from films. Let's skip the obvious sources. No war movies, biopics, or sports flicks. Those genres are rich with leadership examples, but let's dig into the unconventional, the unexpected, and the untrodden, presented here in chronological order. (Spoilers ahead!)

The Manchurian Candidate (1962)

Communist military brass brainwash American troops and return them home to be activated later as unwitting sleeper agents who will help install a pro-Chinese/Soviet president. A parable about McCarthyism, the film ends with the hero snapping out of his daze and destroying the Americans conspiring with the Chinese.

Leadership Lessons

While few security professionals will ever be brainwashed (if anyone can be), some may find themselves actively or passively helping their company commit fraud, conceal or destroy evidence, abuse

DOI: 10.1201/9781003646488-4

staff, or otherwise run afoul of their legal or ethical responsibilities. Sometimes you have to snap out of your stupor and do the right thing.

Moreover, with the abundance of misinformation and disinformation circulating today, we risk buying into appealing but false premises, falling for casuistry, or entombing ourselves in our prejudices. The movie reminds us to break out of such mental traps.

Deliverance (1972)

Maybe the only thing worse than being up the river without a paddle is being up Class IV+ rapids while being stalked by predatory locals. Four adventure-seeking Atlantans fight off their attackers and escape legal consequences, but the three survivors are forever haunted by their experience and the possibility of the truth coming out.

Leadership Lessons

The film is a lesson in crisis management when the options range from bad to intolerable. Pre-planning, knowing your course of action, creating trusted relationships beforehand, and preparing options in case problems arise are all critical, but sometimes everything goes wrong and you improvise. Like Lewis, the Burt Reynolds character who leads all but one of the friends out of mortal danger, you can do your best, and sometimes even that result is awful.

Dead Poets Society (1989)

Robin Williams' character, John Keating, has the students at his prep school address him as "O Captain, My Captain," in homage to Walt Whitman's poem about one of the greatest American leaders, Abraham Lincoln. Keating defies the hidebound traditions of the school to teach his students about fulfillment and self-actualization.

Leadership Lessons

Sometimes tradition and culture stifle growth and innovation. Security can help an organization pivot to new markets and technologies, such as by leading digital transformation. Moreover, sometimes a catalyst is necessary to spark change—and a catalyst doesn't survive beyond that spark. Keating sacrifices himself for a larger cause, a role that security practitioners are used to.

Groundhog Day (1993)

Bill Murray's weatherman lives countless iterations of February 2 in Punxsutawney, Pennsylvania. From a burnt-out, boorish cynic, he rebuilds himself into the best possible version of himself to ultimately escape the time loop.

Leadership Lessons

No matter how jaded, mechanical, or uninspired you've become, you hold the power within yourself to change at any moment. That means even the most hardline, old-school chief security officers can learn their organization's business, mentor next-generation professionals, master cybersecurity, thrive on social media, and embrace mindfulness.

Pulp Fiction (1994)

Gangsters and their molls shed blood and inhibitions throughout this neo-noir classic. One of the characters with the least screen time, Winston Wolfe, takes the prominent leadership role even among a universe of people who constantly live among crisis. Known as the "cleaner," he responds to crises with sangfroid, speed, and surehandedness.

Leadership Lessons

If you can disregard the lawlessness and cruel efficiency of Wolfe's handiwork, the lesson resides in being the type of leader who can step into a storm with calmness, decisiveness, and authority. This is the person other leaders call when things fall apart.

Fargo (1996)

Leadership comes in all packages, including a pregnant police chief from central Minnesota. Frances McDormand's Marge Gunderson unravels the plot behind a kidnap-for-hire that goes awry via a route that takes us from a used-car lot to a woodchipper.

Leadership Lessons

Gunderson leads with empathy and down-home simplicity, gently helping her lug-headed deputy decipher clues in the case and unflappably doing her job even in the harsh Minnesota winter. Empathy and disarming kindness, combined with vision and perception, are more effective than constant confrontation and belittlement of direct reports.

Erin Brockovich (2000)

Based on a true story, Erin, a legal assistant without formal training, uncovers a water contamination scandal and forces a major corporation to pay restitution.

Leadership Lessons

You don't need a title to lead. Passion, persistence, and moral clarity can carry you far, especially in risk roles that involve advocacy, compliance, or ESG. Erin's unpolished yet unrelenting approach reminds us that sometimes courage matters more than credentials.

Leadership lessons don't only come from boardrooms or biographies. They show up in canoes, classrooms, and diners with hitmen. For security professionals, these films offer more than entertainment—they reveal how courage, humility, resilience, and empathy shape the choices we make and the cultures we build.

3
Leadership Styles in Action

Chapter Objectives

- Understand the evolution of leadership thought and its impact on contemporary risk leadership practices.
- Examine various leadership styles, including values-based, holistic, crisis, visionary, and others, to identify their unique characteristics and applications.
- Analyze the effectiveness of different risk leadership styles in various organizational contexts and situations.
- Develop the ability to adapt and apply appropriate leadership styles to enhance team performance and organizational outcomes.

History of Leadership Thought

Today's world moves lightning fast. The 24-hour news cycle has diminished to the time it takes to refresh a website. Technology becomes obsolete the moment it comes out on the market. Fortunes are won and lost on Wall Street by one computer outjockeying another by nanoseconds.

But are our notions of leadership keeping up with the times? Or are we tethered to leadership theories that don't serve the modern world?

Leadership studies can be traced back to the 1840s with the emergence of the *Great Man Theory*. Originated by Scottish philosopher Thomas Carlyle, this philosophy contends that leaders are born, not made.

We still see remnants of this thinking throughout business today, when executives are chosen by pedigree or title. That might include a company hiring a decorated and well-respected military official or government bigwig with no business acumen or emotional intelligence as the new CSO.

DOI: 10.1201/9781003646488-5

Early in the 20th century, *Trait Theory* emerged. Trait Theory posits that people can become great leaders by improving skills typically found in leaders. Those characteristics include intelligence, self-confidence, initiative, and persistence among others.

Among the problems with this theory is that no one could agree on the specific leadership traits, other leadership factors are ignored, and no tests exist to measure these traits or how well they perform. Trait Theory in security today may take the form of identifying, grooming, and coaching young professionals for leadership positions based on observing specific characteristics commonly associated with leadership.

Developed in response to the shortcomings of Trait Theory, *Behavioral Leadership Theory*, developed in the 1940s and 1950s, focus on what leaders do rather than what traits they have. Behavioral frameworks help explain the different styles seen in leaders of GSOC teams vs. field operations or policy-focused CSOs, for example.

In the 1970s, Paul Hersey and Ken Blanchard's *Situational Leadership Theory* gained currency. This theory says that no single style of leadership is optimal; leadership must be adapted to both the people who need to be influenced and the task that needs to be accomplished.

Hersey and Blanchard viewed leadership as falling into one of four behavioral styles: delegating, participating, selling, or telling. For all Situational Leadership's advantages, such as flexibility, not all leaders can adapt in the way prescribed. In addition, shifting between leadership styles can confuse followers or reporting staff. In security, which is often compliance-based, Situational Leadership can come across as flaky or inconsistent.

Around the same time, Robert House built upon the scholarship of Max Weber to proclaim a theory of *Charismatic Leadership.* According to that theory, "leaders transform the needs, values, preferences, desires, and aspirations of followers from self-interests to collective interests. Further, they cause followers to become highly committed to the leader's mission, to make significant personal sacrifices in the interest of the mission, and to perform above and beyond the call of duty."

Though I never met him, Rick Rescorla might meet that definition. As director of security at Morgan Stanley on 9/11, he helped evacuate thousands of people from the Twin Towers, before perishing in the collapse. He had anticipated attacks on the towers and had prepared his staff through training and drills. When the attacks occurred, he jumped into action, singing songs, calming panicked employees, and continually climbing up and down the stairs to rescue more people. His vision, confidence, and emotional inspiration certainly qualify as charismatic.

Bridging the 1970s and 1980s, *Leader-Member Exchange (LMX) Theory* emerged. LMX focuses on one-on-one relationships between leaders and subordinates. Its essence is that effective leadership involves developing high-quality, trust-based relationships with direct reports. In the security context, LMX explains why a threat-intelligence team might be motivated and loyal, while an executive protection team might be disengaged or disgruntled, even under the same leader.

Transactional Leadership, which gained popularity in the early 1980s, is a structured method for optimizing staff performance that relies on the carrot and stick approach to motivate employees. Leaders do not actively engage their staff; they intervene only when an issue arises.

Transactional Leadership may be found in security departments that are under pressure to reduce or minimize costs. Expected to achieve an ongoing sequence of short-term goals, these leaders set specific tasks for their staff and entice them with rewards.

Another style is *Transformational Leadership*, which emerged around the same time. With Transformational Leadership, leaders inspire their staff to collaborate toward a shared vision.

Servant Leadership stands traditional leadership on its head. With servant leadership, leaders serve those who report to them, ensuring that they develop, have necessary resources, feel empowered, and otherwise thrive.

Although the theory hatched 50 years ago, Servant Leadership has truly blossomed since the turn of the millennium. Focusing on empathy and transparency, it remains one of the most prominent leadership approaches today. One of its most ardent practitioners and advocates is Mike Howard, the former CSO of Microsoft and author of "The Art of Ronin Leadership."

Adaptive Leadership, introduced by Ronald Heifetz in the 1990s, offers a critical lens for modern security professionals. It distinguishes between technical problems, ones with known solutions, and adaptive challenges, which require experimentation and stakeholder engagement. In the security realm, adaptive leadership performs well with insider threats, supply chain instability, and systemic bias in surveillance. These problems cannot be solved by issuing a policy or upgrading hardware. They demand learning, flexibility, and coalition-building across disciplines and departments.

In the 2000s and beyond, several new models have emerged, including *Authentic Leadership* (centered on self-awareness and ethical grounding), *Distributed Leadership* (shared influence across teams), and *Digital Leadership* (focused on navigating AI, tech disruption, and data ethics). This quick hopscotch through the history of leadership theory omits several other philosophies that have found favor, but they all overlap and coexist in many ways.

What's clear is that there is no magic formula for security leadership, or any leadership for that matter. While the Great Man Theory might be considered archaic today, it's a good thing that leadership principles don't change at the speed of Google. Being a leader is a lifelong process (Table 3.1).

As Mike Howard puts it in the first chapter of "The Art of Ronin Leadership," "In the … journey to becoming a great strategic leader, I always like to say you must crawl, walk and then run."

The following pages explore some of these and related leadership styles and philosophies.

Values-Based Leadership

At the SECURITY 500 Conference in November 2022, former FBI Assistant Director for Counterintelligence and NBC News National Security Analyst Frank Figliuzzi spoke about what he calls the "Seven Cs of Values-Based Leadership." All seven are pertinent, but just like there really aren't Seven Seas (today we count about 50 different seas in the world), there are several more Cs that I submit are critical to leadership. (Don't worry. I'm suggesting three more Cs, not 43.)

Figliuzzi identified the seven Cs as code, conservancy, clarity, consequences, compassion, credibility, and consistency.

Code means understanding how you and your team conduct yourselves: what you do and what you don't do, and how you do it. Figliuzzi explained that Code emanates from the eight core values

Table 3.1 Leadership Theories, Unbound

ERA	THEORY	CORE IDEA	RELEVANCE TO SECURITY
1840s	Great Man Theory	Leaders are born, not made	Legacy thinking in CSO hiring
Early 1900s	Trait Theory	Leaders exhibit specific traits	Used in grooming future security leaders
1940s–1950s	Behavioral Theory	Leadership is defined by actions, not traits	Explains variance in team-level leadership styles
1970s	Situational Leadership	Leadership style depends on follower readiness	Useful in security training and team dynamics
1970s	Charismatic Leadership	Visionary leaders inspire through emotion	Embodied by figures like Rick Rescorla
1970s–1980s	LMX Theory	High-quality leader–member relationships drive performance	Explains inconsistencies in team engagement
1980s	Transactional Leadership	Rewards/punishments to manage performance	Common in cost-focused security departments
1980s	Transformational Leadership	Inspire teams toward a shared vision	Vital for security culture change
1970s–2000s	Servant Leadership	Leaders serve their people first	Seen in empathetic, transparent CSOs like Mike Howard
1990s	Adaptive Leadership	Tackle complex, evolving challenges collaboratively	Critical for insider threats, social instability, AI ethics
1990s–present	Strategic Leadership	Long-term vision aligned with organizational goals	Guides enterprise risk strategy and resource planning
1990s–present	Ethical Leadership	Lead through integrity, fairness, and legal compliance	Promotes trust, avoids liability, supports regulatory resilience
1990s–present	Values-Based Leadership	Lead according to clearly defined core values	Anchors risk, ethics, and culture; vital in decision-making under stress (e.g. Frank Figliuzzi)
2000s–present	Authentic Leadership	Leading with integrity, self-awareness	Builds trust in volatile environments
2000s–present	Distributed Leadership	Leadership is shared, not hierarchical	Relevant in GSOCs, crisis teams, agile orgs
2000s–present	Cross-Cultural Leadership	Adapts leadership across cultural boundaries	Crucial for global security teams and international operations
2010s–present	Digital Leadership	Navigating AI, tech disruption, and digital risks	Vital for converged security environments
2010s–present	Holistic Leadership	Integrates personal, organizational, and societal well-being	Aligns resilience, wellness, and mission in complex systems

of the FBI, including respect, integrity, accountability, fairness, and "rigorous obedience to the Constitution."

Conservancy is the collective effort to preserve and protect the inherent value of an environment. In values-based leadership, Figliuzzi emphasized, you "are the steward of something greater than yourself." If you want to go into management at the FBI, you have to do a stint in internal affairs investigations. This ensures that new managers will understand that everyone is accountable to someone else.

The third C, clarity, means that if you are going to expect people to adhere to specific values, you must clearly communicate them and enforce them.

When rules are broken, the fourth C comes into play: consequences. Figliuzzi noted that there has to be a price to pay for violations, even if carrying out those consequences hurts you or the organization in the short term. Those consequences, especially if they are harsh, should be meted out with compassion, the fifth C.

The final two Cs are credibility and consistency. Credibility comes from your personal brand and reputation, which in turn flows from your personal value system. Figliuzzi posited that "the ultimate credibility is being able to investigate yourself." Finally, consistency means not throwing out time-tested rules when faced with something new. "Stick with the values that got you this far," Figliuzzi said.

Although values-based leadership is not my construct, I would respectfully offer three additional Cs: culture, change management, and civility.

Culture, Peter Drucker is said (ad nauseum) to have declared, eats strategy for breakfast. If strategy is incompatible with the corporate culture, it gets regurgitated. Culture derives from behaviors that are modeled from the top as well as behaviors from anywhere in the organization that are rewarded or even tolerated. Characteristics of healthy cultures include a clear mission and values, transparency, staff development, diversity, high staff retention, regular communications, and employee recognition.

After his speech, I told Figliuzzi that the 7 Cs seemed to promote stasis, especially conservancy (retaining the status quo) and consistency, which might suggest rigidity. What about change management, which I would include as an additional C? Figliuzzi agreed, emphasizing that both consistency and conservancy shouldn't lock organizations into inaction or stifle development.

My final suggestion is civility. Politics and social issues have permeated every part of our lives, even in the workplace. In addition, tempers can run high even when staff focus purely on business issues. Fostering an environment of respect and civility means staff won't be intimidated from making valuable suggestions or threatened by someone whose social or political views differ.

That makes ten. But ten isn't a magic number, either. I'm sure you can come up with many other relevant C terms.

The "10 Cs of Values-Based Leadership" doesn't roll off the tongue like the 7 Cs does, nor am I suggesting that Figliuzzi change the name. Perhaps specific organizations can define their own 7 Cs of values-based leadership out of a larger pool of Cs. That would give a whole new meaning to the term "C-suite."

Servant Leadership

Among the security and risk profession, servant leadership may be the most popular type of leadership today. It's certainly in its heyday. If it's not the most popular in practice, it's likely the style that's most claimed by professionals. The very word servant resonates with protectors, with its suggestion of assistance and sacrifice.

Hallmarks of servant leadership are:

- Putting people first (including empathy and accessibility)
- Listening over speaking (including processing information before acting)
- Developing staff (including creating new leaders)
- Humility
- Ethics
- Creating a culture of belonging (including mentoring and volunteering)

Servant leaders lead by example and get their hands dirty. When I was running a CSO Roundtable event for ASIS with dozens of security executives in attendance, I once encountered some logistical difficulties. Steve Braden, then of Capital One and now with Flex, jumped in to work with me shoulder to shoulder. That's servant leadership. For Gigi Agassini, a consultant in cybersecurity, AI, and privacy risk, servant leadership has meant supporting a struggling junior colleague without sidelining him after a pentest he conducted for a client went awry. The pentest revealed multiple vulnerabilities, and the client called her in a lather. She realized that the technical issues were minor. The real issue was managing the panicked client. "If I had left him to handle it alone, both his confidence and the client's trust would have been badly shaken," she recounts. She collaborated with the young colleague to bring in an expert team to reassure the client. The colleague shared in the credit of resolving the problem while learning how to manage a knotty issue. "We turned the situation into a teaching moment and showed the team that mistakes are not the end, but opportunities to build resilience," she says.

It can be very difficult to be a pure servant leader. Servant leadership is often an ideal, or north star, rather than something practiced all the time. It's a mindset that comes naturally to many people but can be hard to sustain.

Here's how to inch closer to pure servant leadership:

- Think in terms of "we" instead of "I"
- Support your people publicly (praise in public, course correct—not blame—privately)
- Shut up and let others talk, and when your time comes, thoughtfully address the comments you've heard instead of just pivoting to your original comments
- Continually check your motives: Are you selfish or team oriented?
- Elevate staff by supporting development activities and increasing their responsibilities
- Do the little things that others would feel to be "below" their station (e.g. clean off the table and organize chairs after a meeting; come to the office on a weekend to help a staff member change offices; relieve an executive protection agent who needs a short break)
- Continually ask staff what they need and how you can help them succeed

Servant leadership often reveals itself not in grand gestures but in quiet, purposeful actions that elevate others. As I was wrapping up this manuscript, I took on a role as interim security director at a facility recently hit by a high-profile violent incident. That's where I met a protection agent who, to my mind, exemplified servant leadership in action.

In this role, I worked with many excellent contracted security agents on all aspects of security, including perimeter protection, weapons detection, mail screening, visitor management, public-private liaison, countersurveillance, staff security awareness, crisis management, social media monitoring, and more.

I hadn't, however, had a chance to meet with the building's facility manager, who was also a contractor. One day I met Brandon Bowe, one of the agents at the elite protection firm Soteria's who had been assigned to the site. On his own initiative, and with the approval of organizational leadership, he had spent two hours with the facility manager walking the entire premises after hours, looking for vulnerable areas, hardened locations for safe rooms, potential threats, and other aspects of potential concern or utility.

More impressive than a protection agent assuming that responsibility was the approach that he took with the young facility manager. Instead of just leading him in and around the building pointing out items such as loose flagstones, locks whose keys couldn't be identified, and unsafe storage situations, Bowe presented the tour as a mentoring and learning opportunity. And he didn't monopolize the conversation.

During the inspection, Bowe noticed a gold star on the facility manager's hand, which had been placed there by his young daughter. "When I asked about the gold star, he just lit up," recalls Bowe, which helped him establish a connection. They built a rapport by making a competition of who could find expired or defective fire extinguishers.

Towards the end of the site survey, they ended up on the roof, where other service providers had left trash, including empty bottles and used air filters. The facility manager was going to ignore the refuse until Bowe told him that the items could turn into projectiles during a storm and damage the building.

"That's when it hit me that he didn't put the frappuccino bottle there, he hadn't dumped the filters on the roof," Bowe said. He wanted to encourage the facility manager without seeming to chide him. Having built a rapport, Bowe asked him about his plans and tied in the issue of the trash.

The young man said he wanted to eventually work at a bigger building but didn't have a plan for doing so. He would just keep trying to do a good job. "I recalled his pride about the gold star," Bowe says, and appealed to that pride in his work life. "I said, 'You need to own the building. You need to take pride in it and keep it pristine. You need to inspect the building after someone comes to inspect the generator, change an HVAC filter, or work on the plumbing. You need to know every nook and cranny. If you want to excel, get very familiar with this building, quick.'"

Bowe advised the manager that he had two bosses: the supervisor at the facility management company and the tenants in the building. Bowe coached him to make sure that they both knew he cared about the facility. For example, one room, which could be repurposed as a place of refuge, was filled with paint cans. Bowe suggested sending a memo to the tenants, with a photo attached, identifying the issue and suggesting they acquire a paint locker. The same photo could go to his boss, letting him know that he identified a problem and proposed a solution to the tenant.

"That's how you get ahead," Bowe stresses. "It shows you are competent and proficient. You are handling needs they never thought about."

Bowe hopes the message takes root. "I genuinely care for the young man. When I get another chance to interact with him, I'll ask about his daughter and family. I'll ask about the paint cans. Hopefully he sees me as someone who wants the best for him."

Bowe's interaction checks every box on the servant leadership list. He built trust, listened more than he spoke, used mentorship to develop another professional, and found a way to elevate both the person and the mission, without ego or fanfare. He didn't take control; he cultivated pride, ownership, and growth in someone else. That's the essence of servant leadership: not being the hero but helping someone else become one.

Crisis Leadership

Risk practitioners must be prepared for their crisis-leadership moment. If you deal with security or risk, you will face a reckoning. An issue, event, person, or threat will force you into an uncomfortable or even career-defining decision or action. You may even be in the public spotlight. Choose your role models wisely. Ukrainian President Volodymyr Zelenskyy presents an intriguing example.

Zelenskyy caught the attention of the public in a way the world hadn't seen since perhaps Winston Churchill. Admittedly, with some high-profile exceptions, the comedian turned world leader has been lauded for his leadership for standing up to his Russian neighbor and valiantly joining his compatriots to fight off the Kremlin's invasion of his country.

Let's look at what Zelenskyy's example offers security leaders.

Take Your Shot

Eminem emphasized owning "the moment." He rapped, "You own it, you better never let it go/You only get one shot, do not miss your chance to blow/This opportunity comes once in a lifetime." Zelenskyy's reputation was imprinted when, on behalf of his fledgling democracy, he stood up to an autocrat seeking to restore the post-World War II Soviet regime. He took his one shot and made it.

Security professionals may also get only a single shot to define themselves. For some, it may have been during the COVID-19 crisis. For Chris Krebs, former Director of Department of Homeland Security's Cybersecurity and Infrastructure Security Agency (CISA), his moment came when, in the face of tremendous pressure, he rebuffed President Trump's claims that voting machines were compromised. He has faced tremendous consequences but remains steadfast in his stance.

Follow Your Moral Compass

Sometimes security professionals find themselves in ethical dilemmas. As in Krebs' case, it may cost you your job or your friends, but not your reputation or values.

R.C. Miles, who has led security teams at multiple organizations, once had to confront executives who were installing surveillance cameras to monitor people doing their jobs. He brought his concerns to the CEO, who agreed that this type of use contravened the values of the organization. He got them to turn the cameras off. In another role, despite significant pushback, he called out staff who were assuming aliases to spy on other organizations, pointing out that the practice violated accepted principles of scientific research as well as the company's own ethical guidelines.

If security professionals do stand on principle, they have to be prepared to pay the price. "It's at that moment when you're truly tested," Miles says.

Lead by Example

Zelenskyy backed up his tough talk with action. While he could have taken refuge in other countries, he stayed behind, donned military gear, and took to the streets to fight for his people. His exampled inspired tens of thousands of countrymen and women to follow his lead. Ukrainian expatriates flooded back to the mother country to join the cause, as did many non-Ukrainians. Legions of cyberwarriors rushed to the country's aid, trying to disrupt Russian infrastructure.

Leading by example can take many forms. Credo Cyber Consulting Founder Antoinette King was blown away when, after having just met Andrew Lanning a couple of weeks earlier, he asked her to appear on his program to discuss her industry experience. "I was floored that he asked me," she recalls, since she hadn't presented before. "I asked him, 'Why me?' and his answer has stuck with me ever since." Lanning had publicly committed to championing diversity and representation on his show and in the industry at large. "He didn't just wave the flag of diversity," King says. "His company actually adheres to that principle above everything else."

Mind Your Image

Zelenskyy, leveraging his entertainment background, has mastered his image. Videos, pictures and memes show him looking fit, bravely protecting the streets with fellow soldiers or remotely addressing overseas presidents and legislators. Contrast these with the aloof, sallow images of Putin, perhaps best represented by a photo of him talking to French President Macron across a long table. The memes are endless. People have rendered the table as an airport baggage carousel, a sushi conveyor belt, and a ping pong table. In the vast space between the two men, jokesters have inserted the figures from da Vinci's Last Supper, pairs of figure skaters, and Bernie Sanders in mittens.

Security professionals are unlikely to appear on the world stage, but image counts just as much on the factory floor, at a trade show, or in the board room. It speaks volumes when security leaders stand shoulder-to-shoulder with their colleagues during a crisis.

Communicate Clearly

"I need ammunition, not a ride," retorted Zelenskyy when the United States offered to evacuate him from Ukraine. Those simple, crystal-clear words painted an indelible picture of a man refusing to abandon his nation. Simple language is more forceful, inspiring, and memorable.

Nelson Mandela called democracy an ideal "for which I am prepared to die." He didn't say, "It is incumbent on me to strive to achieve a democratic society, succumb though I may." Martin Luther King, Jr., had a dream. He didn't postulate alternative futures. Keep it easy and memorable.

You'll probably never get the opportunity to stand up to a Russian dictator. But Zelenskyy's blueprint for leadership works well at any scale. Take your shot and own it.

Years before Zelenskyy came to power, McLean Essiene took his shot. Better said, he didn't take a "shot" at all; he laid down his arms in a volatile situation and chose communication over conflict.

We've known each other since 2018, where I learned about his role in brokering peace among rival gangs in Nigeria and featured his story among other extraordinary leaders' experiences at the opening of ASIS's GSX conference.

Here's how McLean tells it:

In 2016, the Ahoada region of Rivers State, Nigeria (about an hour's drive northwest of Port Harcourt), stood at a dangerous crossroads. Infamous cult factions had become the face of terror across Ahoada West and East, orchestrating waves of kidnappings, killings, and criminal intimidation that profoundly destabilized the area.

At the time, I served as the Chief Security Officer of Ahoada Local Government, supporting the Local Government Chairman and directly engaging the security complexities on the ground. Earlier that year, I had contributed to the coordination of a state-level amnesty initiative designed to disarm and reintegrate violent actors into civil society. While the program initially saw some success, including the symbolic disarmament of prominent cult figures, peace proved fragile. Several of these individuals later returned to violent activities, undermining public trust in the initiative.

The state government issued a public bounty on key perpetrators as the crisis escalated. However, for those of us on the front lines, it was evident that force alone would not deliver sustainable peace. A different approach was needed—one that blended strategic intelligence, human empathy, and the willingness to take personal risk.

In a decision many would consider reckless, I entered the hideouts of some of these violent actors—unarmed and without military escort—to open channels of communication. These were not controlled meetings in safe zones, but face-to-face encounters in unpredictable, high-risk terrain. My only assurance to them was that no security forces were lying in wait, and that our intent was not ambush, but dialogue.

Backed by trusted community intermediaries—youth leaders, clergy, repentant ex-militants, and traditional authorities—we created a negotiation process prioritizing dignity over humiliation. Our approach treated the perpetrators not as enemies to be crushed, but as disillusioned stakeholders who could still be redeemed and reintroduced into the community rebuilding process.

Through strategic empathy, calm persuasion, and the trust built during the earlier amnesty, we convinced many gangs to drop their arms and sheath their swords. This was not a coerced surrender, but a consensual and honorable return to peace, rooted in mutual survival.

The outcome was powerful. Bloodshed declined, civil order returned, and confidence in community-based conflict resolution was restored. More importantly, we reinforced a model of security leadership that values restoration over retribution.

That season taught me that authentic crisis leadership is not about volume or visibility but moral courage and quiet influence. It means standing in the operational and ethical gap when others retreat. It also requires believing that even the hands that once unleashed violence can help rebuild peace—if only someone is willing to reach out first.

I've learned that leadership is not always about standing at the front. Sometimes, it is about being the unseen scaffold behind peace—the Silent Architect of Impacts.

I can't add to that.

Visionary Leadership

Visionary leadership is the ability to cast a compelling picture of a future state and gain buy-in from stakeholders to make that vision a reality. It requires imagination, clarity, influence, and the follow-through to help others reach that imagined destination. As James MacGregor Burns argued in *Leadership* (1978), transformational leaders engage others by appealing to higher ideals and moral values, motivating them to exceed their own expectations and those of the organization.

Chris Stitt exemplifies this form of leadership. Early in his career, he instinctively identified ways to improve underperforming systems and overlooked services. His ability to spot inefficiencies and envision better solutions, whether through modernizing emergency planning or redesigning operational tools, led to increasing influence and recognition. His consulting firm, CrisisLead, embodies this mindset. Even its tagline—"Helping You Navigate Risk… And Prepare for What's Next"—reflects a visionary orientation: identifying risks, anticipating needs, and helping others arrive at a better future.

Visionary leadership can also be intuitive and empathetic, as Christine Mica, COO of the National District Attorneys Association, reflects. For her, the most effective leaders are those who make people feel seen and considered. She recalls one university president who made time every December to visit staff and thank them in person, small gestures that conveyed vision through care. Conversely, she recounts missed opportunities: a leader who failed to acknowledge a difficult layoff openly with staff, or an executive director whose departure on parental leave went unaddressed beyond an out-of-office reply. Vision, in this sense, is about inclusion as much as foresight.

Of course, not every vision comes to pass. Not all of mine have. Many leaders articulate ambitious futures that fail to materialize, due to timing, resistance, lack of alignment, or flawed execution. What separates effective visionary leaders is their capacity to adapt. They refine the vision in real time, adjust course when necessary, and listen actively to stakeholders to ensure the future they envision is one people genuinely want to inhabit.

Visionaries don't just forecast the future. They invite others to build it. And they make the journey feel like a shared adventure, not a dictated destination.

Epiphanic Leadership

You could stick almost any adjective before "Leadership" and land on a style or approach that someone has described. But as far as I can tell, "epiphanic leadership" is nowhere in the research literature, isn't used in academia, and can't even be found in a Google search. It's something I made up after I asked a friend of mine, Olivia Arnauts, to describe her leadership journey.

Epiphanic leadership is born of sudden clarity—realizations forged through hardship, moral conflict, or life-altering decisions. It's the leadership that emerges when old paradigms shatter and new truths take their place. While some leaders follow a linear path, epiphanic leaders are shaped by rupture, recovery, and reinvention.

Olivia and her husband, Ralph, are amazing people, and about as pure of heart as you can get. I met them when I was working on a documentary about the white supremacist threat, and accompanying troll storm, to the small Jewish community in Whitefish, Montana. We were looking for investigators who could track the man who had ordered the bombardment of hateful and threatening phone messages, emails, texts, and memes, which ruined the lives of the victims. A real-time pursuit of the man would add contemporary relevance to a documentary that recounted events from 2017.

We had talked to several candidates for the search, but Olivia and Ralph blew us away. They were young, dynamic, authentic, and tatted up. Best of all, they were altruistic and idealist. No cynical, superannuated Nazi-hunters here. Skilled in cyber investigations, Olivia would track the target virtually. Ralph would lead a team on the ground to physically locate him. He could turn up anywhere in the world.

And, somehow, they were raising two young girls at the same time.

Though the documentary still hasn't been produced, the couple became my friends. I've watched them as they have built a brand based on service and heart, ZFIS Protective Intelligence, which offers due diligence, asset tracing, litigation support, and intelligence reporting.

Olivia and Ralph have an extraordinary story of resilience and empathy, especially Olivia, and I asked her to describe it in terms of her leadership journey. After reading it, I created the term "epiphanic leadership." Not in the sense of religious awakening (though that could be relevant to the story), but as a sudden insight or inspiration.

She had been inculcated with a perception of leadership that was titular and unyielding, a belief that vanished as she escaped a stultifying environment. Here's her story, in her words:

They say you can't change the hand you're dealt, but you can choose how you play the game. Leadership means something different when you've experienced the extremes of life – in my life this is exemplified by growing up in a religious cult, surviving and fighting for the prosecution of my abuser, leaving for the U.S. Army at 17, and building a company rooted in justice, safety, and integrity. My growth into leadership hasn't been easy; it's a testament to resilience, personal growth, and the unyielding pursuit of a cause that's bigger than myself.

I was born into a cult in a small town in Utah, a world where leadership was defined by control. I didn't know it at the time, but that environment would teach me a brutal lesson: leadership can be twisted and abused. I was taught that real leaders were above reproach, not because of their wisdom or compassion, but because of their power and the fear they instilled in others.

Growing up in the cult, I witnessed firsthand how power could be wielded to subjugate, manipulate, and isolate people from their true selves. The leaders in that world taught that the ends justified the means, that control was essential for "the greater good." Yet what they failed to realize—and what I had to come to understand the hard way—was that true leadership doesn't thrive on fear or subjugation. True leadership is about empowering others, not controlling them.

At 17, I made the toughest decision of my life: I walked away from everything I ever knew. With no real understanding of the outside world, I joined the U.S. Army as a Signals Intelligence Analyst and flew to Hawaii, about as far away as possible. It was my chance to break free, to reclaim my sense of agency, and to see if I could lead in a world that was different than anything I'd ever known. The Army was where I began to learn about real leadership—the kind that doesn't depend on manipulation or fear, but on accountability, integrity, and sacrifice.

The military taught me discipline and the importance of working as a unit, where your strength was defined by how well you supported the people around you. One truth stood out: leaders in the Army earned respect through actions, not titles. They didn't just bark orders; they led by example, taking responsibility for their decisions and putting the welfare of others above their own.

It was a sharp contrast to the environment I had left, and for the first time, I saw leadership as an opportunity for service, not dominance. After leaving the military I could have taken many paths, but I chose to build a company. Not just any company, but one that stands for justice, safety, and fighting for the vulnerable. The transition hasn't been easy, and It has been filled with the same struggles I faced after leaving the cult—self-doubt, the fear of failure, the weight of responsibility—but I remembered what I learned in the Army: leadership is about showing up, being accountable, and forging on when things get hard.

When you're running a company that aims to fight for justice—while earning enough to pay the bills—you face challenges on a daily basis, and sometimes the problems seem insurmountable. It's in those moments of difficulty that the core values I learned along the way have been tested. Hard work, self-discipline, and compassion have become the foundation of everything I do, and the mission I fight for make it all worthwhile. These values are essential not only for building a business but for building a culture of leadership that inspires others to join you in the fight for what's right.

Building my company hasn't been quick or simple. There were days when I wanted to quit. There still are. We fight against large scale fraud, investigate human trafficking rings, and expose abuse in institutions like religious organizations and the troubled-teen industry. Our work threatens powerful institutions with a lot to lose. The pressure of trying to make a difference, to do the right thing while still keeping a business afloat, is overwhelming, but hard work keeps me going, day after day.

I used to think that leadership meant being tough and never showing weakness. I witnessed leaders that saw compassion as a weakness, but over time I've realized that empathy is a cornerstone of true leadership. It's the ability to understand the struggles of others, to lead with kindness, and to make decisions that consider the well-being of everyone involved. In the world I came from, emotions were suppressed, and, for a leader, vulnerability was seen as a threat to authority. However, in the real world, especially in business, compassion is what connects leaders to their teams and to the people they aim to serve. It's about listening, understanding, and lifting others up rather than tearing them down. It's the ability to turn pain into something constructive and to use your experiences to help others avoid the same pitfalls.

Perhaps the most important lesson I've learned is that adversity doesn't break you—it shapes you or, as my dad would say, it adds character. Every setback, every failure, and every challenge is an opportunity to grow, to refine your leadership, and to evolve. Life hasn't been kind to me in many ways, but I've learned to use every hardship as fuel for my mission. The mistakes and bad things that have happened to me—whether it was leaving behind the only world I knew or facing the hardship of building a company from scratch—have made me the leader I am today. They've taught me resilience, they've taught me to never give up on what I believe in, and they've taught me that leadership isn't about being perfect; it's about being able to rise after you fall and to inspire others to do the same. Leadership is a journey—a journey that requires a willingness to confront your past, embrace your flaws, and push forward toward something better.

I've learned that true leadership is not about exerting control over others. It's about empowering them to rise above their circumstances, to overcome their struggles, and to work together for a common goal. It's working with them to do the dirty work when no one else will.

Leadership, at its core, is about making a difference—not just for yourself, but for the world around you. That difference is born from the hard work, self-discipline, and compassion that help turn the pain of the past into a powerful force for good.

Olivia's journey embodies epiphanic leadership. Her clarity came not from coursework or conferences, but from lived rupture—the trauma of a controlling system, the discipline of military service, and the pressure of building something just and sustainable from scratch. Her leadership isn't theoretical; it's born of stakes, scars, and purpose.

Epiphanic leaders aren't born that way. They arrive through disruption and the hard work of reimagining the self. They challenge what leadership looks like, often replacing dominance with empathy, and hierarchy with humanity.

Leadership forged this way isn't about legacy or charisma. It's about service, responsibility, and helping others break free, too.

Teleological Leadership

If "Epiphanic Leadership" wasn't too esoteric for you, I'll raise you my next example of jerry-built jargon: "Teleological Leadership." I use that phrase to mean the type of leadership that feels destined, a form of leadership that emerges when a person's deepest skills, values, and life path converge at a moment of urgent purpose. It's not assigned, appointed, or even chosen. It arrives when everything you've done suddenly finds its meaning. In Yiddish, it's "bashert," or meant to be. In Mexico, it's encapsulated by the phrase, "al que nace p'a tamal, del cielo le caen las hojas" ("If you are born to be a tamale, leaves will fall from the sky."

In John Irving's novel *A Prayer for Owen Meany*, the titular character makes his friend, the narrator, practice a basketball move they call "The Shot." The maneuver involves the narrator lifting the diminutive Owen in the air so he can dunk the basketball. They practice obsessively for years, refining the timing and execution.

Years later, Owen, now a U.S. Army soldier, is escorting a group of small Vietnamese children through an airport when a deranged man tosses a grenade. In a flash, the years of practice pay off. The narrator lifts Owen, who places the grenade high on a windowsill where it detonates, saving the children but killing Owen.

Although fiction, it's a brilliant example of teleological leadership, and a pretty good Gospel allegory as well. Owen's life pointed toward that moment. His skills, preparation, and conviction converged in an instant of purpose.

It happens in real life, too. Jeff Slotnick's story is a profound example of leadership forged through purpose. Here it is:

I have had a long career as both a United States Army Combat Engineer First Sergeant and a security professional. I've witnessed almost every threat and incident possible, until December 19, 2016, forced me to take stock of who I was as an American, as a Jew, as a security professional, and as a human being. I ended up calling upon every professional and personal skill in my toolbox.

That day, he learned of a psychological terror campaign targeting the Jewish community of Whitefish, Montana, where a troll storm incited by white supremacists had overwhelmed families with vile messages, death threats, and Holocaust imagery. Flights were grounded in a snowstorm, and Slotnick, based in Seattle, was the only responder within reach. He packed tactical gear, food, and communications tools, and drove 532 miles through the mountains.

At the rabbi's house, I received a warm welcome from an anguished family. The children described the hate and betrayal they were experiencing in their schools and social lives. Together with the support of a national nonprofit, we developed an implementation plan, strategy, and mission imperatives.

Over several days, Slotnick met with law enforcement at multiple levels, briefed the FBI and the Governor of Montana, trained targeted families in self-defense, conducted risk assessments of homes, schools, and businesses, and helped set up physical security systems, cybersecurity protocols, and safe rooms.

I spent time with a family who had received the most virulent hate I'd ever witnessed: images of their children photoshopped into gas chambers and ovens. I taught the kids de-escalation and how to respond if physically confronted.

He concluded his stay by leading a three-hour community meeting and strategizing around a threatened neo-Nazi march on Whitefish.

Never in my life did I anticipate being a focal point of knowledge and strength for an entire community under siege. I had to internalize my emotions and be strong for them. When I returned home and said Shabbat blessings with my family, I broke down. I've seen the worst things one human can do to another, but this—this was personal. That experience changed me. I recommitted myself to fighting hate in all forms.

Every facet of Slotnick's past—from his military leadership to his security expertise to his Jewish identity—converged in that moment. He didn't seek it. But when the moment came, he rose. That's teleological leadership.

Jeff's reflection upon returning home is searing. He saw this not as just another operation—but as his purpose. A moment that gave retroactive meaning to a lifetime of preparation. And sealed him as a bona fide mensch.

Teleological leadership doesn't always involve life-or-death stakes, religious symbolism, or heroic sacrifice. But it *does* feel like everything has led to this moment. It's when the past converges with the present to fulfill something bigger than yourself.

Not all of us have a grenade or a hate-fueled rampage in our origin story. But many of us can recall a time when we were *the only one* positioned to act, to decide, or to stand up. If epiphanic leadership is born of insight, teleological leadership is born of culmination.

You probably noticed that both the Owen Meany and Jeff Slotnick stories center on religion and protecting children—subjects that strike at the core of identity and values. But teleological leadership can spring from any telos: a passion for justice, a call to serve, the defense of truth, the advancement of knowledge, or the fierce loyalty to community, family, or country.

Whatever the source, the pattern is the same: preparation meets purpose. And the leader, whether ready or not, rises to meet it.

Chapter Takeaways

- Leadership styles have evolved over time, reflecting changes in societal values, organizational structures, and workforce expectations.
- Each leadership style offers distinct advantages and challenges; understanding these can help leaders choose the most effective approach for a given situation.
- Flexibility in leadership style is crucial; effective leaders adapt their approach to meet the needs of their team and the demands of the environment.
- Self-awareness and continuous learning are key to developing and refining one's leadership style for maximum impact.

From the Lips of Gips: "A servant leader is the person who unclogs the toilet without making a speech about it."

BREAKAWAY II
Risk Leadership Lessons from Streaming Series

Welcome to the second Breakaway, where we move from movies of prior generations to recent or modern-day streaming series.

Streaming series, with their extended arcs and character complexity, offer fertile ground for leadership insights. Unlike two-hour films, these shows let us observe how leaders grow, falter, and evolve under pressure. The following examples, presented alphabetically, blend great storytelling with surprisingly sharp leadership lessons.

Better Call Saul (2015–2022, AMC/Netflix)

We see Saul Goodman. the sleazy but endearing dime-store attorney in *Breaking Bad*, in his formative years as "Slippin" Jimmy McGill. He's too clever and ambitious by half, representing common criminals, drug cartels, and miscellaneous low-lifes as he schemes to vanquish the white-shoe law firm that rebuffed him.

DOI: 10.1201/9781003646488-6

Leadership Lessons

Jimmy's charm, ingenuity, and underdog grit make him a must-watch. And we witness where his slow erosion of ethics will lead him. The show explores how identity, branding, and ambition can lead a promising leader down a path of self-sabotage.

The Bear (2022–, FX/Hulu)

A fine-dining chef inherits his family's failing sandwich shop in Chicago and tries to turn it around amid chaos, debt, and family trauma. And that episode with barely any dialogue? Excruciating, yet delicious.

Leadership Lessons

A raw depiction of leadership in transition. Carmy must transform not just the business but the culture, earning trust and reshaping norms while confronting sorrow and his own perfectionism. It's leadership through grease and grief.

The Diplomat (2023–, Netflix)

Kate Wyler, a veteran, no-frills diplomat, is thrust into the high-profile role of U.S. ambassador to the UK amid a global crisis, while managing a crumbling marriage to her husband, a more senior and ethically compromised political operator. And she may be tapped as the next Vice President.

Leadership Lessons

A study in influence beyond authority. Kate navigates institutional complexity, global stakes, and marital tension with pragmatism and restraint, reminding us that leadership often means holding things together when everything is coming apart.

The Last of Us (2023–, HBO)

In a post-apocalyptic America ravaged by a fungal pandemic, a hardened smuggler must escort a teenage girl who may hold the key to humanity's survival.

Leadership Lessons

What begins as an escort mission becomes a slow-burning exploration of trust, sacrifice, and emotional vulnerability. The smuggler's leadership isn't traditionally heroic, but it's real, flawed, and shaped by moral complexity.

Quarterback (2023, Netflix)

Who knew how complicated it was to call signals in the NFL and that Kirk Cousins uses neurofeedback? Or that Patrick Mahomes goes to a special gym after practice to train on off-balance or improvised throws? This sports documentary follows NFL quarterbacks Mahomes, Cousins, and Marcus Mariota through the 2022 season, revealing how they handle pressure, fame, and leadership both on and off the field.

Leadership Lessons

You see vastly different leadership styles: Mahomes leading with improvisational flair and cockiness, Cousins with methodical calm, and Mariota with resilience amid career uncertainty. What unites them is their clarity under pressure, commitment to the team, and capacity to reset quickly.

Severance (2022–, Apple TV+)

Employees at the mysterious and bizarre (melon bar, anyone?) Lumon Corporation undergo a surgical procedure that separates their work and personal memories, effectively splitting them into two selves.

Leadership Lessons

A phantasmagoric case study in corporate control, *Severance* warns against workplaces that demand total compliance at the expense of humanity. The series explores psychological safety, holistic leadership, and what happens when workers become mere functions.

Slow Horses (2022–, Apple TV+)

A group of MI5 misfits relegated to the agency's "Slough House" are routinely given menial work, until they uncover real threats that force them into action.

Leadership Lessons

Beneath the cynicism and grime, even has-beens can shine under pressure. Humility, creativity, and unconventional leadership beats bureaucratic bloat.

Succession (2018–2023, HBO)

Led by an imperious but ailing patriarch who sets his traumatized children against one another, the series chronicles the backstabbing and manipulation in a global media empire. Degradation, hypocrisy, and alliance-shifting run rampant as the children battle for control of the company. The "Boar on the Floor" scene is a masterclass in the interplay of unbridled power and wanton humiliation.

Leadership Lessons

It's all here: toxic succession planning, reputation-destroying power plays, the emotional immaturity of unchecked privilege, and leadership defined by fear and chaos.

Suits (2011–2019, Peacock/Netflix)

A college dropout with a photographic memory fakes his way into a prestigious law firm, mentored by a high-powered closer while navigating the risks of exposure. The setting may feel familiar to anyone who's worked in high-pressure legal environments.

Leadership Lessons

The series explores informal influence and mentorship under pressure. It also serves as a primer on institutional compromise: how loyalty, ambition, and ethical shortcuts can clash in high-stakes environments.

Ted Lasso (2020–2023, Apple TV+)

A relentlessly positive American football coach is hired to lead a struggling English soccer team, despite no experience with the sport or the culture. His cornball sayings and motivational methods, though naïve and discordant on the surface, end up being pitch perfect.

Leadership Lessons

What begins as a fish-out-of-water story unspools into a lesson in servant leadership. Ted shows how humility, empathy, and belief in others can shift culture and build resilience—even as he's ridiculed as "Ronald [f-in'} McDonald."

Taken together, these series illustrate that leadership isn't limited to corner offices or command centers. It's forged in kitchens, courtrooms, bunkers, and boardrooms. Great storytelling, like great leadership, thrives on complexity, contradiction, and transformation.

4

What Great Leaders Are Made of, Part I

Chapters 4–6 Objectives

- Identify the key traits that distinguish effective security and risk leaders, such as humility, empathy, courage, and curiosity.
- Understand how to wield these traits strategically but authentically.
- Understand how soft skills, often underestimated, can determine team cohesion, credibility, and influence.
- Explore how communication and service-oriented leadership foster trust, engagement, and mission clarity.
- Learn how decision-making under uncertainty, confidence, and accountability enable leadership in volatile or ambiguous environments.
- Reflect on the balance between introspection and action in developing and sustaining essential leadership habits.

Cultural Knowledge and Awareness

Unless you are isolated geographically (e.g. Tuvalu, Bhutan), economically (e.g. North Korea, Cuba, Sudan), or culturally (e.g. South Korea, Norway), you likely interact with clients, customers, and business professionals from many different cultures. Facility in dealing across multiple cultures is a foundational leadership trait today.

I've been fortunate to live in multiple cities in both the United States and Spain. I've also done work in Canada, Latin America (Mexico, Panama, Peru, Brazil, Costa Rica), Europe (UK, France, Spain, Switzerland, Germany, Poland, Sweden, Netherlands, Turkey), Oceania (Australia), and Asia/Middle East (China, Malaysia, India, UAE, Kuwait, Israel, Bahrain, Oman). I've contracted with organizations in West Africa and South Africa, though I haven't set foot in the continent.

DOI: 10.1201/9781003646488-7

As a senior security and risk executive, it's not unusual to travel around the world providing assessments, counsel, and strategic oversight. Knowing a bit of the language, etiquette, and basic cultural norms is a start, but it isn't enough.

Today's risk leaders must be able to recognize, respect, and navigate differences in values, communication styles, approaches to risk and opportunity, and decision-making philosophies. This requires adapting to and working with prevailing cultural norms.

It's not just when you travel to a different country. A security risk leader working for a Germany-based chemical company likely has staff, partners, investors, clients, suppliers, or customers throughout Europe and beyond. BASF, for example, while headquartered in Germany, has subsidiaries and joint ventures in 80 other countries.

Luca Tenzi is a Switzerland-based security risk management consultant whom I met in 2008 when he was International Security Director for Prudential Financial, based in Rio de Janeiro. Besides Switzerland and Brazil, he has also lived and worked in Italy, Austria, Kosovo, Qatar, and the United States. An avid skier, he has slalomed through myriad cultural issues.

For instance, the fervor with which people of various backgrounds treat traditions, holidays, and customs can seem overzealous. Super Bowl Sunday is treated almost as reverentially in the United States. It barely registers in much of the rest of the world.

"Having managed teams in the Middle East," recalls Tenzi, "I had to be sensitive to Ramadan or the Sabbath." In parts of Asia, it's disrespectful to ask a question before the most senior person in the room speaks. "Without this awareness, it's easy to make wrong assumptions," he says.

Recently, he served in Kosovo as a deputy commander of a battalion where he reported to Italian leaders and commanded officers from 14 different nations, including Hungary, Latvia, and Germany.

"Understanding Italian, I could understand what the Italian commander wanted, but I had to switch to English to communicate to my officers," Tenzi says. "Even knowing Italian culture, I would have to translate it to the German or Austrian officer who wanted to work in a specific way. Understanding culture and speaking the language are two different things."

Lisa Gans has operated in some of the world's most hostile areas, where cultural sensitivity plays an outsized role in risk leadership. Gans, a U.S. citizen and human rights and democracy specialist, was working on an elections project in Afghanistan in 2008. She was managing the work of several local firms and coordinating with the Afghan Chamber of Commerce and Industries, a government-led entity. She noticed that the local firm leaders seemed reluctant to participate in meetings and recognized that she was likely missing information about risks to the project.

She describes the situation:

> *So, I invited the leaders of the local firms to a series of meetings, telling the government officials that the purpose was administrative and that their attendance was not necessary. In the first meeting, I explained that my job was to help them, the local firms, succeed and asked them to share their concerns and how I could be helpful. At first, they were cautious, and we mostly discussed logistics. But as time went on and we built up trust, they explained that they were fearful of providing transparent feedback about the elections process because of the reach of powerful people in the Afghan government who had an interest in the election outcomes. They said that they were afraid of reprisals against their firms and even their families.*
>
> *To manage these risks and concerns together, we set up a private channel through which they could submit reports as a way to convey information directly without having to share their findings with members of the government. I learned that people will often share critical information if given the opportunity and the space, and leaders in high-risk environments can learn a lot by creating the trust needed for people to explain their exposure and needs.*

That's Afghanistan, but being culturally adroit starts at home. I've consulted for houses of worship and religious institutions in the Washington, D.C, area where members, staff, and clergy shared a religion but represented many different communities and cultures: Dominican, Salvadoran, Mexican, Pacific Islander, African, and more.

Cultural awareness can't be mere lip service or simply knowing the holidays or etiquette of a foreign country. It's the capacity to recognize, respect, and navigate differences in values, communication styles, perceptions of risk and opportunity, and decision-making approaches. Culturally aware leaders adjust their approaches to align with others' worldviews and aim to minimize bias.

This trait is particularly relevant in security and risk leadership because our remit often includes dealing empathetically with a broad array of cultures, such as conducting cross-border investigations, running executive protection details around the world, or even dealing with, say, cultural clashes on a factory floor or at a construction site.

In addition, threat perception can be cultural. Consider a workplace theft interview with an American subject who avoids eye contact and keeps his head down. He may be exhibiting signs of evasiveness or deception. The same behavior by a Japanese subject, however, might be a sign of respect or humility.

I once consulted for a university serving a Native American community. Administrators and I were discussing the 2005 shooting at Red Lake Senior High School, which took place on the Red Lake Indian Reservation in northern Minnesota. They had observed that the media had portrayed the killings as a "massacre," while school shootings not involving Native Americans were rarely described with that language. Learning about their perception of Native Americans being associated, even subliminally, with massacres helped me understand my clients and better serve them. While this understanding didn't specifically help me or the school administrators manage a concrete risk, it helped us develop tools for the university to communicate with the media on university safety and security through the Red Lake lens. The lesson is that something benign in one culture can be a red flag or taboo in another.

Later in my career, I supervised an investigation in a West African country, though I didn't personally travel there. Facing the investigators on the ground, and me as their manager, was a kaleidoscope of cultural, gender, political, social, and workforce issues.

The assignment was to identify an employee who was providing valuable and incendiary inside information to outside agitators. The investigators were white males from the United States and South Africa, while the employee population was black African, from a variety of tribes. The investigators' arrival immediately put the staff on notice that something was amiss, and they became suspicious and noncompliant.

A strict hierarchy existed from the leadership to the lowest-level staff, with each executive having his own fiefdom and creating his own culture, which produced rivalries with other departments. Coaching and development of staff were rare.

As it turned out, identifying the leaker was the easiest part of the job. The investigators identified a trove of issues just under the surface, involving conflict between staff of different genders, tribes, departments, levels, political leanings, and classes. Those issues were far more than they could address in two weeks on the ground, and it would take at least months or years to even adequately understand the underlying dynamics.

SIDEBAR: BUILDING CULTURAL AWARENESS: PRACTICAL STEPS FOR RISK MANAGERS

1. **Engage in cultural self-assessment.** What assumptions do you bring to the table? What's your cultural "default in your approach to risk leadership?
2. **Diversify your inputs.** Read beyond your region. Listen to global voices in risk, security, and business.
3. **Practice radical curiosity.** Ask team members, "How would this look from your perspective?" and really listen. Don't scoff when someone from a different culture tells you they never lock their door.
4. **Adapt your leadership style.** The "right" tone, speed, and level of directness varies by culture, especially in the context of risk. Different cultures may have different approaches to risk and risk appetite.
5. **Learn from mistakes.** Cultural missteps are inevitable. What distinguishes strong leaders is how they recover and evolve. A cultural faux pas regarding risk or security can lead to an international incident. Because of confusing signage, a male colleague of mine almost wandered into the lady's room in a large mosque in a Middle Eastern country. Thank goodness he stopped to ask.

Communication

Fueled by mis- and disinformation, political and social cohesion in the United States have been fractured. That dissonance infects the workplace as well. How do you work with someone who seems to represent everything you distrust? It takes extraordinary leadership to navigate these divisions, including understanding your culture, knowing what your organization represents, and ensuring that everyone feels valued.

Like most things, that's easier said than done.

I witnessed three examples of that leadership when I traveled to Poland in May 2024 for the March of the Living (MOTL) along with a delegation of about 20 law enforcement officers, under the auspices of Paul Goldenberg and Mark Genatempo of the Miller Center for Policing and Community Resilience at Rutgers University. We were part of an international crowd of students, dignitaries, educators, Holocaust survivors, historians and witnesses who marched the two miles between the Auschwitz and Birkenau concentration camps. Begun in 1988, MOTL memorializes the horrors of the Holocaust, flipping the Nazi death marches at the end of World War II on their head to drive home the resilience and survival of the Jewish people.

Our delegation of law enforcement officials from Louisiana, Nevada, Ottawa, New Jersey and elsewhere had come to bear witness to the remnants of the atrocities of 80 years before. This was the second such delegation; in 2023, a slightly larger group of international law enforcement officers, including some on this year's mission, presented a formal declaration at MOTL that acknowledged the complicity of police in the Holocaust and vowed to operationalize the phrase "Never again." They would do so by creating training programs that would help police prevent and address bias, dehumanization and hate that can transform into violence and hate crimes , and even genocide. That training would roll out at MOTL 2024.

Then Hamas struck Israel on October 7, 2023, dividing workplaces around the world and threatening to politicize an event that is designed to further peace and understanding.

Many workplaces ignored the political tensions in the workplace, but not the New Jersey State Police (NJSP).

NJSP's Col. Patrick Callahan, who attended both marches, consulted with some of his troopers and decided to assemble a group of six Muslim troopers and six Jewish troopers so they could express their feelings and continue to work together without suspicion. Among them were Mudduser Malik, a Muslim, and Marc Zislin, a Jew, who are good friends. Callahan suspected that these two men would model collaborative behavior and let the 12 troopers talk candidly and without recrimination.

It worked. "He brought us together to express concerns, hash out issues, and really let us clear the air," recalls Zislin. "We all knew and respected each other, most of us had worked together and relied on one another, so we were a good group to start the conversation," he adds.

Malik points out that because there are relatively few Muslim and Jewish troopers, who are key to reaching out to their populations, it was particularly important to connect. "The connection to our communities is critical, he says. They see us as their representatives and champions, and if we can enable conversations and enhance understanding, we've done a great service to our diverse populations."

"It showed that the New Jersey State Police is on the side of humanity," Col. Callahan says.

The three men took part in MOTL 2024 and were humbled by the experience—both in witnessing some of the grim apparatus of the Holocaust and in receiving gratitude from fellow marchers for their presence. On behalf of the New Jersey Police delegation, Malik even planted a stake honoring the victims of the Holocaust along the now disused train tracks that once carried millions to their death on cattle cars.

Those are three examples of superb leadership that we all should emulate.

SIDEBAR: PRACTICAL LESSONS FROM GETTYSBURG

At the foot of the monument marking the site of the Gettysburg Address, 20 security professionals, a battlefield guide, and Wharton professor Michael Useem gathered to explore timeless leadership lessons drawn from Lincoln's speech and the pivotal Civil War battle that helped turn the tide for the Union.

It turns out that challenges forged in war have surprising parallels to those faced in modern organizations. Why didn't Confederate General Richard S. Ewell seize the high ground, including Little Round Top, when he had the chance? How did Union General George Meade quickly earn the trust of his officers just three days after assuming command? And how did Union Colonel Joshua Chamberlain convince disgraced and hostile mutineers to return to the ranks?

Such questions bear directly on the kinds of leadership security professionals must practice: earning trust quickly, motivating the disillusioned, and acting decisively amid uncertainty. According to Useem, essential skills such as clear communication, mentoring, emotional intelligence, and mission-driven leadership are timeless and battlefield-tested.

One participant, a military veteran, spoke about the power of camaraderie and the advantage of liking the people you work with. Loyalty, he explained, follows connection. Loyal teams will go to great lengths for the leaders they trust. Another attendee noted that some of the biggest challenges arise unexpectedly. The Union and Confederate forces collided at Gettysburg by accident, and a strong leader must be able to assess and adapt on the fly rather than waste time lamenting the circumstances.

A third student drew insight from Chamberlain's treatment of the 120 mutineers from the 2nd Maine Infantry. Scorned, abused, and starved, they arrived at Gettysburg demoralized. Instead of punishing them, Chamberlain made a bold wager on humanity: he fed them, treated them with respect, and invited them into the mission. Nearly all joined his charge.

Perhaps the most striking lesson came from a communication breakdown. General Lee ordered Ewell to take the Union position on Cemetery Hill and Culp's Hill "if practicable." Ewell interpreted that as a suggestion, not a command. Stonewall Jackson, whose death led to Ewell's promotion, would have taken the same language as an imperative, Useem explained. One takeaway: vague expectations lead to inaction. Another: mentoring matters. Jackson never trained Ewell. That gap in leadership development may have cost the Confederacy the battle—and the war.

Humor in Leadership? Funny You Should Ask

Sometimes it's better to disarm than to arm. Put another way, humor can be both a powerful leadership and tactical tool for security.

Humor is tricky business in the security world. Briefing staff on warning signs of workplace violence, precursors to terrorist attacks, contingency plans for natural disasters, and methods of corporate espionage doesn't exactly lend itself to one-liners. Most security incidents aren't a laughing matter. Moreover, a security professional who cracks jokes—or even shows a lighter side on the job—risks being viewed as unprofessional.

Yet humor has a powerful role in leadership, even in security leadership. Not inappropriate or off-color humor, or barbs at the expense of direct reports. But mild self-deprecation, droll commentary on unusual situations, and lighthearted remarks that puncture stressful moments can yield huge benefits. According to an article in *Harvard Business Review*—citing research from Wharton, MIT, and London Business School—"every chuckle or guffaw brings with it a host of business benefits. Laughter relieves stress and boredom, boosts engagement and well-being, and spurs not only creativity and collaboration but also analytic precision and productivity."

This finding aligns with research by Jennifer Aaker and Naomi Bagdonas, authors of *Humor, Seriously*, who argue that humor increases influence, improves retention, and signals authenticity, which are critical traits in any effective leader.

Brian Reich, who has led security programs at several financial institutions, can attest to these findings. Reich used to be a stand-up comic, and he still practices comedy to keep his management skills sharp. "The ability to connect with people is truly the art of comedy—and by extension, communication," he explains. "Being funny is a byproduct of connecting with people. To be impactful, comedy has to be believable and relatable, and the presenter likable."

Another naturally funny security executive who wields humor strategically is Torsten Wolf, Head of Group Security Operations at Zurich Insurance Company. "Humor comes to me naturally," he says, but he emphasizes that timing is critical. He uses humor to "defuse tense discussions or situations" and builds it into presentations to put people at ease or win them over.

I can attest to his success. His humor helped get us through a hairy situation with vendors on the streets of Kowloon when we were in Hong Kong for a conference.

Many of the qualities of humor overlap with the building blocks of leadership, including humility, communication, balance, accessibility, authenticity, influence, trust, social intelligence, and conflict management. For example, Reich says that gaining trust when taking over new teams depends on connection and likability, and humor can be a powerful way to win over a skeptical audience.

Of course, most security executives aren't stand-up comedians. Heavy-handed attempts at humor often misfire, offending staff or making superiors question your judgment. Humor can be "dangerous," says Wolf. "Not everybody shares your sense of humor or understands it. Therefore, in terms of strategy, I also think carefully about when it's better not to use it."

Cross-cultural humor can be a landmine, agrees Luca Tenzi, a security professional who has worked globally. "What makes one team laugh might puzzle or even offend another," he says, and even more so "in remote settings where you can't pick up facial expressions or body language easily." He adds that humor is time sensitive. "Something that was funny yesterday might sound weird tomorrow."

For those reasons, it's critical to gauge the culture of the organization or event and leadership's attitude toward humor. Equally important is knowing your audience. Authentic humor that reflects your personality and stays within those guardrails can be extremely powerful. So, when the time is right, "disarming and funny" beats "armed and dangerous."

Here's an example, albeit in a low-stakes venue: When I was an executive at ASIS, I was presenting with my boss, CEO Peter O'Neil, to the ASIS Mumbai Chapter. An opportunity arose to make a timely and resonant joke, but I would be navigating a cultural divide. I had seen an article in a local newspaper announcing the death of a Bollywood superstar, legendary in India for uttering an indelible phrase in the 1975 classic *Deewaar*, the Bollywood equivalent of something like "I coulda been a contender" or "Frankly my dear, I don't give a damn."

The movie is about two brothers raised by a single mother in the slums. One becomes a crime boss, the other a police officer. In a pivotal scene, the mob brother says (roughly translated): "Today I have a building, property, money in the bank, a bungalow, a car … What do you have?" The upright brother answers, "Mere paas ma hai" ("I have my mother").

After Peter spoke, I poked fun at myself for being second banana at ASIS and in the presentation: "Peter's the boss with the big title, authority, esteem, power, and budget but ... mere paas ma hai."

That brought down the house. I had asked friend and CSO Prasun Dixit beforehand how to pronounce the phrase correctly, and the joke worked because it was self-deprecating as well as a respectful nod to a cultural touchstone and the actor's recent passing.

The moment reminded me of one of the themes of this book: that leadership doesn't always follow procedure, protocol, or even instinct. Sometimes, like humor, it's learned in motion, practiced in real time, and refined in unexpected places. It's not in the manual.

Beyond self-deprecation, humor can even lend insight into risk management. One of my favorite books is *Plato and a Platypus Walk Into a Bar: Understanding Philosophy Through Jokes.* As the title suggests, it explains abstruse philosophical theories through (often well-known) jokes. Here's one from the book that happens to deal with security:

> *If you're getting on a commercial airliner, for safety's sake, take a bomb with you ... because the overwhelming odds are that there won't be two guys on the same plane with a bomb.*

The joke exemplifies the Monte Carlo fallacy—the mistaken belief that past events influence future outcomes. It's why roulette players bet big on red after six straight spins of black.

I apologize in advance for the explanations that follow, which may strip the humor from the jokes—but not, I hope, the leadership lessons.

On Risk Management and Business Development

I was going to start a risk management business until I realized everything that could go wrong.

This joke skewers the mindset of total risk aversion. Security executives aren't meant to eliminate risk, but to guide their organizations in managing it intelligently and accepting some risk in pursuit of greater reward.

On Staff Training and Contingency Planning

The life-safety team interviewed me on fire-safety protocols today. They asked me what steps I'd take in a fire. I said, "Great big ones."

This joke underscores a training gap. In real emergencies, panic may override reason, and staff must fall back on drilled behavior. Without proper preparation, even clever answers won't save lives.

On Staff Development

A CISO returns from a staff development seminar full of new ideas. He calls his team together and tells them that his door is always open. Soon, a young security software engineer shyly enters and admits he has a problem. The CSO says, "There are no problems here, only opportunities." The engineer hesitates, then replies, "OK, I have a drinking opportunity."

While the punchline lands with irreverence, the point remains: encouraging openness without offering support can lead to missed chances for real leadership.

On Crisis Management and Accountability

A departing CSO gives her successor three envelopes and tells her to open one each time a crisis occurs.
The first crisis hits—a major security lapse. Envelope #1 says: "Blame your predecessor."
The second crisis: drug trafficking at a distribution facility. Envelope #2: "Blame insufficient resources."
The third: a massive insider breach. Envelope #3: "Prepare three envelopes."

Security leaders are expected to anticipate improbable crises with limited budgets. After the second disaster, no one wants to hear excuses. What matters is preparation, response, and recovery. The joke also warns that habitual blame only defers, not deflects, accountability.

On Ethics

Four risk executives emerge from an ethics conference.
The *first says, "We carry the weight of every ethical dilemma in our companies. Let's confide in each other."*
The second says, "I've been ignoring the CEO embezzling millions."
The third: "I falsified my résumé to get past screening software."
The fourth: "I've been quietly enforcing an age cap on hiring."
The fifth: "I can't keep a secret."

Ethics are nonnegotiable. Security leaders who feel ethically compromised should speak with general counsel or a trusted superior. Just make sure they're not the fifth CSO in the joke.

Key Takeaways: Humor as a Leadership Tool

- Humor, when used authentically and thoughtfully, builds trust, diffuses tension, and humanizes leadership.
- Mild self-deprecation and dry wit, especially in high-pressure environments, can help security leaders appear more approachable and emotionally intelligent.
- Know your audience and your organization's humor threshold. Humor that feels forced or risky can undermine credibility.
- Don't try to be funny; try to be real. Humor grows naturally from connection.

SIDEBAR: A MODEST LEADERSHIP PROPOSAL

It is a melancholy object to those, who ply this great trade of security, when they see the companies, the agencies, the facilities crowded with practitioners of our profession, followed by three, four, or six direct reports, all in confusion, and importuning every colleague for a guiding hand.

If you don't recognize the writing style in the previous paragraph, I'll remind you of the great essayist Jonathan Swift, who devised an "ingenious" idea that simultaneously addressed food scarcity, overpopulation, malnourishment, and urban blight: eating unwanted children.

In a similar vein, I humbly posit a modest (and satirical) proposal to address the need for leadership in security. This suggestion will improve efficiency, increase motivation, play to individuals' strengths, and fortify security.

By now, Security as a Service (SECaaS) is well-entrenched, and its benefits have been documented over time. Typically, subscription-based, SECaaS provides greater expertise, avoids heavy up-front costs, shifts maintenance to the provider, includes regular updates and upgrades, outsources administrative tasks, and offers a web interface for a holistic look at security activities. SECaaS has been so successful that it has spawned offshoots such as Access Control as a Service, Video Surveillance as a Service, Network Security as a Service, and Business Continuity as a Service.

So, isn't it time for Risk Leadership as a Service (RLaaS)?

The SECaaS benefits apply equally, if not more so, to RLaaS. Let's take a look.

Greater expertise. No matter how good your people are, they are probably not proven professional leaders in the mold of Abraham Lincoln, Martin Luther King or Julius Caesar. Using RLaaS, when the need arises for direction or inspiration, just dial up or call in trained leaders who've experienced everything before and know the right clichés to use and hackneyed motivational tactics to deploy. Many have memorized classic motivational speeches from history. For the security industry, they would specialize in Sun Tzu, Napoleon, and MacArthur.

Lower upfront costs. Why train everyone to lead when most of that training will be wasted? Many people are not cut out for that type of responsibility. Face it; it takes time, effort and resources to develop leadership abilities. This is valuable time being taken away from more important tasks that have a tangible impact on the bottom line, such as detecting fraud or protecting cargo shipments.

Maintenance. Keeping leaders polished and relevant is hard work. RLaaS providers would incur the responsibility of refreshing training, sharpening oratory skills, and ingraining the latest business jargon.

Updates and upgrades. A bad leader can taint a whole enterprise, and replacing that leader entails time and expense. RLaaS puts the responsibility in the provider's hands. They hire and fire and put people out to pasture. Furthermore, imagine if your staff had to learn soft skills and emotional intelligence. They wouldn't be able to show their face again in the security industry.

Administration. Just like SECaaS pawns off administrivia on service providers, so does RLaaS shuttle leadership to the margins where it belongs most of the time. While the important work of security gets done, leadership stays on the periphery until the time for platitudes and hollow exhortations arises.

Web interface. RLaaS providers can fit leaders with trackers, so when they are embedded in an organization, the company can see where they are at all times. This allows a holistic look at where leadership is being applied, particularly so management can keep them from interfering with operations.

Everyone should agree that I've made a resounding case for RLaaS. For my next book, I will offer an equally irrefutable argument for why the CSO should report to the mailroom intern.

Humility

Humility isn't the absence of confidence. It's the refusal to let confidence harden into arrogance. I didn't fully understand this until I enrolled in a seven-day executive protection (EP) course outside of Baltimore and realized, within hours, that no amount of intelligence, education, or knowhow could substitute for attention to detail, adaptability, and the willingness to look foolish in the name of growth.

Confidence leavened by humility is the winning combination, as I learned when I attempted to make the leap from security journalist to security professional nearly two decades ago. I enrolled in an intensive 7-Day Executive Protection Course run by one of the godfathers of EP, Bob Oatman, in Towson, Maryland. This was in the days before iPhones, Waze, and social media.

I was on my first mission, and it was going horribly wrong.

Thanks to a misplaced jacket, a broken elevator, my indecipherable handwriting, and my teammate's thick Caribbean accent, I had already lost my principal before the assignment even began.

Along with 36 other security professionals and hopefuls, I was nearing the end of an 80-hour executive protection training. The course was clear from day one: corporate EP was more personal service than Secret Service, more clock management than Glock management.

On the fifth day, we were placed in protective details. My team included Dave, an ex-cop from St. Louis; Doc, his terse Kentucky colleague; Andrew, a soft-spoken Trinidadian from that country's Ministry of National Security; and me. Bob Oatman himself played our principal.

I was supposed to lead the principal's vehicle, a Cadillac. But I had left my sports jacket in my hotel room. We had been instructed to mirror our principal's appearance, and Oatman was always dressed sharply. I dashed back to retrieve it.

Big mistake.

The elevator was broken, so I took the stairs from the outside of the building. I reached my room on the sixth floor, grabbed my jacket, sprinted down, turned the corner, and ... the Cadillac was gone.

Andrew, waiting in my car, calmly said, "They left."

I had already failed. I had lost my principal.

We scrambled to catch up, using directions I had hastily scribbled down. Andrew began reading them aloud, but between the engine noise and his accent, I couldn't make them out. "Go 29 miles on 955," he said.

There is no Route 955.

I remembered: it was 2.9 miles on I-95 South. We were already on the edge of disaster. Andrew couldn't read my handwriting, I couldn't decipher his voice, and he wasn't licensed to drive in the U.S.

I was learning what every leader eventually does—the smallest failure of preparation can feel enormous when the stakes are high. Owning that mistake, rather than excusing it, was a small but necessary act of humility.

Every detail matters in EP. Every inconvenience is magnified. For example, I had copied directions from MapQuest by hand because the hotel had no printer. When we hit the road, median strips and no-turn signs invalidated multiple instructions.

We eventually caught up to the lead car, though not without possibly violating a few traffic laws. But the lesson stuck: fully understand your assignment, double-check your tools, and if you're writing directions, make sure your partner can read them.

When we reconvened at the hotel the next day, Oatman immediately began grilling us on aspects of our environment we had failed to observe:

"Is there a fire extinguisher on your principal's floor?" "How many doors to the exit?" "Is the front desk open 24/7?"

Each student hesitated or guessed.

It brought me right back to the first week of law school, when the professor's finger hovered over a large cardboard seating chart, then dive-bombed onto the desk labeled "Gips." I was asked to recite the facts and holding of Fortune v. NCR. I fumbled the difference between contract and quantum meruit and felt a hundred hands fly up to correct me. Once again, I was on the defensive, exposed, and considering bluffing my way through something I should have just prepared for.

Later, when tasked with protecting Oatman, our four-person team assumed we didn't have time for an advance. Another mistake. We squandered resources, annoyed our principal, and took inefficient routes, including a detour through a mall parking lot that wasted valuable time. Even if we hadn't had time for a full advance, we could have asked the hotel concierge or a local delivery driver for tips.

Good leaders ask for help. Humble ones do it early.

On the return trip, a classmate from the Maryland Transportation Administration offered us a more efficient route. His advice worked beautifully. Oatman praised our return.

Another humility lesson: locals and insiders often know more than you. Listen.

The most high-profile part of EP involves protective operations: countersurveillance, driving, facilitating logistics, and extracting the principal. But even here, the ego must take a back seat.

We practiced countersurveillance by observing suspicious individuals. Some students misidentified obvious threats; others missed people completely. One memorable exercise had us shown a photo for three seconds. One student swore the foreground car was blue. It was bright yellow.

The lesson: observation is a skill, not a reflex. Assume you're missing something until proven otherwise.

In one simulation, we had to extract a dummy/our injured principal ("Alice") from an attack scene. Alice weighed 90 pounds. In the rain, she might as well have weighed 900.

None of us could get her into the car solo. Not the ex-military guy. Not the fittest agent. No one.

We had to put aside the arrogance that any one of us could handle the task alone. Humility meant recognizing the limits of strength and training.

EP isn't about bravado. It's about facilitation and unobtrusive service. We provided our protectees with water bottles, newspapers, and ideal car temperatures. We kept quiet, alert, and in the background.

Henry Kissinger once advised his protection team: stay "close enough to protect me, but not so close I have to introduce you." That's humility in motion: indispensable, invisible, and egoless.

During mall protection drills, I lost the principal multiple times—once because I took a call, another time because I overcorrected after squeezing too close in a crowd. When I misjudged a threat and startled the executive, he snapped at me for nearly spilling his coffee.

Humility isn't just knowing your role but also knowing when you're getting in the way.

That week taught me more about leadership than a year in an office ever could. In EP, there's a reason it's called a "detail." And in leadership, there's a reason humility endures while arrogance fails.

Leaders don't need to dwell in the details. But they should never consider themselves above them.

From the Lips of Gips: "Disarming and humorous beats armed and dangerous."

5
What Great Leaders Are Made of, Part II

Influence

Most CSOs will never have the formal authority of a COO or CFO. They often lack direct control over significant budgets, policy enforcement, or enterprise decision-making. But the most effective ones don't rely on title or power. They lead through influence earned over time, built on trust, and exercised with nuance.

Influence is the ability to persuade and guide rather than command and coerce. In security leadership, this is essential. Most of a security executive's effectiveness comes from influence, not formal authority.

Salesforce CSO Keith White puts it this way: "It's a bit of a misnomer to say that if you don't have a straight-line reporting relationship to the CEO, you're not working directly with them, taking direction, or giving advice." White has regular access to the CEO despite reporting through other channels, and he's learned to embrace soft power. "CEOs often want to talk to a subject matter expert unfiltered, and anyone in between on the reporting line has to accept that."

Roy Lemons, CSO of International Paper, is even more direct: "The number one tool the CSO has is influence. If you are a trusted partner, you can influence things that happen in a company, regardless of your place on the org chart."

How Influence Is Built

Influence isn't granted with a job title. It must be earned, demonstrated, and sustained. Here are five ways high-performing security executives build and wield influence.

DOI: 10.1201/9781003646488-8

1. Build Relationships

   Strong relationships form the foundation of influence. Steve Georgas, CSO of Levy Restaurants, notes the delicate balance required: CSOs may be called upon to investigate colleagues, which can strain trust. "Your allegiance belongs to the organization," he says. Influence depends on being respected as fair, principled, and discreet.

   Security executive R.C. Miles, agrees. In a former role, he reported to the SVP of Operations, but would meet weekly with the CEO and present to the board. "It's about the relationship more than the position," he says. But relationships aren't automatic. "What derails many CSOs is coming in with the attitude of, 'I'm the CSO, and you have to listen to me.' No, you have to earn it."
2. Know the Business

   Security leaders who understand the full spectrum of the business—operations, finance, culture, and personalities—can anticipate concerns, align with strategy, and offer more effective counsel. "Know the business cold," advises Steve Antoine, a security executive who has worked at multiple corporations across industries. When you understand the company better than your peers, influence follows.
3. Speak Their Language

   Executives don't respond to security jargon. To influence them, you must translate risk into business terms. One automotive CSO creates tailored metrics for short-, medium-, and long-term goals. Lemons reinforces the point: "Security is about one percent of a business. We have to speak their language, not the other way around."
4. Offer Options, Not Just Obstacles

   Security leaders are sometimes stereotyped as running the "Department of No." Run the "Department of Know" instead. Become the most informed person about the workings of the company, and influence will follow. Using this mastery, influential CSOs work with business leaders to find risk-managed paths forward. Antoine offers an example: food delivery companies traditionally refused to drop off orders at parks or beaches for safety reasons. By partnering with security, some platforms found creative ways to serve those areas safely. "Security helps deliver profit and becomes a growth driver," he notes.

5. Identify Advocates

   Having powerful allies who will champion your work behind closed doors is essential. White recalls a high-ranking executive he rarely interacted with becoming one of his most vocal supporters, winning security new resources. Miles emphasizes engaging trusted stakeholders: "You have to identify key stakeholders that your boss trusts and win their trust. Engage people who surround the decision makers in a way that solves their problems, and they will help solve yours."

Consider these scenarios:

- A CSO with no formal control over facilities convinces the real estate team to install CPTED upgrades by reframing it as a brand enhancement project.
- A security director persuades Legal to add duty-of-care clauses in vendor contracts after using a recent incident to show potential liability.
- A cybersecurity leader partners with IT and marketing to delay the launch of a vulnerable new app feature, not by invoking fear, but by showing how a breach could undermine customer trust and long-term brand value.

None of these required rank. All required influence.

Security leaders rarely win by fiat. They succeed through credibility, curiosity, clarity, and connection. Influence is not a side effect of leadership. In most security organizations, it is the job.

The best CSOs don't demand a seat at the table. They become the person everyone wants sitting next to them.

The Curious Case of Curiosity

"Barbecue sauce."

That's the phrase Ted Lasso utters before hitting a bullseye in a high-stakes darts game in the eponymous TV series. It's his calming mantra and a quiet nod to his upbringing. But what sticks with viewers isn't just his accuracy and sangfroid. It's the satisfaction of seeing the arrogant team owner, who has mocked Ted as a backwoods American, get his comeuppance. And it's the brief speech Ted gives before that final shot:

> "Be curious, not judgmental."

Ted credits the quote to Walt Whitman (incorrectly, but it still resonates). It's a lesson for leaders, especially those in the risk and security space: when you lead with curiosity, you see things others dismiss. You ask instead of assume. You invite collaboration instead of defensiveness.

I'm preternaturally, compulsively, curious. My CliftonStrengths profile proves it: Input, Ideation, Learner, and Intellection all land in my top five. If someone on the radio mentions Feynman and quantum superfluidity, I need to know more. If a friend mentions a Victorian duke who built 24 kilometers of tunnels under his estate, I will learn his story. (Both real examples.)

Even walking my dog, I'm glued to my phone chasing some new thread of insight. Neighbors have commented—jokingly, I think—on how rare it is to see me walk without reading. And, yes, I know, that's impairing my situational awareness, but I've made my risk calculation.

That kind of curiosity fuels innovation, but it can become indulgent or unmoored from impact. For leaders, curiosity works best when it's not inward or abstract, but directed outward: toward people, systems, and challenges.

Curiosity helps leaders:

- Identify the root causes behind data trends, such as an increase in staff data security violations, not just react to symptoms
- Ask why a procedure like changing passwords every 30 days exists, rather than just enforce it
- Engage with functions outside their domain—legal, HR, operations, finance—to better understand organizational context
- Connect with frontline employees whose insights rarely reach the C-suite

Curiosity in a security context might mean learning how marketing's incentives could increase social engineering risks. Or investigating the behaviors behind repeat access control violations rather than just disciplining the offender.

Curiosity isn't a fixed trait. It can be developed like any other leadership muscle.

- Ask questions you don't already know the answer to.
- Rotate who you sit next to at lunch or during offsites.
- Replace the phrase "I already know" with "Tell me more."

But a word of caution: fake curiosity backfires. Feigned interest is easy to spot and erodes trust quickly. Authentic curiosity, on the other hand, earns loyalty. People feel seen when leaders ask real questions and care about the answers.

Security and risk leaders don't need to have all the answers. But they do need to care about what others know. Curiosity bridges silos. It builds rapport. And it prepares leaders to spot subtle shifts in behavior, policy, or risk.

My own curiosity helps me spot patterns, link seemingly unrelated ideas, and pose questions no one else has thought to ask. That's not a personal eccentricity. It's a professional advantage.

So, the next time you feel tempted to judge, pause instead. Ask a question.

Be curious, not judgmental.

Developing Others

Great leaders multiply. In the corporate security and risk world, that means developing deputies, mentoring proteges, and creating environments where others rise. But does the security and risk industry have anything akin to the NFL's celebrated coaching trees?

Consider Bill Parcells, who trained 14 head coaches including Bill Belichick, whose influence now extends to generations of NFL leadership. Or Andy Reid, whose former assistants have had top coaching jobs across the league. These trees symbolize a leader's deeper legacy: the elevation of others.

In security, the trees aren't as obvious, but they exist.

Russ Cancilla at Baker Hughes built one of the most impressive set of branches in recent memory. He recruited and mentored deputies who went on to become top security leaders at Jacobs, Amazon, Stripe, NRG, and more. Cancilla didn't just build a team; he launched careers.

Capital One is another example. Under CSOs Tim Janes and Timothy Rigg, the bank produced executives who took top roles at PayPal, McKesson, Flex, and other major businesses.

Target under Brad Brekke did the same: developing staff who took the reins at MetLife, Meta, and elsewhere.

Yet such trees remain the exception. Why?

Scott Lindahl, CSO at Kellanova and past ISMA (International Security Management Association) president, notes that many CSOs come from second careers—FBI, military, or Secret Service—and may not prioritize succession planning.

Executive recruiter Jerry Brennan points to structural hurdles: security executives lack the influence NFL head coaches have. Companies often overhaul departments once a CSO leaves, or promote someone outside security. Some CSOs may even neglect or suppress deputies, intentionally or not.

Unlike football, success in security is harder to quantify. Wins and losses are tangible. Prevented incidents, subtle risks managed, and reputational capital built? Less so.

Still, there are patterns among those who develop others:

- They understand the business beyond security.
- They provide visibility for their team members.
- They help deputies build enterprise relationships.

Jacobs CSO Joe Olivarez recalls that his boss Russ Cancilla arranged for him to regularly brief business leaders. That exposure positioned Olivarez to eventually influence Jacobs' COO and CEO on centralizing HSE operations. "It wasn't just my boss. It was the COO and CEO who bought in," he says.

"CSOs need to prepare people to compete," Olivarez emphasizes. That means more than technical know-how. It means teaching them how to influence, build relationships, and think like an executive.

For decades, women were glaringly underrepresented in senior security roles. A few trailblazers carved out space in a male-dominated field. But it took the founding of groups like ASIS Women in Security in 2011 to provide community, sponsorship, and momentum.

Sasha Larkin, now head of intelligence for FIFA and formerly a senior officer with Las Vegas Metro PD, says mentoring women is essential. "I try to personally mentor anyone I can. I'm working with one woman who I'm sure will be the first woman in SWAT."

The 2025 documentary *The Women in Security Documentary* captures the power and persistence of female leaders in the field. From post-9/11 shifts to barriers like strip-club meetings and inappropriate comments, it chronicles both progress and what remains to be done.

Richard Ticho, a former ASIS events producer, led the five-year effort to make the film. His advisory board included me, a longtime supporter of women in the profession. Credit also goes to Jenny Hartman, who went beyond her administrative role at ASIS in 2011 to take the reins in launching the Women in Security program, as well as many inaugural members and advocates who defied skepticism or indifference.

Sometimes, leadership development happens at home.

Paul Goldenberg, a longtime leader in law enforcement and homeland security circles, recalls a meeting with Royal Canadian Mounted Police officials during a law enforcement exchange program. As he sat down across from several deputy commissioners, he assumed they recognized his name due to his own international law enforcement work. But one of the deputies said, "Yes, we know Alex Goldenberg. We've read a lot of material by him." Paul was momentarily surprised, and then delighted, to realize they were referring to his son, not him. Alex, now an analyst and researcher quoted in major media, has testified before Congress and uses digital forensics to track online extremism. Paul notes that while he once read graffiti to assess threats, Alex now uses technology to do the same and more.

By age 12, Saran Purcell was working for her father, Wilbur Purcell, who ran the largest security company in Antigua and Barbuda. She started as a receptionist, dealing with customers and absorbing the language of guarding, CCTV, cash in transit, and canine operations. "My dad is stern," she says with a laugh. "He told me that every second counts when it comes to security. I thought, 'I can't mess up!'" After attending Florida International University, she returned home to lead and modernize the business. She managed six departments, implemented SOPs and contracts, and introduced new technologies like guard tour systems. Now Port Security Manager at Antigua Cruise Port, she says, "His leadership helped me propel the company forward," but adds that her approach brings a new, more modern lens to the work they both love.

Sean Komendat grew up watching his father, Dave Komendat, former Chief Security Officer at Boeing, work late into the night and travel the world. "I was intrigued by his work. It was serious, global, and purposeful," Sean recalls. After managing supply chain security at a large tech firm, he became a cybersecurity architect at Kirkland & Ellis, the world's largest law firm. He remembers attending a major security event with his father: "It filled my heart to see him in his element. I thought, 'This is exactly where I want to be.'" His father modeled daily leadership behaviors—greeting everyone, prioritizing people, and creating a strong professional brand. While Dave helped connect Sean with mentors, he encouraged him to find his own path. Now Sean bridges cyber and physical security, even helping his father with tech. "Because of him, I'm a student and people leader first. I try to be the calmest person in the room. His demeanor, his way of connecting, the strong brand he creates. I want to emulate that."

From coaching trees to organized mentoring networks to family role models, the principle is the same: great leaders build more leaders. They provide stretch opportunities, champion behind the scenes, and develop more than skill: they develop vision.

That's the legacy that outlives titles.

SIDEBAR: KINDLING THE SECURITY SPARK IN STUDENTS

(A Conversation with Ron Martin)

Ron Martin, a Vietnam veteran and former police officer, runs The Consullition Consultancy Coalition, a security consultancy based in Shreveport, Louisiana. He credits his early success to senior Army officers who pushed him to join ASIS International and earn his CPP. That push changed his life. "These guys put me in a position to excel," Martin says. "They all said, 'Don't forget the people who come up behind you.'"

He hasn't. Martin sponsors 40–45 students for ASIS membership annually, often out of his own pocket, and helps guide them into the security profession. "I'm very blessed," he says. "I like to give back."

He's a longtime supporter of the International Organization of Black Security Executives (IOBSE), which was formed when groups like ASIS were harder to access for women and people of color. Martin supports student programs at IOBSE events and makes connections. At one event, he introduced a student to the then-CSO of Microsoft, who offered her an internship on the spot. Another student, interested in policy, connected with the Security Industry Association's CEO and landed a similar opportunity.

Martin also walks students through the U.S. Department of Labor's (DOL) security career competency model. "Pick a field," he tells them. "Then go to the DOL occupational handbook and figure out what it takes to succeed in it." That becomes the basis for building their resume.

Through his nonprofit, he also runs a student affiliate program that introduces young people to security technologies like identity, credential, and access management as well as physical-logical access integration. One high school student he mentored designed a complete access control system as part of a hands-on lab project. When government visitors and systems integrators saw her explain the setup and respond to their technical questions, they were so impressed they offered her a job. She later graduated from Stanford and joined a Fortune 100 company.

Martin even earned a PhD in Technology in 2020 to motivate his granddaughters to pursue advanced education. "I didn't need it. I'm retired. But they told me, 'Well, you don't have one.' So, I got it—for bragging rights."

His message is simple: mentoring matters. "If I can sponsor 40 students, anyone can sponsor one."

Recognizing Others

The risk professions love awards. ASIS, SIA, the Electronic Security Association, and other associations bestow a bevy of awards annually to distinguished professionals and organizations. Martin Gill's OSPAs (the Outstanding Security Performance Awards) recognize exceptional managers, consultants, officers, manufacturers, and others across numerous countries. The Life Safety Alliance, where I've served as President for several years, celebrates the Top 40 Thought Leaders in Security and Life Safety. Multiple publications and associations spotlight rising young stars, outstanding women, and other standout professionals.

And let's not forget the Security Vanguard Awards, the British Security Awards, the Australian Security Awards, and countless cybersecurity honors.

Hollywood ain't got nothing on the security profession.

And that's not a bad thing.

The film, television, and music industries often take heat for their self-congratulatory nature. But most award recipients in those spaces are already celebrated by box office numbers, downloads, and ratings. The security industry, by contrast, works largely in the shadows—until something goes wrong. If any profession deserves to cheer itself on, even if few outsiders notice, it's security.

Awards in this space are more than vanity. They're a collective thank you. A recognition of work often done for emotional reward, not financial compensation.

I've nominated several colleagues for awards over the years. In 2025, I nominated a well-known and deserving colleague who had been passed over for previous awards. He was struggling with health issues at the time. When he learned that I nominated him, he called me and thanked me profusely, his voice quivering. Just nominating him meant so much to him. When colleagues win, it's immensely gratifying. But I get just as much satisfaction from simply hitting 'submit.' I'm proud of the honors I've received, but I'm even prouder of those I've helped recognize. Seeing a peer I admire get spotlighted, especially if they didn't see it coming, brings unmatched joy.

Mike Brzozowski, a corporate security executive for a major tech company, exemplifies the leadership it takes to support a nominee through the evaluation process. He has seen strong candidates lose on technicalities, or the perception that the person "isn't one of us" or came to the profession by an unusual route. Yet he redoubles his efforts to craft even more compelling nomination narratives. "We fall back on convenience," Brzozowski says. "We need to hold ourselves accountable for recognizing the best of our profession and not revert to a 'boys club' mentality," he says.

Brzozowski understands that the power of recognition is well documented. Gallup research links praise and acknowledgment to higher productivity, loyalty, engagement, and tenure. And in the security world, there's no higher praise than nominating a colleague or direct report for a respected award.

Of course, not all awards are equal. Avoid pay-to-play schemes that send you a trophy invoice along with the congratulations. (To be fair, many legitimate competitions charge entry fees to cover judging, logistics, and award materials.)

Some skeptics say awards are just logrolling or power plays. And yes, they can be—especially when the same small circle nominates and judges year after year. But the solution isn't cynicism. It's contribution. Leaders don't just critique; they elevate the process. They expand the pool, recommend diverse voices, and push for transparency. They improve systems from within.

That's why in 2024, the Life Safety Alliance launched a new kind of award: the Top 40 Thought Leaders in Security and Life Safety. It's not a popularity contest or a writing competition. It's based entirely on objective criteria: courses taught, articles published, keynotes delivered, board positions held, fellowships earned, and so on. Each is scored with a point system, then ranked by a proprietary algorithm. (More on the Top 40 later in this chapter.)

When considering candidates who deserve formal recognition, keep in mind that not every worthy contributor holds a C-suite title. Sometimes it's the analyst who caught a subtle breach, the officer who de-escalated a volatile situation, or the program manager who kept everything from falling apart. We need to trumpet those people—the professionals, teams, solutions, and innovations—who make our field better. The security and risk industries are evolving fast, and new talent emerges every year. As I was finalizing this manuscript, I nominated colleagues both the U.S. OSPAs and SecurityInfoWatch's Security Innovator Award.

Do likewise. Even if you're. Several won not sure your nomination will win, it tells someone their work matters. Recognizing others is a gift—to them, to the field, and to yourself. And sometimes the greatest satisfaction is nominating someone quietly, without their knowledge, then watching their name get called. Just be sure they're okay with the spotlight.

Recognition doesn't pay the rent, but it fuels the recipient and lifts up the profession.

Knowing Your Limits

As mentioned previously, security has the reputation of being the "Department of 'No.'" No, that risk is too great. No, we can't take the chance. No, the likelihood of failure is too high. But many of us in the profession believe that the role of the security executive is not to say "no," but to lay out the risks, costs, organizational appetite, and other relevant factors, and then let the business or asset owner make an informed decision whether to proceed.

But when it comes to our own decisions—about our time, energy, and capacity—sometimes "no" is exactly the right answer.

We are innate helpers, protectors, and doers. We want to prove our value, pull our weight, support the team. But saying no appropriately and strategically goes to the heart of sustainable leadership.

I should know. I've never mastered it. At one point, over a few days, I was writing four articles (for four different publications), prepping a keynote to deliver in Spanish, helping to publish an industry standard, advising a colleague on opening a business, and helping two security professionals wordsmith their resumes and find job prospects, all while running my own security consulting business and trying to fit in a workout routine. I delivered, but afterward I needed a full weekend to decompress: NFL football, silence, and zero obligations.

When can you turn down a professional request? I asked two colleagues to weigh in: a C-suite advisor and a corporate security executive.

"I have to admit, I also struggle with saying no," says Angela Scalpello, a corporate advisor who works closely with security leaders. She's developed a system for evaluating requests. "I ask for more time. Then I sit with the feeling of 'how will I feel if I say yes?' If it's overwhelmed, or stressed, or slightly resentful, I know I need to say no." She pauses again before making the final call. "Then I sit again, and if I feel I need to make time, I feel more guided."

What about guilt? The fear of letting someone down?

"Sometimes I think, 'Why is everyone else allowed to say no except me?'". But the ability to choose wisely makes us more effective in the things we say yes to."

Farhad Tajali, a security executive at Creative Artists Agency, acknowledges that saying yes is often viewed as collaborative and business friendly. But boundaries matter. "Saying no may be a way to uphold standards and protocols, prevent overextension of resources, and protect against security threats that may arise from taking on too many projects and commitments," he says. "It also helps maintain strategic focus, ensuring the organization's security posture aligns with its goals and risk tolerance."

Saying yes to everyone and everything takes a toll. "Self-care, especially in [the security and risk management] professions, is really important," Scalpello emphasizes. "Saying yes to yourself is critical, and you only have time to say that if you give yourself permission to say no to others."

Letting someone down is easier if you don't make it personal. If your boss asks you to take on a project outside your core responsibilities, try framing your response this way: express concern that you might not be able to deliver at your usual level of excellence given other priorities. In that case, saying no actually protects the department and the organization.

For external requests—co-presenting at a conference, job search help, mentoring—Scalpello offers this guiding question: "Do I really believe in the person and the purpose, and do I really have the bandwidth to do this?"

Knowing your limits doesn't diminish your leadership. It defines it.

Self-Care

Self care merits its own discussion as an essential aspect of effective leadership. In fact, two of the four domains of Daniel Goleman's emotional intelligence involve self-care: self-awareness and self-management. Goleman contends that you can't be emotionally intelligent if you can't recognize and regulate your own feelings.

Meet Tanya Spencer, a security consultant and trainer extraordinaire whom I met in Montreux, Switzerland, in 2009 at the ASIS Europe Conference. She was a dynamic and engaging presenter, an American woman of color living in Denmark, winning over a crowd of buttoned-up European men.

We crossed paths again at ASIS Europe in London, where she gave a presentation on communicating security without fear. Though we lost touch, her style and message stuck with me.

Fast forward to the COVID-19 pandemic, when I was posting Kindness Games videos highlighting people who had inspired me. In a video dedicated to colleagues from Scandinavia, I called out Tanya. She messaged me days later, deeply touched. Her business had stalled, and she was personally struggling.

With Tanya's permission and feedback, I assembled her story in her own words. They speak for themselves.

I felt like I was burning out but my skin was holding me up.

I started in human rights and peacebuilding in the 1980s, which brought me into security. During the war in Yugoslavia, while leading a team raising awareness of human rights issues in Kosovo, I was interrogated by five policemen and expelled from the country.

After that, I joined a training on nonviolence and convinced the facilitators to let me lead a 12-hour role play on security for peace workers. It was so successful, they hired me. I began working with Peace Brigades International and other organizations.

After getting a master's, I joined the Overseas Development Institute. A colleague there was writing a book on NGO security, focused on physical gear. But no one discussed what I specialized in: active listening, de-escalation, and community relations.

By the time emotional intelligence became trendy, I was already training in it. My background wasn't military or police—I approached security through human rights.

In 2000, I returned to Denmark with my husband and launched my training and consulting business. I became well known in NGO circles and gradually began working with governments and the UN. I traveled constantly, training in capitals around the world.

But I pushed too hard for too long. In 2013, while writing my second book, I began to spiral. Secretly, I started chain-smoking. I traveled for work up to nine months a year, while my family life disintegrated.

When I was home, I performed the role of responsible parent and spouse. When alone, I unraveled.

I'd drive on the freeway and close my eyes to see how fast I could go. I got up to 150 kph (90 mph). I'd dare myself to turn the wheel without looking. It made me feel something.

When I asked for a divorce, I did it through a bullet-point meeting agenda. I boxed my things and walked out.

My social network vanished. All my friends were through my husband. With more time, I worked harder—and crashed harder.

I was depressed. I'd crawl into bed after work and stay there. On my birthday, I shut down my business and filed for unemployment. I sobbed.

I re-opened and closed the business multiple times. I went back to school and earned a second master's in intercultural communication, hoping to pursue a PhD. Then the pandemic hit, and scholarship opportunities vanished.

I felt stuck.

Toward the end of 2024, I was overwhelmed. I was doing consulting to pay the bills while trying to launch a coaching company. The pressure became too much. My resilience rituals slipped.

Then I hit a wall.

A coach friend gave me a choice: give up or rebuild. "The pain is coming from your indecision," she said. That line stayed with me.

Around that time, I was diagnosed with Attention Deficit Disorder. It explained the highs and crashes. My usual coping strategies weren't working. I needed new foundations.

So I built them. Slowly. I cut alcohol, changed my sleep, limited social media. I cleaned my space and quieted my mind. I journaled daily and repeated affirmations. I said no to draining obligations.

It was a hard climb. But necessary.

Tanya's Nonnegotiables for Recovery

- Daily affirmations
- Clean, organized home environment
- Limited social media
- Alcohol-free lifestyle
- Restorative, consistent sleep routine
- Daily journaling
- Morning visualization
- Walking and regular movement
- Ruthless elimination of energy-draining obligations

Here was someone I admired as a world-class leader. Yet at her lowest, she could barely lead herself to the toilet.

Her story is a warning and an inspiration. Many high-functioning leaders in security and risk operate on empty tanks, masking exhaustion as excellence. But if they fall, everything around them—their missions, teams, and companies—suffers too.

Tanya isn't finished yet. She's rebuilding, coaching, and reemerging. And if she was that impactful before, just imagine the force she'll be now.

Because in the end, no leader can give their best to others if they're running on empty.

From the Lips of Gips: "Curiosity killed the cat. So what? It's got eight more lives."

6
What Great Leaders Are Made of, Part III

Critical Thinking

In his 2005 book *Thinking for a Change: 11 Ways Highly Successful People Approach Life and Work,* John Maxwell articulates six types of critical thinking skills:

- Big Picture Thinking: Moving beyond your specific issue and considering the broader ramifications.
- Realistic Thinking: Grounding thinking in truth and possibility.
- Strategic Thinking: Having a plan to think through relevant issues and themes.
- Focused Thinking: Concentrating your thinking on the most important issues and removing distractions.
- Unselfish Thinking: Focusing on adding value to others.
- Bottom-Line Thinking: Thinking about what has to occur to accomplish your ultimate goals.

In the age of disinformation, when algorithms feeding us half-truths, exaggerations, and specious information divebomb us via social media and the Internet, perhaps we should add a seventh critical thinking skill to Maxwell's typology: BS-Detection Thinking.

Security Management Resources CEO Jerry Brennan has been tracking leadership traits of security executives for decades, and he says critical thinking has fallen by the wayside. "We don't train people growing up to do this," he says. "And we are bombarding them with BS on social media. They are learning to get their information in ways that are fundamentally flawed."

When I look at my Reels on Facebook, it feeds me a steady stream of material that it knows I like. I see detailed arguments or discussions that only reinforce my existing point of view and further embed me in my echo chamber.

DOI: 10.1201/9781003646488-9

If you dare to conduct your own research, watch out. "You have to ask the right questions, even if you are a trained investigator," says Brennan. The kicker, he says, is "You are now interviewing the algorithms of AI." It's critical to validate the sources you use, as well as the sources of those sources, the sources of those sources of those sources, and so on.

Security is largely about people and the psychology of people. It's about anticipating human behavior and how it will affect your organization. That requires critical thinking to know what information you need, where to obtain it from, and how to assess it.

Here's how to sharpen your critical thinking:

- Ask where information is coming from and why
  - What is the source of the information?
  - How is the information being conveyed?
  - What is the motive of the author/provider?
  - How reliable is the source?
  - Why is the information being conveyed at this specific time?
- Verify digital content with independent sources
- Create a culture of healthy skepticism
- Gather and assess multilevel intelligence
  - HUMINT
  - OSINT
  - SIGINT
  - Behavioral
  - Technical analysis, such as forensics
- Train your team in critical thinking and cognitive biases

As veteran CSO Don Taussig puts it, "Your greatest asset as a security director isn't your badge, your clearance, or your tech stack. It's your ability to think clearly in chaos, to ask better questions, and to lead your team through the noise."

Inspiration: Speeches, Messaging, and Momentum

> We shall fight on the beaches, we shall fight on the landing grounds, we shall fight in the fields and in the streets, we shall fight in the hills; we shall never surrender.
>
> *Winston Churchill (1940)*

> I have never lost an American in space, sure as hell aren't going to lose one now. This crew is coming home. You got to believe it. Your team must believe it. And we must make it happen.
>
> *Gene Kranz (1970)*

> Mr. Gorbachev, open this gate! Mr. Gorbachev, tear down this wall!
>
> *Ronald Reagan (1987)*

Three classic examples of oratory that make you want to run through a wall for the speaker—the Berlin Wall, in the final example.

Security leaders aren't expected to be poets, but words can save lives, restore morale, and realign teams. From Churchill to Kranz to Reagan, we remember the great speeches because they didn't just fill a room. They moved people to act.

So how and when should a security or risk professional rally their team with words without sounding performative, hollow, or bombastic? Below are eight principles offered by seasoned security professionals who've both delivered and received powerful messages.

Use Speeches Sparingly, Not Routinely

Motivational speeches lose their force if overused. "A good pep talk is best when it's actually needed, like at the start of a big project or when the team is under pressure," says Farah Benis, managing director of a security company in the United Kingdom. Former pharmaceutical CSO Rich Widup adds, "You can overdo motivational speeches to the point they don't resonate anymore."

Cadisha Miceli, senior security coordinator at the City of Toronto, keeps speeches rare, but motivation constant. "I'm always praising their work. I hardly ever work from home. I'm there day to day, reinforcing values and giving them feedback," she says.

Root It in Who You Are

The best speeches are extensions of the speaker's true beliefs. "If you're just trying to manufacture a 'motivational moment,' people will see right through it," says Benis. "Speak with conviction, and back it up with action." GardaWorld Regional Manager Chris Anquist echoes: "If you don't mean it, don't say it."

Tell the Truth, Even When It Hurts

Authenticity isn't just tone, it's content. "People skew speeches to cover up what's lurking in the background," Widup says. "If the topic is negative, acknowledge the reality. Don't whitewash it."

Earn the Right to Inspire

Dr. Gavriel Schneider, CEO of Risk 2 Solution, recalls delivering a pep talk after winning a contract during the waning days of COVID-19. His speech landed because he'd built trust and credibility during the pandemic. That's leadership capital earned by showing fairness, empathy, and consistency over time.

Script with Soul, Not Stiffness

"You have to be disciplined. Never improvise complex speeches," says Anquist. But beware of over-rehearsing. Oratory works when it blends message with mood. If you have the natural ability to speak with passion and tell stories, use it, Schneider advises.

Benis prefers to stay light on planning: "If you know your team and understand what drives them, you can speak to what actually matters."

Read the Room

Addressing security officers is different from addressing a boardroom—or a volunteer team at a professional organization. Know what matters to your audience, Widup urges.

Schneider references the Tribal Leadership model. Motivational speeches resonate most with staff in "Stage 4" ("we're great") and "Stage 5" ("life is great"). At lower stages, where people feel disengaged or self-important, speeches often fall flat. Recognition or individual attention may work better.

Mission Is the Message

"Why are we doing this?" is a crucial component of every good speech. Anquist teaches leaders to focus on three elements: (1) What's the main problem? (2) What do we do about it? (3) Why does it matter? The last one is about mission. "That's the hill you die on," he says.

Honor the Work and the Road Ahead

Effective speeches respect the audience's effort and reality. "It's not about sugarcoating," says Benis. "It's about giving people confidence they can finish the job."

Praising team efforts, acknowledging the challenges ahead, and reminding people of the bigger picture builds connection and resilience.

And me? I've delivered my share of speeches in tough times. But I still wait for the golden opportunity to end one with:

> And the last thing he said to me—'Rock,' he said—'sometime, when the team is up against it—and the breaks are beating the boys—tell them to go out there with all they got and win just one for the Gipper.'
>
> *Knute Rockne (1928)*

Day-to-Day Inspiration

Motivational speeches work best when they punctuate, not replace, a regular rhythm of vision, values, and reinforcement. As Columbia Business School Professor Adam Galinsky points out, repetition of core messages builds trust and clarity.

In a Stanford study cited in *Harvard Business Review* (March–April 2025), leaders were found to be 10 times more likely to be criticized for undercommunicating than for overcommunicating. The lesson? Say the right things often. Say them clearly. And mean them every time.

Day-to-day inspiration is not about fanfare. It's about being a leader whose presence, visible or virtual, reminds the team what matters.

Here are a few ways that seasoned leaders maintain motivation through everyday behaviors:

> I take 15 minutes every Monday to call someone on my team and tell them something they did well the week before. It's personal, it's specific, and it builds loyalty more than any teamwide email ever could.

***

Every shift, I walk the floor. Not to micromanage, but to be visible. If I miss a day, I hear about it. That tells me it matters.

***

During onboarding, I ask new team members what motivates them—recognition, challenges, stability, career growth—and I write it down. I try to tailor how I interact with them based on that.

***

Once a quarter, I share a failure of mine with the team and what I learned from it. It shows them it's okay to stumble, and that resilience is part of the job.

These aren't dramatic moments, but they inspire by showing consistency, attention, humility, and care. When the moment does come for a rallying cry, you won't need to force it. You'll have earned it.

Kindness/Empathy

To paraphrase Niccolò Machiavelli, it's better to be feared than to be loved, if one cannot be both. Five centuries later, that philosophy persists in parts of the security world. Historically drawn from law enforcement or the military, many corporate security leaders transferred their intimidating command-and-control approach to the private sector. Being too nice could get you labeled "soft" or "weak."

But that mindset is changing. In fact, research by psychologist Daniel Goleman identifies empathy as one of the core components of emotional intelligence—a skillset tied to leadership effectiveness, trust, and long-term performance. Kindness, far from being a liability, is now recognized as a leadership differentiator.

Yet, resistance persists. Perhaps the one exception to the rule of guarded professionalism is the five or so weeks between Thanksgiving and New Year's, when everyone is expected to be grateful and pleasant at minimum. What if that could be the case year-round?

Newer leadership principles that prize attributes such as empathy have eroded the old hardline approach to management somewhat. But plenty of managers and leaders still warily eye colleagues who seem too friendly or upbeat.

Witness some of the backlash to an initiative called The Kindness Games, in which practitioners of security and other fields publicly praise colleagues, notably in videos posted on LinkedIn. (I participated in The Kindness Games, having posted more than 60 videos.) No one said a single negative thing to me about my posts (except for the occasional joke about how colleagues couldn't escape my face on LinkedIn), but others were warned that such behavior is bad for their career. And most of those cautioned, from what I have heard, have been young women.

Perhaps it's the stereotype that young women are eager to please in a male-dominated profession, or that they will be seen as too irresolute to deal with difficult situations such as angry employees or underperforming direct reports.

Kelsey Carnell, one of the founders of The Kindness Games and a regional sales manager for a major surveillance camera manufacturer, has faced criticism for her buoyant personality. "People ask whether you're forsaking your job or they think that you are being insincere to make a sale," she says. "There's a whole connotation that kindness is sunshine, rainbows and unicorns, and that it is fake." But for her, an outgoing, positive attitude represents a major part of her so-called "authentic self."

Carnell knows of two female colleagues whose bosses advised them not to partake in the games. They took that admonition to heart for fear of their jobs.

Young professionals of all genders have been asked rhetorically, "Do you really want to be known as a kind security professional?" says Tim Wenzel, a work colleague of mine and another original member of the group that introduced the games. "The implication is that if you value your career, you'll stop."

A third cofounder, Mexico-based security risk management executive Lee Oughton, worries about a profession that drives out budding superstars. "You shouldn't be demoralizing your talent," he warns. "It infuses a narcissistic and toxic environment."

Oughton adds that by muzzling kindness, security businesses are passing up revenue and security departments are depriving themselves of an effective tool. For example, Oughton notes that Carnell's personality helped make her the top salesperson in her region. And Wenzel says that kindness and empathy during the termination process make the departing employee feel much less aggrieved, reducing the potential for violence and helping departing staff members feel they've been treated respectfully.

"Kindness is not fluffy," Wenzel insists. "We need to manage situations by looking at how can we serve people with empathy."

And The Kindness Games has expanded beyond its roots in the security field, which the founders see as an antidote to today's toxicity and culture wars. "We are in the middle of an 'ideological Hunger Games,'" Wenzel contends. "Kindness transcends that. The philosophy of leading with kindness is game changing for anyone in the professional world."

The movement developed during the Great Resignation, as the world's workers reconsidered their priorities in light of the COVID-19 pandemic, and many workers are holding fast to these changes. Years after the pandemic ended, many offices are still half empty. Companies that reimpose yesterday's rules and attitudes risk losing their burgeoning talent to organizations that will listen to their voices.

But kindness and empathy in the workplace didn't begin, or end, with a social media initiative. Danielle Weddepohl, head of public safety at a college in Toronto, reminds us that kindness used to be part of the daily rhythm of work, not a special event or public gesture.

"Some acts of kindness are an offshoot of us being polite, others are larger and more impactful," she notes, "but they all mean taking time for another person."

Weddepohl reflects on her early years working 12-hour shifts in security. What she remembers most isn't the tedium or the protocols. It's the warmth of those long shifts: sharing chats, coffee, and homemade food with thoughtful people from different cultures. "It broadened our understanding of the world, and humanity in general," she recalls. Those connections not only built friendships, but they also strengthened team cohesion and the drive to protect others.

She laments the loss of spontaneous connection in today's fast-paced workplace. "We have moved away from shooting the breeze… do most businesses even have watercoolers anymore?" In the past, watercooler talk didn't just fill time. It fostered informal learning, built empathy, and sparked creativity. "Some of the best ideas percolated there."

Rather than labeling small thoughtful gestures and conversations as extraordinary acts of kindness, Weddepohl suggests we reclaim them as essential. "This practice of caring about other people's lives and finding commonalities ... should be part of a normal day."

Especially in diverse security teams, these conversations help dismantle bias, navigate trauma, and build community. "It's important for your team to see shooting the breeze as an important and regular activity which not only makes kindness blossom but also helps them in developing their investigative and customer service skills," she says. Not insignificantly, a warm, inquisitive team is more likely to uncover the truth in sensitive cases.

For security professionals still skeptical, empathy doesn't mean coddling. It means understanding people's perspectives, reading emotional cues, and adjusting your response in a way that reinforces trust.

Examples of empathetic leadership include:

- Recognizing personal milestones like birthdays or life events.
- Asking "How are you?" and pausing long enough to hear the answer.
- Framing critical feedback in terms of growth rather than failure.
- Modeling vulnerability by admitting mistakes.

These aren't signs of weakness. They're signs of confidence and emotional maturity.

The most respected leaders today don't separate high standards from human connection. They tie them together. Because when employees feel seen, heard, and respected, they perform better, stay longer, and speak more candidly. And in the security field, that candor could make all the difference.

You're never too young to be an empathetic leader. Consider the case of Ria Sethi, who between her freshman and junior years at Monta Vista High School in California, created an organization called Cyber for Youth. It isn't a collection of coding aficionados. It's a group dedicated to raising awareness of and eliminating cyberbullying.

Sethi tells me that she was cyberbullied on social media during her freshman year before finals, including comments on her appearance. "It was an anonymous account under the school's name," she says, "and it would post anything." It even posted her home address and urged students to shoot her.

When the account started going after her younger brother, Sethi had had enough. Even though she was discouraged by the school administration and law enforcement, she jumped into action, determined to create her own anti-cyberbullying initiative even before the particulars had crystallized in her mind.

The initiative immediately received backlash, with classmates saying that she was bringing the bullying on herself. At that point, "I saw that the community didn't recognize this as a real problem, and that had to change," she says.

The program, launched in August 2024, is completely teenager-led, tailoring its messages to different demographics, including elementary school students, parents, and senior citizens.

I asked her if she considered herself a natural leader and what her leadership superpower is. "My leadership is being able to empathize but not being super-loud about things but helping other people share," she says.

No way would I have had the wherewithal, strength, or ability to do the same at her age.

SIDEBAR: THE PREDICATE TO KINDNESS: CARING

True kindness is impossible without caring. Caring about people, experiences, concerns, criticisms, reputation, performance, quality. And when I think of caring in the security and risk fields, one name jumps to mind: Paul Moxness.

Why? His motto is "Always care," and he proves it every day. His 2021 book *Spin the Bottle Service: Hospitality in the Age of AI*, cowritten with his wife Kirsten, doesn't have the word "leadership" in the title, or in much of the text, for that matter. But it's a brilliant, example-laden primer on leadership in the hospitality industry, covering many of the issues I address in this book: teams, recognition, cultural differences, communication, and gratitude. (By the way, the title has nothing to do with the teen kissing game popular in the second half of last century. It refers to how a waiter in Brussels would deftly twist a beer bottle so the diner could read the label.)

Kirsten and Paul end the book with the line, "Hospitality: It's about the people, period." That's a good way of looking at risk management, too.

Future Focus

The final chapter in this book addresses leading into the future, which naturally would include focusing on future possibilities, trends, and developments. But focusing on the future is an essential attribute for today's leaders as well, which is why it appears here.

Recent history is littered with examples of thriving companies secure in their market position with a reactive, myopic approach to business. Kodak dug in on their film business as digital photography was about to take off. Blockbuster spurned Netflix's overture to be acquired for a mere $50 million. Nokia shrugged off the onset of smartphones with touchscreens and app ecosystems. Sears, Toys "R" Us, and Borders stuck with brick and mortar over "click and order."

"The future doesn't always knock politely," says Dave Cohen, Sydney, Australia-based deputy CEO of Risk 2 Solution. "Sometimes, it shows up in jeans with a pitch deck, and you laugh. Future scanning isn't about predicting the next trend. It's about cultivating a mindset that questions assumptions, explores signals, and bets on change before it becomes obvious."

That's a good description, but it's also exceedingly difficult to accomplish. For example, it seems like a safe bet to invest in AI—but when, how, and to what extent? How quickly or completely do you transition? In hindsight, it seems obvious that e-commerce would rival physical retail stores, that rideshares would challenge—and, in some places, all but replace—taxi cabs, and that cloud-based platforms would displace on-premises software and applications. But if it were that obvious, thousands of companies would have pivoted and still be in business today.

I asked Dave how to succeed at future planning and future scanning.

"First, let's not confuse horizon scanning with future scanning," he says. "Horizon scanning focuses on identifying what's coming. Future scanning goes further. It's about building the capacity to act before change arrives."

He says that future scanning demands curiosity, imagination, and risk intelligence, a term coined by Dr. Gavriel Schneider. "Risk intelligence is a living skill, one that must constantly evolve to keep pace with changing environments, and an applied attribute. Adopting a future scanning mindset also helps us distinguish weak signals from background noise, allowing us to detect small shifts early—shifts we can act on before they become major disruptions. It's the concept of zooming out to zoom in: instead of fixating on KPIs, isolated risks, or local issues, we look at broader forces: global trends, technological change, geopolitical developments, social movements, and environmental signals."

Of course, that's a mere mental exercise absent action. "Future scanning must inform strategic choices, scenario planning, and capability development. Without linking insight to execution, we're no better off than when we started," Cohen emphasizes.

To my mind, future focus doesn't mean predicting the future. I'm not that foolish. It means being attuned to emerging technologies, social trends, scientific discoveries, economic factors, population shifts, political movements, communication tools, and rising leaders. It's being curious, knowledgeable, thoughtful, and agile and putting yourself in a situation where you can imagine multiple future states and act accordingly.

Ethical Grounding

In what has to be one of the most bizarre and disturbing cases involving corporate security in the history of that function, in 2020 security executives at eBay pled guilty to charges involving cyberstalking, intimidating, and strongarming a Natick, Massachusetts, couple. The couple had been publishing a newsletter about online auctions that had criticized eBay.

Here's the Department of Justice's description of eBay security's activity. Remember, this was carried out by eBay's Senior Director of Safety and Security and six other members of the department in a multibillion-dollar corporation, not by an organized crime group or gang:

> [The director of safety and security and his staff's] campaign included sending anonymous and disturbing deliveries to the victims' home, including a book on surviving the death of a spouse, a bloody pig mask, a fetal pig and a funeral wreath and live insects; sending private Twitter messages and public tweets criticizing the newsletter's content and threatening to visit the victims in Natick; and traveling to Natick to

> surveil the victims and install a GPS tracking device on their car. The harassment also featured Craigslist posts inviting the public for sexual encounters at the victims' home.

Media reports also said that pornographic magazines, including *Hustler: Barely Legal*, with the husband's name on them were intentionally sent to neighbors' addresses. The couple also suddenly began receiving dozens of publications with names like *Sin City Fetish Night Newsletter* and *Irritable Bowel Syndrome News*, and a company running sex-toy stores called after being told that the couple were interested in opening a franchise.

The online auction company ended up forking over $3 million to the victims, and the culprits received criminal sentences ranging from a year of home confinement to 57 months in federal prison.

Not all unethical behavior is that drastic, but it's not hard to find, either. Jerry Brennan, who has been in security for almost 50 years, most of it as a recruiter, believes unethical behavior has been increasing in recent decades. He says that the most common transgressions are fraud, sexual harassment, kickbacks, resume padding and misrepresentation, and just poor ethical choices.

Consider the case of Apple, which in 2011 was dealing with the disappearance of a confidential iPhone prototype ahead of a major product launch. The company's security team located the device at a private residence and conducted what many described as an intimidating recovery operation. Reports claimed Apple's team may have misrepresented themselves as law enforcement and offered hush money in cash.

The prototype was retrieved, but the questionable means of doing so led to significant fallout. Shortly after, Apple's security leadership saw internal shakeups and departures.

It may be a cliché, but corporate ethics flows down from the top. Executives who cut corners or operate in ethically murky zones develop or attract underlings who do likewise. As longtime CSO Don Taussig puts it, "The question isn't whether your team will face ethical dilemmas. It's whether you've built a culture strong enough to handle them with integrity."

In at least the eBay case, security acted with Machiavellian ends-justify-the means arrogance. Lack of oversight in each example led to abuse of power, so that the department charged with managing risk became the source of risk itself.

Brennan, Taussig, and others offer the following lessons in security and risk ethics.

1. **You Are Stewards of Trust, Not Enforcers of Ego**
   Security leaders are entrusted with authority. How you use it defines your credibility. Your job is to protect, not intimidate.
2. **The Ends Never Justify Unethical Means**
   Whether it's protecting IP, the brand, or executives, once you cross legal or ethical lines, you become a threat to the organization.
3. **Power Without Accountability Leads to Crisis**
   Most scandals happen not because of poor policies but because no one asked tough questions or dared to say "no." Build systems that check your own power.
4. **Legal ≠ Ethical**
   Just because you *can* do something doesn't mean you *should.* Ethics fills the gap between the letter of the law and doing what's right.
5. **The Culture You Tolerate Is the Culture You Own**
   If your team sees unethical shortcuts rewarded or misconduct ignored, don't be surprised when small violations turn into big scandals.
6. **Internal Oversight Is Your Best Defense**
   Collaborate with Legal, HR, and Compliance. Ethical security leadership requires cross-functional guardrails and real-time accountability.
7. **Reputation Is a Security Asset**
   An ethical failure in security damages more than operations; it shatters trust with employees, regulators, and the public.
8. **Lead by Example, Especially under Pressure**
   When tensions are high (data leaks, whistleblowers, bad press), your response sets the tone for your entire department. Choose ethics, not expediency.

Learning from Failure

George Washington, the father of the United States, was a fraud. Not really, but over the centuries we have whitewashed the shortcomings of perhaps America's greatest president, general, and citizen. He surrendered at Fort Necessity during the French and Indian War. He succumbed in a string of battles early in the Revolutionary War, including losing New York to the British. He struggled with public oratory. He was known as a poor tactician. But he obviously learned from his mistakes and became the exemplar we know today.

All the greatest leaders in history have had forgettable or disgraceful episodes. Many of them are documented in hilarious and erudite fashion in the long-running web series *Epic Rap Battles of History*, where the likes of Shaka Zulu, Julius Caesar, Abraham Lincoln, and Che Guevara square off to humiliate each other using inventive freestyle verse.

Here's an excerpt from an episode with Mansa Musa and Jeff Bezos:

Mansa: I expanded horizons with libraries and mosques/While you chopped the top off of all the mom and pop shops/All you widened was the gap between the haves and have-nots/Now they ordering a living in your cardboard box!

Jeff: You're overrated like you leave economies inflated/You're about to taste some of that salt that you traded/.../Three years to trek to Mecca? Man, you must be trippin'/One click, I'll get you there overnight with free shippin'!

And from Richard the Lionheart vs. Ragnar Lodbrok:

Richard: Your own story ended worse than Game of Thrones/Your son killed your ex, your ex killed your wife/I'm the Lion King, man, but that's a messed up circle of life.

Ragnar: You went from chainmail to chained up in jail / 'Til Mommy drained England to pay for your bail!

The point is: Even the most legendary figures got things wrong. Some people say you must fail to succeed. I'm not convinced of that.

Phrases like "fail fast, fail often" have become common mantras in business, especially in tech circles. But they often miss the mark. No one sets out to fail—we set out to try something bold and hope it works. When it doesn't, we learn. So yes, we should take informed risks, iterate quickly, and grow from setbacks. But let's not romanticize failure for its own sake.

Failure is only useful when it leads to learning and change. The goal isn't to fail fast. It's to learn fast. That's what distinguishes resilient leadership from reckless risk-taking.

Early in my security journalism career, I wrote a case study about a major U.S. railroad that was using a tool to forecast localized weather incidents. I interviewed the railroad's personnel, who were enthusiastic about the product. But I chose not to interview the product provider.

Why? I was concerned they'd try to influence the editorial process or request to review the story before publication, a line we would not cross. I feared they'd push for glowing treatment. So I excluded them. I wrote what I thought was a vivid, accurate narrative based on the end user's experience, and the piece landed on the cover.

Then the phone rang.

My editor received a furious call from the provider. The article had relied on the railroad's terminology and understanding of the tool, which turned out to be flawed. It used imprecise language like "cloudburst" and mischaracterized key features. The provider had been left out of their own story. Left out in the cold and rain, so to speak.

We had to run a correction, nearly three-quarters of a page long. For a publication where errata rarely exceeded a paragraph, it was a professional black eye.

My mistake was clear: in trying not to be manipulated, I had overcorrected and disrespected the provider's expertise. I put faith in secondhand technical understanding when I should have confirmed the details with the people who built the product.

There was a middle path, and I missed it. I could have engaged them respectfully, clarified expectations, and ensured accuracy, without giving up editorial control.

That experience stuck with me. Since then, I've committed to having the hard conversations up front, inviting input from all relevant parties, and never letting fear or expediency make my decisions for me.

SIDEBAR: RULES, LISTS, AND LEADERSHIP LORE: USE WITH CAUTION

Say this, not that. Read that, not this. Do this, not that.

You too can become a great leader if you simply follow the endless exhortations of online leadership lists.

The web is awash in advice: the five phrases great leaders never say, the eight habits of highly productive executives, the 17 best leadership books, the ten foods, seven hats, or 12 catchphrases that will unlock your inner CEO. These lists can be penetratingly wise, breezily entertaining, or infuriatingly dogmatic, sometimes all at once. Most are subjective, ahistorical, devoid of context, or just clickbait.

Still, people cling to them. We crave clarity. We like commandments.

So let's examine the "rules," both informal and enshrined, and what happens when they collide with real-world leadership.

"Phrases Leaders Should Never Say"—Really?

Take these alleged leadership verbal missteps:

- "I don't know"

  Critics say it makes leaders look unprepared or weak. But used sparingly and strategically, "I don't know" can be powerful: honest, disarming, even inspiring. It invites collaboration and shows humility.
- "I'll do it myself"

  Often dismissed as micromanaging or impatient. But when spoken calmly with the right intonation, especially for scut work or unclaimed tasks, it can be servant leadership at its best. Some security executives fill in for absent officers during overnight shifts after a full workday.
- "It's good enough"

  Supposedly a concession to mediocrity. But it can also reflect strategic pragmatism. "Don't let perfect be the enemy of the good" is a more generous translation, and often the wiser path when chasing perfection means wasting time, morale, or money.

These phrases aren't inherently weak. Like all languages, their impact depends on tone, timing, and trust.

The Ten Commandments of Leadership

If leadership had a sacred tablet, it might include these:

1. Lead via influence, not authority
2. Display a bias for action
3. Credit success to others, accept blame personally
4. Act with integrity
5. Have a vision and inspire others with it
6. Trust and empower your team

7. Practice and encourage continuous learning
8. Keep things simple
9. Embrace failure
10. Surround yourself with people smarter than you

They're sensible. Inspirational. I've devoted whole chapters to some of them. But are they always right?

- "Surround yourself with people smarter than you"
  Ideal in theory. In practice, some executives fear being outshone. One risk management VP confided, "If my boss sees they're smarter than me, I could be replaced." He hired bright talent, but only in non-core areas.
- "Credit success to others, accept blame yourself"
  Noble. But sometimes weaponized. A cybersecurity VP named Lydia took blame for minor staff errors and praised her team's wins. Her rival used this to poison her reputation with the CEO. Lydia left; the rival was eventually fired, but the damage stuck.
- "Bias for action"
  Fast, decisive, entrepreneurial, great in the right context. But it can also be a cognitive bias, driving impulsive decisions absent good data. one major retailer learned this when a theft-prevention system backfired: shopping carts locked mid-parking-lot, and the viral video backlash cost them reputational capital.

Leadership principles, like George Orwell's six rules of writing, are useful until they become dogma. Orwell's final rule:

"Break any of these rules sooner than say anything outright barbarous."

Chapters 4–6 Takeaways: Leadership Qualities and Styles

- Risk leadership success depends as much on emotional intelligence and integrity as it does on technical skills or domain expertise.
- Effective communicators inspire clarity and unity of purpose, even in crisis or complexity.
- Curiosity and humility fuel personal growth, inclusive leadership, and the capacity to admit and learn from failure.
- Courage and conviction empower risk leaders to make tough calls, champion ethical choices, and shoulder responsibility.

- Building trust through empathy, service, and consistent behavior fosters loyalty, performance, and a culture of accountability.
- Humor can humanize risk leaders and foster trust, but must be used judiciously.
- Influence is often more powerful than formal authority, requiring trust, strategic relationships, and business fluency.
- Leadership trees matter—like in sports, security and risk leaders leave a legacy by mentoring rising professionals.
- Leaders must protect staff from being paralyzed by failure, fostering psychological safety while holding accountability.
- Saying "no" strategically is a leadership skill that preserves effectiveness and prevents burnout.
- Inspirational speeches must be rare, real, and resonant, rooted in authenticity and mission rather than rhetoric.
- Empathy and kindness are powerful leadership tools, not liabilities, even in high-stakes professions like security.
- Leadership includes knowing how to assess, challenge, and apply advice, even questioning truisms like "fail fast" or "hire smarter."

From the Lips of Gips: "Leadership is 1% inspiration, 1% perspiration, and 98% tribulation."

BREAKAWAY III
Risk Leadership Lessons in Television Ads

I hate TV commercials until I don't. Some are high art and are better than the shows they disrupt. Among the best are those that demonstrate the most powerful lessons in leadership. They are worth showing to aspiring leaders; the ads may even serve as templates for your own leadership messages and media. Here, in ascending order, are my top ten.

10. Barbie, "You Can Be Anything" (2023–2024)

Description

A little girl gives a pep talk to a football team. Another lectures a college classroom. A third brushes dust from a dinosaur skull. The camera lingers just long enough for us to realize that none of this is pretend. These girls are doing the things they've imagined, things they've rehearsed in bedrooms and backyards for years, and the inspiration was 11 inches tall, plastic, and improbably proportioned. The ad ends with the quiet assertion that Barbie has held over 200 careers, and her influence is just beginning.

DOI: 10.1201/9781003646488-10

Leadership Lessons

Representation doesn't just reflect the world; it reshapes it. We talk about leadership pipelines, but this is where they start. Leaders who inspire others to dream, even before they know what leadership is, leave the deepest mark.

9. Uber, "Thank You for Not Riding" (2020)

Description

It opens on an empty city. Streets that once bustled are still. Then: a boy builds a fort out of couch cushions. A woman celebrates her birthday alone with a slice of cake and a video call. Neighbors wave across rooftops. Couples slow-dance in their kitchens. Grandparents peer out from windows. The ad ends with the simplest, strangest message a business can deliver: "Thank you for not riding with Uber."

Leadership Lessons

True leadership means putting principle over profit. Uber told us not to use its service—because it was the right thing to do. That's not savvy marketing. That's stewardship. In crisis, good leaders ask, "What do people need?" And sometimes, the answer is: not us.

8. Apple, "1984" (1984)

Description

Rows of expressionless workers march through a dystopian industrial corridor. A massive screen looms ahead, where a Big Brother figure preaches obedience. Then: a lone woman in red shorts and a track suit, sprinting with a sledgehammer. Guards chase her, but she hurls the hammer into the screen, shattering the system and the spell. A title card: "And you'll see why 1984 won't be like *1984*."

Leadership Lessons

Innovation; courage; disruption. Apple didn't just advertise a product. It declared a worldview. Leaders don't wait to be invited. They challenge the premise, break the screen, and give people back their agency.

7. Nike, "Just Do It" (1988)

Description

A man identified as 80 years old jogs across the Golden Gate Bridge. His voiceover says that he runs 17 miles every morning. Then he says, "People ask me how I keep my teeth from chattering in the wintertime. I leave them in my locker." A title card appears saying, "Just Do It."

Leadership Lessons

Vision; values; bias toward action; humor. The man isn't pitching athleticism but modeling mindset. Leaders don't wait for the perfect time or conditions. They act, improvise, and move forward anyway. "Just Do It" crystallizes this ethic with charm and simplicity.

6. Partnership for a Drug-Free America, "Frying Pan" (1987)

Description

A hand holds up an egg. "This is your brain." The egg cracks into a hot skillet. It hisses and sizzles. "This is your brain on drugs." A beat. "Any questions?"

Leadership Lessons

Simplicity is power. Great leaders don't need to shout to be heard. They need to be clear. This ad landed like a mallet because it skipped the nuance and trusted the audience to get the message.

5. Budweiser, "One Team" (2020)

Description

Stadiums sit empty. A voice says, "This Bud's for the Reds," but instead of a ballclub, we see a Red Cross worker. "This Bud's for the Trailblazers": a lab team, hunched over test tubes. "This Bud's for the Braves": a delivery driver in a mask. The ad ends with a quiet rallying cry: "This Bud's for the home team."

Leadership Lessons

The best leaders don't confuse visibility with importance. During a time when the usual heroes were sidelined, Budweiser rewrote the playbook. Leadership meant showing up, even if no one was cheering.

4. Coca-Cola, "Hey Kid, Catch!" (1979)

Description

Legendary Pittsburgh Steelers defensive tackle Mean Joe Greene limps down the tunnel after a game, bruised and silent. A young boy follows at a distance, clutching a bottle of Coke. He shyly offers it to Greene, who takes the offering, drains it, and turns to trudge away. The boy starts to walk off, crestfallen. Then Greene stops, smiles, and says, "Hey kid, catch!" He tosses the boy his game-worn jersey.

Leadership Lessons

Humility; gratitude; creating legacy. For the boy, it's more than a jersey, it's a moment in grace from a hero he'll never forget.

3. NFL, "Run With It" (2023 Super Bowl)

Description

Interviewing Diana Flores, the quarterback of Mexico's national flag football team, a sideline reporter tries to pull one of her flags. Flores takes off, and what follows is a dazzling 90-second display of speed and agility as she evades a legion of pursuers (including NFL players Sauce Gardner and Davante Adams in a mascot getup) in the bowels of the stadium, through the parking lot, into a shopping mall, over rooftops, and into a hotel, until she finally makes it home to her mother. As the mother goes in for a protective hug she reaches for the flag, and Flores is off running again. With its fun, frenetic pace and a legion of cameos (Billie Jean King throws a car-door block!), the commercial shows that a new generation is embracing American football, and it's not necessarily male or from the United States.

Leadership Lessons

Diana Flores isn't just outrunning defenders, she's outrunning the constraints of what leadership is supposed to look like. The ad celebrates a female athlete's prowess in a traditionally male-dominated sport, highlighting the importance of recognizing and promoting diverse leadership.

2. Monster.com, "When I Grow Up" (1999)

Description

A child stares straight at the camera: "When I grow up, I want to file all day." Cut to another: "I want to climb my way up to middle management." Then another: "... and be replaced on a whim." A grim parade of kids speak their career "dreams" with deadpan sincerity. The ad closes with a single question: "What did you want to be?"

Leadership Lessons

Humor; listening; vision; truth-telling. Monster skewers the soulless drift of corporate life, reminding us that leadership should inspire, not disillusion. The best leaders help people find both jobs and purpose.

1. United Airlines, "Speech" (1990)

Description

A business executive addresses a packed conference room. His tone is somber—a longtime client has just left, and the company lost them by forgetting the human connection. He holds up a paper airline ticket and says they're going back to face-to-face meetings. One by one, he hands out tickets. When someone objects that they have clients in more than 200 cities, the boss replies, "I don't care." He keeps handing them out. Then he says he's off to visit the client who fired them.

Leadership Lessons

Humility; accountability; leading from the front. The executive doesn't just admit failure: he mobilizes around it. He puts values into motion. Good leaders don't delegate the hard part.

7
Becoming a Thought Leader

Chapter Objectives

- Understand the value of thought leadership in building credibility, visibility, and influence within the security and risk domains.
- Identify opportunities and platforms to showcase thought leadership, including podcasts, publications, and awards.
- Learn how to engage audiences through impactful presentations, compelling storytelling, and authentic public speaking.
- Explore the strategic use of podcasts, webinars, and online content to share expertise and build a personal brand.
- Develop writing and publishing skills to produce articles, reports, or books that reflect subject-matter authority.
- Examine how generative AI and social media can amplify thought leadership efforts while maintaining authenticity and trust.

Methods of exhibiting thought leadership abound. You can present in person at conferences or symposia. You can write blog or social media posts, newsletters, articles, or research papers. You can appear on videos, podcasts, and webinars. And so much more. Here's a sample.

Presenting: From Staff Meetings to the Main Stage

As a risk professional, you likely have a story to tell: a perspective, an insight, an experience. Sharing that story with clarity, substance, and style is the essence of thought leadership. And one of the most visible ways to do it is through public speaking.

Whether you're addressing a handful of coworkers or a packed ballroom, presenting sharpens your thinking, builds credibility, and broadens your impact. But don't expect to keynote RSA, RIMS, Black Hat, DEF CON, or GSX right out of the gate.

DOI: 10.1201/9781003646488-11

Most recognized speakers in the risk and security field got their start in modest venues, such as Toastmasters meetings, community events, or even talks at their local church or condo board. Presenting to small groups at your own organization can also build confidence and skill. From there, expand to virtual formats like webinars or podcasts, which are abundant and allow you to present from the comfort of your home or office.

Want to speak at GSX? It's highly competitive. A more accessible path might be your local ASIS chapter (or, in this virtual age, any chapter), which needs regular speakers for monthly meetings. Don't limit yourself to security audiences. You'll often have more impact speaking to those outside the field.

In my own experience, I've presented to state bankers' associations, travel groups, retailers' alliances, religious and cultural institutions, chambers of commerce, and law enforcement organizations. These audiences often welcome security expertise as something novel and valuable. Colleges and universities are another great venue. Instructors are always looking to bring in fresh voices and perspectives from the field.

For example:

- I've guest lectured for Adjunct Professor James DeMeo's class on Sport/Event Security at Tulane University.
- I've spoken for Julio Fumigalli Macrae's lecture series on Human and Multidimensional Security at the Universidad del Museo Social de Argentina.
- Senior security executive R.C. Miles began his speaking journey by sharing his canine security experience in a criminal justice class at Texas State University.
- Lisa Oliveri, who has moved from NGO security to running a GSOC for a leading customer engagement platform company, began speaking in small, volunteer-led settings as a subject matter expert. Gaining confidence through practice and diverse experiences, including insurance and risk conferences, she expanded her reach and was later invited to speak as a panelist and moderator at larger events like the OSAC Annual Briefing, GSX, and Security LeadHER.

If you're already a practiced speaker, consider mentoring those who are new to the platform. Invite a colleague to co-present, especially if they bring a fresh perspective.

I've invited several new speakers to present with me at conferences and webinars, even assisting with their content. Some people have warned me that doing so diminishes my authority, but I don't see it that way. In fact, they often motivate me to up my game.

Conversely, if you're new to presenting, reach out to more seasoned speakers to co-present. Many experienced professionals are eager to give back to the field and help elevate emerging voices. They can also provide a confidence boost.

Hari Pratap Shekhawat did exactly that in 2021 when he reached out to me looking to jumpstart his speaking career. I paired with him to present virtually to the Greater Atlanta Chapter of ASIS on the topic of overlooked insider threats. Just a year later, Shekhawat was invited to keynote the "Campus to Corporate" workshop at Sardar Patel University of Police, Security and Criminal Justice in India.

And if you're concerned that your skills might not match those of professionals in other fields, don't be. I've delivered media and presentation training to hundreds of executives in verticals including finance, higher education, defense contracting, aerospace, law, and high tech, and no profession is inherently more gifted than another in these skills, though they may well be more practiced. I've also coached experienced speakers who had cemented bad practices over the years, such as robotic delivery, overreliance on notes, and lack of personality. Know your material, don't suppress your personality, and let your enthusiasm for the subject enchant your audience.

To Become a Thought Leader

- Start local: Internal briefings, community groups, and local chapters are ideal launchpads.
- Virtual counts: Webinars and podcasts build your presence and polish without requiring travel. You may be able to discreetly refer to your notes.
- Elevate others: Co-presenting can spotlight emerging voices and deepen your own credibility.
- Accept help: Co-presenting with a mentor accelerates development and builds connections.

Speaking in Podcasts and Webinars: A Mic and a Message

You don't need a keynote slot or a publishing deal to be a thought leader. Some of the most accessible and influential platforms for sharing your expertise are podcasts and webinars, and they offer a low-pressure, high-reach way to test your voice and refine your message.

Security and risk professionals, a group often known for tight-lipped discretion, often open up in these forums. That's part of their appeal. Whether you're telling war stories, walking through frameworks, or sharing lessons learned, these formats give you space to explore and connect.

Why Podcasts and Webinars Matter

- **They're accessible**. You don't need a fancy job title, just something relevant to say.
- **They're flexible**. You can record from home, your car, or even the airport lounge.
- **They stick around**. Podcasts and webinars live on after you speak, offering long-tail exposure.

While many guests are regulars on the speaking circuit, there's always room and appetite for fresh voices. You don't need to be an industry celebrity. You just need an idea, a story, or a unique take.

Choosing Where to Speak, and What to Say

The number of security-related podcasts is staggering. They cover everything from executive protection and threat intelligence to secure coding and surveillance systems. Some sound tactical; others are surprisingly philosophical.

To pick just one security and risk field, I reached out to my LinkedIn network and asked for their favorite risk leadership-focused podcasts, especially ones led by fellow practitioners, not organizations or publications. I received dozens of responses, including heartfelt recommendations, niche gems, and insightful commentary (see sidebar)

SECURITY AND LEADERSHIP PODCASTS WORTH YOUR TIME

The Fearless Mindset Podcast (Hosted by Mark Ledlow)

"Interviews with the Security Industry's best and brightest to learn about the tactics and strategies they use to protect the world's wealthiest families."

Comments: "I can describe his style in one word: courageous." "Compelling."

The Great Conversation (Hosted by Ron Worman, The Sage Group)

"Each conversation seeks to illuminate an idea, a practice, or a movement."

Comments: "Ron is a master interviewer who elevates the conversation to business, not just tactics."

Next Level (Hosted by Jon Harris)

"We focus on professionals in the security industry and empowering you to reach your next level — personally and professionally."

Comments: "He highlights next-gen talent and mixes in mental health and self-improvement themes."

The Security Circle (Hosted by Yolanda Hamblen, IFPO)

"We can highlight the work of heroes in our industry, promote leadership best practice, and provide access to top security professionals."

Comments: "Yolanda is skilled at drawing out a guest's best material. She hears what you're not saying."

The Security Student Podcast (Hosted by Travis Lishok)

"My goal is to educate security practitioners (me included) about the range of sub-fields and roles across the risk management spectrum."

Comments: "Travis is humble, curious, and generous. He shares knowledge without ego."

Security Theater (Hosted by Carlos Francisco and Scot Walker)

"Debunks the myths and misconceptions that surround the security industry."

Comments: "They tackle absurdities with wit. It's smart and a little subversive."

Security Thought Leadership: In Conversation with Martin Gill

"Panel discussions and interviews."

Comments: "Martin is thoughtful and global. It's one of the only truly international security podcasts."

SIDEBAR: BREAK OUT OF THE ECHO CHAMBER

Sometimes, the best leadership lessons come from outside the security bubble. A few security professionals I admire recommended podcasts that touch on resilience, entrepreneurship, team dynamics, mindfulness, and even emergency services—all useful to risk leaders.

- **5 Minutes to Chaos** (Emergency management; Steven Kuhr)
- **Harder Not Smarter** (Career reinvention; Greg VanDyne & Kevin Seiff)
- **Harvard Business Review podcasts** (Leadership, teams, coaching)
- **Last 8% Morning** (Mindfulness, decision-making; JP Pawliw-Fry)
- **Leadership Tea** (Practical leadership; Shelby Smith-Wilson & Belinda Jackson Farrier)
- **RIMScast** (Risk management; Justin Smulison of RIMS)
- **The WiLD Conversation** (Human-centered leadership; Rob McKenna)
- **Executive Checkpoint Podcast** (Security leadership perspectives; Tino Urbina)

Getting on a Podcast

Interested in being a guest? Most hosts aren't looking for perfection but for someone with something to say.

Here's how to increase your chances:

- Be specific: "I'd love to be on your podcast" is vague. Try: "I have a case study on supply chain threat modeling I'd love to walk through."
- Engage first: Comment on the host's posts. Share a favorite episode. Start a genuine conversation.
- Be brief, be bold: When pitching yourself, lead with the idea, not the résumé.
- Support the show: After your episode goes live, promote it. Tag people. Send a thank-you note.
- If you're nervous about going solo, consider asking a mentor or peer to co-guest with you. The best conversations often come from good chemistry.

Key lessons:

- You don't need a stage. Podcasts and webinars are powerful platforms to share insights and sharpen your voice.
- There's a seat at the table for newcomers with niche expertise or strong stories.
- Be intentional about where you show up and how you present yourself.
- Great podcast guests listen as well as they speak: it's a conversation, not a monologue.

Writing: From Blog Posts to Books

Writing is one of the most enduring and versatile ways to express thought leadership. Whether it's a blog post, article, white paper, or full-length book, written work has staying power. It can establish your authority, clarify your thinking, and reach audiences far beyond your professional circle.

Even if you don't consider yourself a writer, you likely have insights that others would value. If only you could get them out of your head and onto the page.

Begin with what you know. Start with bullet points. A short blog post on LinkedIn or your company's intranet based on your professional experience, lessons learned, or a case study is often the easiest on-ramp.

These don't need to be grand or literary. A few paragraphs, a strong point of view, and a dose of clarity go a long way. Blog posts also invite conversation and feedback, which can sharpen your ideas for future writing or speaking opportunities.

Once you've gained confidence, you can move to longer, more structured formats.

Articles for trade publications, association magazines, or peer-reviewed journals require more than opinion. They demand examples, research, sources, and often editorial collaboration.

I took a reverse path from most security professionals. I started as a writer and editor for *Security Management* magazine and learned security through interviews, observation, and osmosis. I relied on countless subject-matter experts who generously walked me through the intricacies of magnetic media forensics, access control technologies, and cyber hygiene, including unforgettable sessions on scanning tunneling microscopy, degaussing, and coercivity.

The point is, you don't need to be the expert in everything, but you do need to write clearly, cite accurately, and know your audience. And if you can wrap it all in a narrative, even better.

In the era of ebooks, self-publishing platforms, and ghostwriters-for-hire, it feels like everyone in security has written a book. The truth? Most haven't. And most never will because it's hard.

Writing a book both signals and demands thought leadership. It conveys discipline, vision, expertise, and follow-through. But it's also a slog.

You will not make much money, if any. It may actually cost you savings if you hire your own writer, editor, or proofreader. You will spend months, maybe years, of late nights, rewrites, last-minute edits, legal reviews, and missed deadlines. Sources will become elusive. You may start questioning your thesis or purpose.

When it's finally published, you will likely be the primary promoter. You will handle your own social media posts, podcast appearances, speaking engagements, book review requests, and maybe even autograph sessions. But if you're ready for the investment, the rewards can be substantial: personal pride, thought leadership credibility, consulting opportunities, and new professional relationships.

SIDEBAR: THE PUBLISHING LANDSCAPE

Book types range from practical how-tos to leadership memoirs to scholarly texts. Consider this sample of recent security-related titles, including a few I've contributed to, to see the breadth of possibility:

- Scholarly: *Strategic Risk and Crisis Management*—Dr. David Rubens (2023)
- Reflective: *The Kindness Games*—Lee Oughton and Tim Wenzel (2023)
- Career Advice: *Yes, S.I.R.*—Chuck Andrews (2022)
- Academic: *The Handbook of Security (3rd ed.)*—Edited by Martin Gill (2022)
- Practical Guide: *The Digital Citizen's Guide to Cybersecurity*—Antoinette King (2022)

- Political analysis: *Attack from Within*—Barbara McQuade (2024)
- Introductory overview: *LinkedIn Guide for Security Pros*—Abraham Desantiago (2025)
- Reference and case compendium: *Terrorism & the Medical Environment*—Louis R. Mizell, Jr., and E. Reed Smith, Jr., M.D. (2016)
- Multidisciplinary analysis: *Security & Crime: Converging Perspectives on a Complex World*—Alison Wakefield (2021)
- Best practices: *Recetas Para Una Operación Productiva Segura*—Herbert Calderon Alemán (2024)

These aren't vanity projects. They serve as business cards, thought leadership platforms, textbooks, field guides, and even provocations.

Thinking about Writing a Book? Try This First

- Contribute a chapter to a collaborative book project.
- Write a longform article that could be expanded into a manuscript.
- Create a recurring column or newsletter to test ideas and tone.

Then talk to authors you admire. They've been through the process, and many will gladly share their experience, challenges, and publishing advice.

Start by asking them how they stared down that first blank page.

Establishing Yourself as an Author

- **Start small**: A thoughtful post can be more influential than a long-winded article.
- **Build rigor**: Longer-form writing requires editing, research, and sometimes humility.
- **Books amplify your brand** but only if you have something meaningful to say.
- **Seek feedback and mentorship**: The writing community within security is more generous than you might think.

Writing with Generative AI: Collaborator, Not Creator

When generative AI first came on the scene, I felt like John Henry, the steel-driving man, hammer in hand, bracing for a race (rage?) against the machine. As a prolific writer, I took pride in the speed, rhythm, and originality of my own work. The idea that a computer could churn out prose faster, and sometimes unsettlingly well, felt like a direct challenge. Generative AI is incredibly, intoxicatingly powerful, which is both its gift and its curse. It can undermine your work, introduce errors, and corrupt meaning. Using generative AI without close oversight is akin to releasing malware into your work product.

But let's be honest: John Henry died. Pride is one thing. Survival, growth, and relevance are another. Wisdom comes not from resisting innovation but from adopting it, iterating on it, and ultimately mastering and improving upon it. Generative AI isn't a rival. It's a tool, a thought partner, and an analyst. The real race isn't against the machine. It's against irrelevance. And the only way to win is to keep evolving. (But I'll keep that steel-driving hammer in the garage … just in case.)

When I began writing this book, generative AI was in its early days but evolving rapidly. Since then, it has become a staple in everything from brainstorming sessions to business proposals. I've incorporated it modestly and strategically, primarily as a sounding board and editorial assistant. The ideas, arguments, and the prose stylings are mine, even as I occasionally had to extinguish ChatGPT's furtive forays into my text, as I describe in detail below.

Today, the best use of this tool is not to create content, but to support the creative process.

AI as Prompt Engine and Drafting Assistant

For many professionals, the hardest part of writing isn't clarity, but momentum. Generative AI can help you:

- Break through writer's block
- Rephrase clunky sentences
- Draft outlines or article structures
- Suggest counterpoints
- Refine tone for different audiences

It's especially helpful for those who don't write frequently. The AI can offer a first draft that's readable and clear, and that can be enough to get you thinking more sharply.

But make no mistake: generative AI can't replicate insight. It assembles language, not ideas.

The Difference between Input and Insight

I've tested AI on several occasions to see how it performs, especially on creative, metaphor-driven pieces. Once, I asked it to write a column drawing leadership lessons from *Peanuts*. It produced a few decent observations, like the value of strong relationships and the importance of communication. But it missed the emotional subtext and contradictory qualities that make the strip rich with meaning. In my own column, I dug into more specific character dynamics, like how Schroeder's respect for Charlie Brown bolstered the lovable loser's authority in subtle but meaningful ways. (See Breakaway 4.)

When prompted with, *"Give me an unexpected pop culture metaphor for security leadership,"* the AI offered:

> "Leadership Lessons from Ted Lasso: Kindness as a Security Strategy."

On-brand, but far from original. That concept has been published in books, blogs, and webinars. Asking for something less obvious yielded:

> "Leadership Lessons from the Great British Bake Off: The Power of Unlikely Partnerships."

An interesting angle, but one already explored in multiple HR and management blogs. Even when the phrasing is new, the idea often isn't. Generative AI can suggest directions, but it rarely breaks new ground.

When AI Works, and When It Doesn't

AI is most useful when you:

- Want a quick way to test phrasing or organization
- Need to summarize, expand, or adapt existing content
- Are trying to consider counterarguments or alternate tones
- Are outlining longer projects or idea trees

But it falls short when you need:

- Original synthesis
- Industry nuance
- Voice and emotional resonance
- Uncommon angles

AI isn't good at capturing the friction, ambiguity, or leadership paradoxes that make our field complex and human.

It also can plant landmines in your work. I ran early drafts of a couple of chapters of this book through ChatGPT, and the AI launched a stealth mission to subtly erode my work. I had asked it to do a check for grammar, flow, and persuasion. It spit out a version that had changed some of my sentence structure, word choices, and even arguments, which drastically changed the tone and message. I even asked the AI to highlight the changes it made, and it skipped mention of the offending material. Only when I asked it whether it changed specific language did it cop to its hatchet job.

Use It with Purpose

Think of AI as your brainstorming partner, not your ghostwriter. It can accelerate drafting and editing, but it shouldn't do your thinking for you. If you rely too heavily on it, your voice flattens, your perspective becomes generic, and your credibility suffers. We all know when someone is using generative AI. Where they once struggled for hours to write a memo, they churn out clean business prose filled with em dashes.

In this book, AI played a minor but helpful role: offering editorial nudges, helping with organization, and occasionally suggesting phrasing I could build on. But every idea, story, and argument reflects real experience, not algorithmic output.

Don't rely on AI, but don't scoff at it either. If you ignore its capabilities, you're missing a tremendous opportunity to enhance your thinking, accelerate your work, and sharpen your leadership message.

SIDEBAR: GENERATIVE AI

- Use AI as a springboard, not a shortcut. It's a tool for structure and clarity, not substance.
- Watch for clichés and factual errors. AI tends to write in well-worn grooves. You may have to query the AI multiple times before it "admits" what it has changed from your original draft.
- Be transparent. If you're using AI in your work, say so, especially when presenting to clients or peers.
- Let your voice lead. AI can assist with the *how,* but only you can deliver the *why.*
- Dismiss AI at your own risk. The tool is evolving rapidly and so are the professionals who use it wisely.

Mastering Social Media

In today's professional world, your social media presence is often your first, and sometimes only, impression. For risk and security leaders, that can be a double-edged sword. It's an opportunity to build your reputation, share your voice, and signal your values. But it's also easy to be misunderstood, misread, or miscast.

Platforms like LinkedIn offer more than résumé-building and congratulatory posts. They're where thought leadership lives and breathes, through how you write, what you share, and who you uplift. Your communication style becomes a reflection of your leadership style.

And like in leadership, there's no one right way to do it.

Three Leaders, Three Distinct Styles

Reading a post by security professional Tyler Schmoker is like reading an e.e. cummings poem. The formatting is jagged and irregular, with frequent line breaks. Emojis pop up throughout the text. His style is "visual, emotional, and literal," as he puts it, designed to mirror how people process ideas psychologically and socially.

While his activity has cooled since his heyday in 2024, his posts often reference the outdoors, endurance racing, and pushing limits. And at the bottom of each one, he includes a few professional credentials, a grounded counterbalance to the free-form structure above. Many others now end their posts with similar biographical shorthand.

So what does this say about Schmoker's leadership style? "I'm pragmatically fluid & I allow it from my people too," he told me. "Less constrained by industry norms, more focused on progress, disruption, and innovation."

His unconventional approach has boosted both his performance metrics and professional visibility. But it's also drawn some criticism. Leadership on social media, like in person, invites feedback, good and bad.

In contrast, Carlos "The Corporate Security Translator" Francisco brings boundless energy to his videos and posts. His animated style draws inspiration from the world of Disney: upbeat, expressive, and relentlessly engaging.

"Drawing from Disney's vibrant spirit," Carlos told me, "I infuse my posts, podcasts and relationships … with enthusiasm, creating what I hope is a contagious energy that reflects my commitment to inspiring and motivating others."

His style is a lesson in consistency, the same Carlos you see on screen is the one you'll get in person. He shares his journey, promotes his podcast, and regularly offers career transition advice to newcomers in corporate security. Empathy and accessibility are threaded through everything he posts.

Then there's Solveiga Jaskunas, an HR professional with a quiet strength. Lithuanian-born and a U.S. resident, she has rebranded herself as "The Immigrant Voice in HR," a rare but resonant perspective in her field.

Her posts rarely center on herself. Instead, she uses her platform to thank mentors, spotlight colleagues, and promote others' podcasts and books. Fittingly, she describes herself as a servant leader.

She's candid about her discomfort being called a leader. "I love putting others in the center of attention, helping them with their careers, mentoring them, seeing the value they can bring to others," she told me. "But I don't like putting myself so much in the center of attention."

And yet, her presence speaks volumes. It's consistent, authentic, and unmistakably hers.

Whether your style is bold and booming or humble and understated, the key is *intentionality*. Schmoker, Francisco, and Jaskunas couldn't be more different, yet each has cultivated a digital presence that reflects their leadership philosophy, values, and voice.

That's the bar to aim for.

It's not about going viral. It's about shaping the narrative around your work and your identity, before someone else does it for you.

Ask yourself:

- Are you sharing insights or just information?
- Are you engaging others or just broadcasting?
- Are you signaling your values or blending in?

MASTERING SOCIAL MEDIA

- **Your social media voice should reflect your leadership voice**, not just your résumé.
- **There's no template**. Effective styles can range from poetic to pragmatic to promotional, as long as they're genuine.

- **Elevating others builds credibility and community**. People remember generosity.
- **Consistency matters**. Your audience should recognize you, in tone, intent, and values, across posts.
- **Silence speaks too**. If you're not shaping your professional persona online, someone else may do it for you.

Recognition and Metrics: How Influence Gets Measured

Thought leadership doesn't require a trophy case, but recognition can be a powerful amplifier. Awards, rankings, and nominations bring visibility, validate effort, and signal credibility to employers, clients, and peers. They also provide a moment to step back and reflect on the impact you're having beyond your immediate circle.

But not all awards are created equal. Some rely on glowing narratives, others on objective metrics. Some celebrate innovation; others reward visibility. Understanding how these systems work, and where you might fit in, is part of managing your professional persona.

WHY RECOGNITION MATTERS

- **Credibility**: Awards offer third-party validation in an often self-promotional landscape.
- **Visibility**: Even local or niche recognition can help expand your network.
- **Opportunity**: Honorees often get invited to speak, publish, or lead.
- **Reflection**: Preparing a nomination forces you to articulate your contributions, something many leaders rarely pause to do.
- That said, awards should be treated as a byproduct of contribution, not the goal itself.

A New Model: The Life Safety Alliance Top 40

In 2024, the Life Safety Alliance (LSA) launched a new recognition program: the Top 40 Thought Leaders in Security and Life Safety. (Full disclosure: I was serving as president of LSA at the time.)

What sets this program apart is its reliance on objective criteria. Unlike most awards that hinge on the strength of a nomination letter or the persuasive powers of a nominator, the LSA Top 40 uses a scoring algorithm based on real-world outputs.

Metrics include, among others:

- Articles published
- Conference presentations
- Webinar and podcast appearances
- Media appearances and citations
- Volunteer leadership roles
- Professorships/fellowships/post-secondary courses taught
- LinkedIn engagement and reach
- Publicly released reports authored
- Corporate board service
- Books and book chapters authored

This system aims to bring transparency, consistency, and rigor to a space that often feels opaque and subjective. And while the methodology isn't perfect, it levels the playing field and encourages broader participation.

It's also adaptive. In its second year, the LSA welcomed Andrew Thorburn to lead the program. Andrew is a highly principled veteran judge of other awards schemes attracted by the objectivity of the Top 40. A New Zealander, Thorburn set out to expand awareness of the program to Oceania and beyond so that the program considers the worthiest candidates no matter where they are in the world. Thorburn immediately added and tweaked categories and helped fine-tune the scoring structure. For example, in the first year of the program, candidates worldwide received a certain number of points based on LinkedIn followers and connections. In its second year, those points adjusted to take into account the candidate's location, since it is typically much more difficult for someone in New Zealand, for instance, to rack up connections as it is for a similar professional in the United States.

A Word on Awards Culture

I've served as a judge in multiple awards programs, and I can say with confidence that most are run with integrity and good intentions. But outcomes often hinge on the strength of the nomination rather than the nominee's body of work.

Sometimes, well-qualified professionals are passed over because their submissions are thin, generic, or rushed. Others win because someone took the time to craft an eloquent and impassioned case.

The LSA Top 40 was designed to reduce that kind of variability, to shift focus from persuasion to production. It's one model among many, but I hope it inspires other programs to think critically about how they measure leadership and influence.

As I discussed, recognizing others, especially through nominations, is one of the most generous and impactful things a leader can do. If someone's work has impressed or influenced you, take the time to help them be seen. Awards may be symbolic, but the act of uplifting someone else's contributions is real leadership.

How Relevant Is Thought Leadership, Anyway?

The term "thought leader" was first coined 30 years ago in *Strategy+Business*, a magazine published by PwC. Since then, it has become one of the most overused labels in the business world. In some circles, it now carries the same skepticism once reserved for "guru" or "visionary."

In mid 2024, Tyler Schmoker, whose creative LinkedIn writing style I discussed earlier in this section, posted that thought leadership "has become cringe in all of its social media excess." He posed a question to his network: *Is thought leadership just repackaging things people already believe but haven't said out loud yet?*

About twenty people responded, including me.

Most agreed that you don't have to invent a new model, theory, or acronym to be a thought leader. You don't need to be Simon Sinek or Brené Brown. Sometimes, the most important voice in the room is the one that puts structure or visibility around ideas others were already thinking.

As brand advisor Cebien Alty posted:

> "Thought leadership to me is more than original concepts or modes of thinking. It's in our ability to put a voice to the topics that interest us to drive conversation and challenge the status quo or assumptions."

Creative project manager Tanya Boyd added:

> "We aren't always able to come up with topics that have never been covered before, but what we can do is reframe them in a unique way... and get the conversation started again."

At the same time, some professionals, like consultant Drew Brown, questioned whether the term has become a trendy bolt-on, like "servant leadership" became a few years before. Others noted that people often call themselves thought leaders before they've done the work to earn that title.

Still, the phrase persists. And in a world where influence matters, for good or ill, the idea behind it remains useful.

Curious how generative AI defines thought leadership? I asked ChatGPT various versions of the following question:

> "Who are the 10 leading thought leaders in corporate security?"

The results were mixed. Some lists skewed cyber-heavy. Others produced a blend of physical security professionals, often depending on how I phrased the question.

I then asked several colleagues to run the same query. The overlap was surprisingly low. While some names appeared repeatedly, many lists featured individuals known only to the person doing the asking.

That's part of the point. AI is highly suggestible. When I had previously entered a list of professionals I considered thought leaders, ChatGPT later returned many of those same names as part of its "objective" answer. The more context you provide, the more the tool echoes your framing. That can reinforce your own biases or assumptions without your realizing it. (And we are back to the bête noire of cognitive bias again.)

So what does that tell us? That the phrase "thought leader" isn't anchored by universal consensus. It's shaped by context, proximity, phrasing, and memory.

That's not necessarily a problem, but it's worth remembering.

Here's a simple experiment:

Open ChatGPT, or your other generative AI tool of choice, and ask, *"Is [Your Name] a thought leader in [your field, e.g. cybersecurity, corporate security, risk management, business continuity]?"*

You might be surprised by the answer, or by how much it resembles what you've already told the tool.

But ultimately, the real test isn't what the algorithm says. It's whether people in your field look to you for clarity, insight, and perspective. If they do, you're already leading.

From the Lips of Gips: "The open secret is that much of 'thought leadership' is really 'thought followership.'"

Chapter takeaways

General Concepts

- Thought leadership isn't about self-promotion. It's about contribution, relevance, and resonance with your professional community.

Presenting

- Start with smaller audiences and build confidence through association chapters, local groups, or webinars.
- Co-presenting with mentors can ease beginners into public speaking and help elevate emerging voices.

Podcasts and Webinars

- These offer accessible platforms for thought leaders to share ideas or learn from others.
- Notable podcasts include *Fearless Mindset*, *The Great Conversation*, and *Security Circle*.
- Listening outside the security echo chamber can broaden leadership insight.

Short-Form Writing

- Generative AI can assist with structure and speed but lacks deep insight, creativity, and accuracy.
- Effective thought leadership writing requires a clear voice, meaningful perspective, and rigorous editing.
- Blog posts, articles, and books all contribute to professional credibility and influence.

Book Authorship

- Writing a book is a major investment of time and effort but can enhance visibility and influence.
- Books can serve as calling cards, guides, memoirs, manifestos, or practical toolkits.
- Reach out to published authors on security and risk topics for mentorship and guidance.

Social Media

- Thought leadership thrives on authenticity, different styles (like those of Tyler Schmoker, Carlos Francisco, and Solveiga Jaskunas) show there's no one-size-fits-all approach.
- An intentional social media strategy can reinforce your professional identity and values.

Recognition and Metrics

- Objective-based awards like LSA's Top 40 Thought Leaders emphasize output over popularity.
- Metrics like presentations, published work, and reach help quantify influence.

The Value of Thought Leadership

- "Thought leader" remains a useful but overused term. What matters is impact, not self-labeling.
- Thought leadership can mean giving voice to widely held but unspoken insights, not just inventing new ideas.
- Self-awareness, consistency, and humility are essential in managing one's professional persona.

8
Leading in Transition and Adversity

Chapter Objectives

- Learn how leadership manifests in times of disruption, from career shifts and job searches to startups and remote work.
- Understand how to build credibility quickly in new roles or unfamiliar organizational cultures.
- Explore the challenges and strengths of solo leadership and leadership without formal authority.
- Examine leadership strategies for turning around underperforming teams or disillusioned staff.
- Recognize the importance of reflection, humility, and adaptability when stepping down or reassessing your leadership path.

Leadership for Nonleaders

"Youth is wasted on the young," goes a popular witticism, which has been ascribed to George Bernard Shaw, Oscar Wilde, Michel de Montaigne, and others. The point is that young people have the vitality and enthusiasm to achieve tremendous things, but they usually lack the wisdom, experience, and maturity to do so.

Equally true is that leadership is wasted on leaders, but for different reasons. It's not that people who are in a position of leadership—CEOs, politicians, coaches, clergy, judges, and so on—necessarily lack any quality that lets them excel as leaders. It's that they are expected to lead and to navigate followers through difficult situations. They signed up for it.

What's truly extraordinary is when someone not in a traditional position of authority steps up to leadership. That could be a security line manager, an auditor, a compliance supervisor, or an intelligence analyst.

DOI: 10.1201/9781003646488-12

Of the 90,000 books on leadership that Amazon.com sells, listed at or near the top (not including sponsored results) is Doris Kearns Goodwin's highly praised 2018 work, *Leadership in Turbulent Times*. Kearns Goodwin chronicles the exploits of four U.S. presidents at their defining moments: Abraham Lincoln through the Civil War leading up to the Emancipation Proclamation; Theodore Roosevelt during the coal strike as the gears of the Industrial Revolution were grinding down workers; Franklin D. Roosevelt and his first 100 days in the heart of the Great Depression; and Lyndon Johnson coming around in his thinking on social justice to push through a civil rights platform.

These men, like most world leaders, were put in the position to lead, were expected to lead, and were regularly presented with situations and issues in which they could exhibit leadership. That history bore out their judgment distinguishes them from their presidential colleagues who were defined by failure, at least during their terms in office: Jimmy Carter for his inability to navigate the nation out of an oil crisis and economic "stagflation" or rescue the American hostages in Iran; James Buchanan for allowing the South to secede; Andrew Johnson, for poor leadership during Reconstruction efforts; and Warren Harding for allowing a culture of corruption to flower around him.

Wharton Professor Michael Useem calls the critical confluence of time, place, situation, and individual the "leadership moment," the title of his 1998 book. (Comparing the "leadership moment" to my homespun teleological and epiphanic leadership, a leadership moment might qualify as either, but not necessarily.) While that book explores nine such leadership moments, from the man who brought Apollo 13 down to Earth to the president of El Salvador who ended his country's civil war, Useem, too, focuses on people in power.

But leadership is much more wondrous and thrilling when it is exercised by someone without a pulpit or even an audience. It's like grass growing in the desert. It's why Todd Beamer, he of "Let's roll" on United Flight 93 on 9/11, resounds as a symbol of bravery and grit in the face of terrorism, why Rosa Parks is synonymous with quiet grace and resolve amid institutionalized discrimination, and why Malala Yousafzai epitomizes how a single person can stand up to a tyrannical regime.

During the pandemic, we all greatly appreciated the tremendous sacrifices made by medical professionals, emergency responders, day-care staff, delivery drivers, and workers in the food and health supply chain. But there's a special place for people whose jobs don't require that kind of sacrifice but who inserted themselves into the fray. Many of them are security professionals.

As a security or risk professional, you almost undoubtedly will face a critical moment that tests your leadership. It could be facing an unprecedented nation-state cyberattack, as Stevan Bernard did as CSO of Sony Pictures Entertainment. Or running a security business while waging an existential war, as Andrii Lukashenko has been doing in Ukraine. Less dramatically, it could be deciding whether to turn in a corrupt CFO, confronting the CEO about a potentially devastating strategic decision, or even leading a successful cybersecurity, physical security, and business continuity convergence initiative.

It's the cybersecurity professionals who created or groups of like-minded practitioners who volunteer their time to send threat data to healthcare institutions to help them prevent cyberattacks and damage to their resources and medical infrastructure.

It's the security executive who took time off to connect self-isolated vulnerable people in his community with volunteers who could support and supply them with basic provisions.

It's the criminal justice major at Northeastern University, who co-oped as a security officer at Boston Medical Center.

It's the professional who, during the COVID-19 pandemic, connected people vetted through the U.K.'s Security Industry Authority to help people in need or at risk due to the pandemic.

You may have encountered your leadership moment. The COVID-19 pandemic that struck in early 2020 challenged the whole world, but security and risk professionals nobly stepped up where others wouldn't: conducting temperature checks at entrances; administering COVID-19 checks to staff; enforcing social distancing mandates; assisting with ergonomics in employees' home offices; studying and adjusting filtration systems. Some of the health and safety duties, as well as an enhanced role on the organization's crisis management team, stuck after the pandemic died down.

Think you missed your leadership moment? Others will come along.

Leading through Career Transitions

FedEx. Google. McKinsey & Company. 3M. Salesforce. Cisco. Pfizer. BNY Mellon. Sounds like the makings of a pretty good investment portfolio, a nice blend of traditional firms and disruptive technology. Yet all of these companies have shed jobs in recent years.

In 2025, as it transitioned to AI, Duolingo said, "So long, farewell, Auf Wiederseh'n, adieu" to its contract staff. Also that year, Winnebago figuratively decamped, leaving 400 former employees behind. Expedia sent 3 percent of its staff packing. Audi kicked 7500 workers to the curb. And British grocery Tesco cashiered several hundred wage earners.

Eclipsing them all, of course, were the several hundred thousand U.S. civil servants RIF'ed at the start of the Trump Administration.

No organization is immune from staffing corrections in a VUCA(D) world. Not even the once impregnable U.S. government, whose Department of Government Efficiency has both excised jobs with a scalpel and lopped them off with a chainsaw.

Among the victims are always security professionals, from guards to CISOs to VPs of Risk Management. If you define yourself by your vocation, and your job is gone, how do you maintain leadership? I posed this question to three security leaders whose former employers made their positions redundant.

Tim Wenzel had spent nine years at Meta, seven as the Head of Protective Intelligence and Technical Countermeasures, when he became a victim of mass layoffs at the tech giant. Before transitioning to a senior role at a major risk advisory firm, he survived his interim experience by leaning into the leadership roles outside of Meta that he had developed earlier in his career.

"I got involved in ASIS's ESRM steering committee, which solidified my subject-matter expert (SME) credibility," he recalls. "It got other people to look at me outside of my company or role." (Incidentally, that's when I met Tim, because I was running ASIS's ESRM initiative at the time.)

He subsequently got involved with the Security Industry Association (SIA), began regularly presenting at its ISC West conference, and worked with a mentor through SIA. He eventually cofounded The

Kindness Games. These opportunities "let me lead outside of my role," Wenzel says.

"This was my first time being laid off as a leader," he reflects. "I thought when I got laid off, I would lose. But people shockingly continued to reach out for advice and guidance, and not necessarily about my previous role or duties."

Wenzel's colleague at Meta, Developer Platform Investigations Manager Altaf Bora, suffered a similar fate, but found a role as Director of Data Center Operations at Metro One Loss Prevention Group within six months. For him, maintaining a leadership role during the layoff lacuna came down to attitude.

"You've been let go—okay. Acknowledge the feelings and accept it. Take some time to process what happened," Bora advises. "The big thing I had to learn is about being a leader even if you don't have a role, you still have people looking at you. I knew people were watching me. I'm going to map out how to bounce back even higher."

In fact, Bora cleverly used the experience to become a leader on how to navigate a layoff. Rather than mope, Bora threw himself into his graduate degree program, physical fitness, speaking engagements, and podcast appearances. "I was using the recovery time to show people, you can still live a healthy life and work 60-70 hours a week."

Key to this journey was Bora's social media presence. "If you don't communicate, people will think you gave up," he says.

Phillip Moldoff, after leaving New Relic, a cloud software company where he served as Head of Global Safety and Physical Security, adopted a similar approach. After his position was eliminated, Moldoff increased his LinkedIn posting frequency to raise his profile and showcase his expertise, with conference speaking opportunities in his sights. He scoured the security press for valuable articles and reports to keep up on trends. He regularly engaged with the 400 or so members of the Silicon Valley Security Group via mentoring, business development, and information sharing.

These three professionals demonstrate that job disruption is not fatal to leadership. In fact, it can even stimulate leadership development in new areas or to different audiences.

As Wenzel puts it, "I don't see my identity in the job title that I have. It's important to be a person with purpose, such as goals and an active community, beyond work."

Leadership isn't granted by a badge or a title. It's affirmed through continued engagement, presence, and purpose. A layoff may be a pause in employment, but it need not be a pause in influence.

Keep that in mind if you are ever trimmed from the Jenny Craig payroll, separated from David's Bridal, or dropped by Dropbox.

Taking the Helm: Leadership with a New Employer

After two decades with the same employer, then 5 years running my own business, I took a job in a well-known risk advisory firm in January 2025. Even as I went full throttle into this opportunity, I considered how to transition my leadership skills and traits to the new position and environment. I'm in no way an actor, so my natural personality and style emerged on day one. Given the new position—which entailed new colleagues, expectations, culture, mission, team dynamics, and duties—I wondered whether and how I should gradually transition my leadership style to accommodate my new surroundings. I turned to experts for advice.

When I spoke with Mike Brzozowski, he was 64 days into a new job in Frankfurt, Germany, at a large high-tech company. He had spent the previous four years as a security director for a financial services company in Canada. Did he adjust his leadership style for a new position, company, city, country, industry, and culture? In what ways?

"I'm a person who just wants to get stuff done," Brzozowski says. "I'm working on being more patient and flexible. I have to force myself to slow down and realize that I don't have to have an answer today."

Rather than charging into leadership, he has focused on learning the culture first. While he is physically in Germany, many of his corporate peers work in other countries across Europe, with customs and mores of their own. He's also a people person, but he can't easily sit down for coffee with coworkers in Copenhagen or Amsterdam to get to know them better. The team is also so closely knit that he feels like an outsider.

"Everyone speaks English, but they come from different cultures. Shared ownership is huge," he continues. "I've put a real focus to make a concerted effort to be more understanding of different approaches. We are all trying to row in the same direction, we are just trying to get the cadence."

Brzozowski also likes to wield humor as a leadership tool, but he has held that in check. "Germans are formal. I'm putting a toe in the water and learning how funny I'm allowed to be."

To help navigate his transition more systematically, Brzozowski turned to a book, *The First 90 Days*, by Michael Watkins, to guide his transition. "It's going well," he reports. "I make a concerted effort to come to the office, where my team is. I want to be here to learn and provide guidance and build relationships across adjacent teams." With remote staff members, he has virtual meetings once a month.

By contrast, David Nicholas transitioned from a mid-level role at the U.S. subsidiary of a European automaker known for precision engineering to the head of security at an NGO in Washington, DC. Prior to the corporate roles, he spent 17 years with the Diplomatic Security Service (DSS), which he credits for making his leadership style flexible. He considers himself a situational leader.

"DSS conditioned me to be culturally adaptable," Nicholas explains. "I changed posts every two to three years: new country, culture, language. We were conditioned to be ready to immerse ourselves in a new environment."

His time in the State Department also taught him patience and observation. "Going into any new post, I first observe and understand the security culture, how the function sits in the larger organizations, does it carry clout, is it seen as a source of confidence and truth or does that have to be reestablished."

At the automaker, the culture stressed attention to detail and precision. When he joined the nonprofit, the emphasis shifted from product to mission. "In a think tank where the product is research and ideas, it's more reflective and deliberative," Nicholas says. "As a security leader, one has to take that context into account when introducing changes. There will be a lot of input. Experts in different areas will weigh in on the security program and the impact on their mission and funding."

So how did he adapt?

"In my first 30 to 60 days, I tried to be in the community as much as possible," Nicholas recalls. "I never said anything negative about past security." Instead, he asked open-ended questions about how security could be improved and what stakeholders would like to see change. Key to his success was delivering for people who showed an interest in improving security. "Some people wanted more security training," he says. "I asked for budget and approval for that training, and that helped me develop credibility and relationships with those staff members."

Some of Nicholas's takeaways:

- Pay attention to what others focus on regarding security and the context for their views.
- Try to understand where people are coming from when they voice a perspective or idea.
- Strategic planning may require working backward from a stated goal to align your process and style.
- Expand your lens from a security focus to a business or mission focus.

Know thyself, advises Jonathan Kassa. That's the first rule of leadership. Kassa recently moved from a tech startup to become the first executive director of ZeroNow, an organization devoted to making "schools safer for good." He worked for large security companies before the startup.

Since the organization is volunteer-driven, Kassa relies on influence far more than actual authority. "How do you get people from just talking to getting buy-in" and get volunteers to put in work? he asks. Kassa's solution is to create accountability by creating KPIs for boards and committees.

Kassa, who views himself as a reflective leader aspiring to visionary leadership, says his previous corporate jobs were transactional, while his current role (and a previous leadership position at The Clery Center) were relational. In fact, his new position has unshackled some of the leadership traits he's had to suppress.

"I had been trying to fit a visionary leadership style in companies that didn't want to transform," he acknowledges. "I had to check myself."

Three leaders, three recent transitions, three sets of adaptations. These leaders thrive, however, because they adjust, they don't metamorphose. At their core, they are their authentic selves in leadership. As Kassa might say, they know thyselves.

Job Hunting and Ghosts: Leadership in the Search Process

Call me Casper.

I've been ghosted so many times in my professional career that I should live in the Haunted Mansion and vacation at the Overlook Hotel of *The Shining* fame. I'll hang out with Slimer, Jacob Marley, Bloody Mary, Inky and Blinky, the Headless Horseman, and Hogwarts' Nearly Headless Nick.

I'm hardly alone. We all know that ghosting has become a professional epidemic. According to Indeed, 40% of job applicants say they have been ghosted by a potential employer after the second or third interview. Twice as many job seekers have admitted to disappearing on companies.

Less well-documented are meeting cancellations that never get rescheduled; unreturned calls, emails, texts, or social media queries; networking requests that go unheeded; business proposals that are met with silence; and follow-ups from recruiters who seek you out then drop off the face of the Earth.

Don't get me wrong. We all get busy or forget. We all suffer calendar glitches, personal emergencies, last-minute board meetings, limited cell service or Wi-Fi, or any of the many other inescapable vagaries of modern business communication.

Nor am I talking about ignoring cold calls, scammers, or anyone who is rude, hostile, or demanding.

However, getting a reputation for not responding to or following up in a timely and professional manner to legitimate business matters is a sure-fire way to erode your credibility. Every week I hear from supremely qualified colleagues who apply for suitable roles and yet never hear back from the company. The recruiter deserves some of the blame, but so does the hiring manager. Yes, you may have received thousands of applications for a single role. But many security job candidates spent hours examining the position and company description, researching the business, tailoring their resume, writing a cover letter, and hopscotching through the online application.

They are invested. Ignoring them is disrespectful.

All it takes is one thoughtfully written response that can be used for every rejected applicant. Take the case of a colleague who applied for a senior security role at a major software company. This person had previously met the executive to whom the position reported, but didn't get an interview. Within two months of applying, he received the following (edited) reply:

> Thank you for taking the time to apply for the role. We're fortunate to have received a lot of interest in this role, resulting in a very competitive selection process and unfortunately, at this time we have decided not to move forward with your application. While it didn't work out this time, we hope you will continue to explore other opportunities with us by visiting our Career Site. Thank you once again for your interest in our company, and we wish you all the best in your search for a suitable position.

Disappointing, but responsive, polite, encouraging, and professional.

It's even worse for your reputation if you ghost as a job seeker. If you skip an interview—or worse, fail to show up after you've been hired—you are likely to obliterate your reputation. Security executives (and recruiters) speak. A cavalier approach to your career or business relationships will stick to you like ectoplasmic slime.

That can turn you into something worse than a ghost: a persona non grata.

The security industry is tight-knit. Your behavior, whether thoughtful or thoughtless, travels through whisper networks, LinkedIn threads, and conference chatter. Job hunting is not just about getting the next role. It's about how you show up when you're not in power.

Startups: Leading at the Edge of Innovation

A need, an idea, a passion, maybe even a patent. A business plan, a credible team, sources of funding and materials, a website, and a path to market. These are fundamentals of a promising startup, whether in security or elsewhere. But even if every box is checked, success often depends on one overlooked factor: leadership that fits the moment.

A 2022 *Forbes* survey of 30 startup CEOs asked for the single most essential leadership quality in a "hypergrowth" environment. Nearly a third said *vision*. Others pointed to *patience and tenacity* (23%), *authenticity* (13%), and *inspiration* (10%).

But what do veterans of the security startup scene say? How does leadership in a startup, particularly a security startup, differ from leadership in other environments? I asked some experts for their opinions.

Whether you're starting your own security firm, building a consulting or training brand, or launching a security or risk function within a larger organization, there are lessons to be learned from those who've already forged new ground.

In a word, the key to security startup leadership is culture.

Culture starts with listening. "What I've learned is that you have to be flexible and listen to other people," says Steve Layne, who in late 2021 launched Red Vector, a software tool that ingests multiple data streams and uses AI to assess insider risk. As much as you want to be a strong leader, he cautions that acting unilaterally is "usually going to get you into more trouble than not. You have to be able to ask good questions, and you have to learn to shut up and listen."

Those traits are crucial in startups both because the operating environment is so fluid and because you are trying to build a passionate and cohesive team that feels respected. Building such a team makes selecting, training, and retaining staff so important.

Steve Reinharz, CEO of security robotics company Robotic Assistance Devices (RAD), is fastidious about team building. At RAD, instilling the right culture starts at the recruiting stage. "We don't ask people to conform to our culture," he says. "We look for people who exhibit elements of the culture." The result is people "who are excited to come to work on Monday, who are invigorated by their jobs … who like their colleagues and environment, put in incredible efforts, and leave feeling energized and supported."

To screen for true fit, RAD uses a rigorous prequalification, interview, and onboarding process. Job candidates meet with four leaders who embody the company's values. Many are asked to complete a custom assignment—a report, a deck, or a creative problem-solving task—to assess their mindset and capabilities. Finally, all applicants read the company's culture manifesto and discuss it directly with Reinharz.

The process is both exhaustive and exhausting. But the results speak for themselves: more than 90% employee retention and a 400% increase in revenue in under two years.

Culture is also carefully cultivated at Swiftlane, a startup focused on mobile and facial recognition-based access control, particularly in the multi-family sector. "Culture is part of our core values," says CEO Saurabh Bajaj. "We talk about examples, we celebrate wins, and we actively discuss culture as an important tenet." That's particularly challenging because two-thirds of Swiftlane's workforce is virtual, "leading people that we don't see," as Bajaj puts it.

The lessons have been transformative. "We used to evaluate a team member based on skill set," Bajaj says. "Over time, I've realized that's not enough. The other axis is trust. Are you building a trusting team where people can lean on [each other]?"

Not all startups are solving known problems with well-worn tools. Some are introducing entirely new paradigms in areas where discomfort or denial reign, such as organizational readiness for extreme, unthinkable threats.

Aric Mutchnick, founder of Experior Group and architect of the Red Ball Drills crisis-training program, speaks candidly about what it means to lead in this space. "We're not just building a business," he explains. "We're asking organizations to admit vulnerabilities they'd rather not face, and then engage in high-stakes, realistic drills to confront them."

That kind of pioneering work comes with challenges few startups face. "When your product is a radical rethinking of crisis management," Mutchnick notes, "you're often ahead of the market, trying to sell the future to a world still processing the last crisis." Leadership, in that context, means holding the line when some decision-makers recoil from the discomfort, when exercises expose inconvenient truths, and when short-term resistance threatens long-term progress.

It's also a test of belief. Convincing clients to move beyond checkbox compliance toward true preparedness requires relentless conviction in the mission, and the nerve to keep pushing even when the terrain gets hostile.

"Leading a company like Experior means being the voice that says: we can be braver, faster, and more self-aware. We're not just selling a product; we're helping shape how entire communities prepare for chaos," he says.

Reinharz, Bajaj, Layne, and Mutchnick all project energy, and that's no accident. "You have to be enthusiastic and exude confidence," Layne says. "You better believe what you are selling."

That belief is often what sustains founders through the inevitable friction of startup life, when the wins are hard-won, the path isn't clear, and the market isn't yet ready.

Startup leadership isn't about having all the answers, but about asking the right questions, building the right culture, and trusting the right people to help you find the way. The most successful founders in the security space aren't just innovators. They're listeners, recruiters of trust, and builders of resilience from day one.

SIDEBAR: THE ACCIDENTAL STARTUP

He's a veteran of five (official) wars. He has worked with Delta Force and SEAL Team Six, prevented scores of terrorist attacks, broken up countless international cartels and gangs, and otherwise served the American public with extraordinary courage and conviction.

But perhaps Louis R. Mizell Jr.'s biggest legacy is his accidental startup: the business that arose out of him trying to maximize his effectiveness as an intelligence agent and operative. Back in the 1970s, intel agencies placed him in global hotspots without much, well, intel. To survive, he cobbled together scraps of information from newspaper articles, government documents, judicial records, clandestine sources, corporate security logs, history books, interviews with captured terrorists, and everything else he could get his hands on. The result is a collection of more than 3 million incidents, organized into 100 "systems" (such as insider threat, bombs and bombers, aviation, maritime) and 80,000 topic chronicles. His algorithm-busting categories include ironic crimes, bombs hidden in sports equipment, criminals with prosthetics, and terrorists who became world leaders.

He has sold databases to intelligence agencies, government bureaus, law enforcement, law firms, security companies, insurers, the media, nonprofits, think tanks, and Fortune 500 corporations. His clients, even with their vast resources for gathering data, are routinely blown away by the scope and quality of his information. Even today's AI can't keep up, because many of his sources are either not on the web, buried in places like a security report filed by a Panamanian company or an article written in Arabic by a Lebanese newspaper.

Some of his best material has come from his own experiences, such as in Lebanon's brutal civil war. In 1979, after working for 30 hours straight and barely able to function, he stumbled into a secluded Beirut inn to get some rest. Fearing he might oversleep, he repeatedly instructed staff to wake him up in three hours. An employee remarked, "You think you have a hard time waking up. The Iranian man in 104 [across the hall] uses 11 alarm clocks!"

The comment barely registering, Lou staggered into his room, collapsed in his 18-pound vest, and crashed hard. Soon after, a thought jerked him awake: *My neighbor must be making bombs.* He relayed the information to a friendly officer, who ended up being promoted for preventing a series of devastating attacks.

In another case, he was assigned to the U.S. embassy in Colombia, where he ended up exposing dozens of terrorists and narcotraffickers that Bogota knew nothing about. He accomplished that by tracking one couple who was always sitting at a bus stop but never boarding a bus.

Lou was behind the Automobile Association of America's 1997 bombshell report that introduced the world to road rage. He was one of my favorite sources as an editor at *Security Management*, providing me 187 cases of people dressed as Santa Claus for a Christmas article, incidents of practical jokes gone wrong from an April Fool's item, and several examples of primitive uses of "drones"—kites, carrier pigeons, balloons, and so on—for a 2002 piece.

"People say I'm good at connecting the dots," Lou says. But I view my greater service to be collecting the dots that need connecting.

Leading People Traumatized by Failure

When you make a mistake in security, or any risk-related field, it can be a big deal. Assets lost, damage done, reputation harmed, maybe lives extinguished. We deal with enormous consequences in our profession. It's often said that the bad guy only has to be right once; we have to be right 100% of the time.

In risk fields, failure can result in loss of self-confidence or ability to respond in a crisis. That's not acceptable.

Failure is inevitable. It inspires some but cripples others. A truly impactful leader doesn't just correct failure, they support their team through it and ensure it doesn't scar them or impair their abilities or confidence.

As a young lawyer in a midsize firm, I witnessed some of my colleagues live in terror of missing a key legal citation, misinterpreting or misapplying a legal principle, or even presenting to certain partners.

One partner would bark at his associates things like, "This is an $80 million dollar case, and it's on you if we blow it!" or "Why don't you tell the client that you singlehandedly cut his chances of prevailing in half?"

In fact, I was eventually assigned to this attorney. When that news became public, a fellow associate pulled me aside and confided that the last six attorneys to work for him had left the firm within a year, some within days—two had quit, four were fired. Those were the most enervating months of my career. I left the firm shortly thereafter.

To understand how a constructive leader approaches mistakes, I turned to a prominent intellectual property lawyer and friend, Erik Kahn. If you substitute "security professional" or "risk professional" for "attorney," his observations ring equally true:

> In a high stakes profession like law, there is an expectation of perfection… With that said, lawyers are human, and mistakes are a product of being human.
>
> How then should a supervising lawyer handle mistakes? Over the years, I have directed all of my energy only on fixing the problem, rather than letting someone know that I am disappointed and on the verge of losing faith in them.
>
> Few leadership actions cause more harm in the development of a professional career than beating down someone who has failed… This consuming fear of replicating failure takes up space in the psyche that could otherwise be used for problem solving, learning, and necessary levels of risk taking.
>
> I have personally seen people whose careers have been entirely sidelined due to a heavy dose of 'tough love'-style abuse heaped on during crisis.

Kahn invoked a powerful sports example to illustrate an effective way to deal with shell-shocked professionals:

> "I recently watched an NFL kicker blow two easy field goals in a row. Each time, the coach gave the kicker a hug and looked that player in the eye, telling them that it was okay—that the past does not define the future (what I imagine the coach may have said) or similar words of encouragement.
>
> To do otherwise would be counterproductive. There are situations where someone is no longer effective or unable to function at a high level on a team. In that case, that person should be counseled out to regroup and try again somewhere else. But in situations where someone adds value and is capable of being helped, providing a supportive team-based approach not only helps the person who has blown the kick; it also helps the team win in the future."

Leaders must model calm, clarity, and compassion when things go wrong. Fear corrodes trust. Blame stifles innovation. But empathy, accountability, and belief in the team build resilience.

Orchestrating Turnarounds

Few organizations in American sports suffered from more corrosive leadership than Washington's NFL franchise under Daniel Snyder. For 25 years, it was a case study in dysfunction: accusations of harassment, financial misconduct, and cultural toxicity. Then, in one of the most dramatic turnarounds in professional sports, during the 2024 season the team came within a game of the Super Bowl, after a wholesale change in leadership, values, and governance. For security leaders trying to steer broken organizations back on course, Washington offers a surprising but instructive model.

What changed? Everything that mattered.

When Snyder sold the team, the toxic culture didn't vanish overnight. But the new ownership group quickly signaled a break from the past. It didn't just fire and replace—it redefined purpose. The new leadership prioritized transparency, rebuilt fractured relationships with fans and players, and emphasized dignity and accountability. Front office decisions, staffing, fan engagement, and even stadium operations began reflecting a human-centered, high-integrity approach.

This shift wasn't just about ethics, but about performance. Dysfunction at the top had rippled through the entire organization: scouts weren't trusted, players weren't protected, and employees weren't empowered. Once a new leadership ethos took hold, productivity and morale rose, talent stayed longer, and results improved, on and off the field.

The lesson for security and risk leaders is that cultural turnaround is possible even after years of degradation. But the spark is always the same: intentional, values-driven leadership.

Patterns across Turnarounds

Turnarounds—whether in sports teams, Fortune 500 companies, or security departments—share recognizable patterns:

- New leadership, not just new leaders: It's not enough to swap personnel. There must be a philosophical shift. Leaders must model the behaviors they want embedded in the culture.
- Symbolic actions matter: The new regime in Washington renamed the franchise, renovated training facilities, and removed visual reminders of the past. Such symbolic gestures aren't superficial; they communicate a clean break and demonstrate concern for the players' well being.
- Middle management is the key hinge: Turnarounds often falter if only the top changes. In Washington, operational leaders (scouting directors, department heads, marketing staff) were aligned with the new leadership vision. That alignment spurred transformation.

Security leaders often inherit broken programs. Perhaps a predecessor overpromised and underdelivered, alienated other business units, or tolerated underperformance. You may walk into a program where trust is low, standards are unclear, and the team is demoralized.

In those moments, remember: you're not just managing people. You're recalibrating a culture.

Here's how:

- Start by listening. Employees in toxic cultures often feel unheard. Conduct one-on-one meetings. Host roundtables. Let people vent but pay attention to patterns.
- Build credibility through action, not slogans. Don't talk about "transparency" and "empowerment" unless you're visibly practicing both.
- Create quick wins. Identify one broken process you can fix fast, such as an outdated travel risk policy prohibiting two staff from flying in the same commercial airliner, and then do it. Early wins create momentum and credibility.
- Don't try to 'out-manage' dysfunction. Replace it with purpose. A culture of compliance and fear can only be supplanted by a culture of clarity, accountability, and mission.

Consider one CSO who took over a corporate security department that hadn't conducted a meaningful training in five years. The prior leader, a former law enforcement officer, ran the team as a command-and-control unit. Creativity was stifled. The team was seen as obstructionist by the business.

The new CSO took a radically different approach. She conducted 30 interviews in her first 60 days, launched a security advisory council with business unit leaders, and restructured the team to include risk analysts and cross-functional liaisons. Within a year, incident reporting rose (a good sign), staff retention improved, and the security function was invited into strategic planning conversations for the first time.

As she told me, "I didn't have to be the smartest person in the room. I just had to be the most curious and the most accountable."

That's turnaround leadership.

Working Alone: Leading Without a Team

Many security practitioners don't lead a team. They may not even be part of a team. Individual consultants, solo business owners, researchers, trainers, coders, and academics often work in isolation. Yet their leadership potential and impact can be just as powerful.

While it's easy to associate leadership with team dynamics and org charts, influence doesn't require infrastructure. Solo professionals still engage with clients, shape perspectives, challenge assumptions, and drive change. Choosing not to lead in these settings isn't humility but abdication.

Consider golf and swimming, two of the most individualistic sports. Swimmers literally compete with their heads down. British golfer Tony Jacklin, despite limited success as a player, became a legendary captain for the European Ryder Cup team. He studied his U.S. rivals, restructured his team's culture, and instilled pride and purpose across national boundaries. Under his leadership, Europe broke a decades-long losing streak.

Likewise, U.S. swimmer Jason Lezak etched his name in Olympic history during the 4 × 100 relay in 2008. Anchoring the U.S. team, he entered the water nearly a full body length behind French swimmer Alain Bernard, the world record holder in the 100-meter freestyle. With astonishing closing speed, Lezak reeled him in over the final 50 meters. As his three teammates and the world watched, he overtook Bernard by just 0.08 seconds to win gold for the United States. Lezak obliterated the previous record split time for that distance, a time he never came close to duplicating in individual events. Part of what drove him was to help Michael Phelps secure a record eighth gold medal in a single Olympic Games.

These examples prove that even the most solitary performers can lead: by preparation, passion, and delivering when it matters most.

Lessons in Solo Leadership

Here are seven leadership strategies for risk professionals who typically work alone:

- **Motivate colleagues and clients**: Solo consultants help clients reimagine risk strategy. Trainers spark growth in students. Thought leaders empower their online networks.
- **Continuously learn**: Stay sharp by absorbing trends, tools, and techniques. Brian Reid of Brison LLC exemplifies this, relentlessly acquiring knowledge in the risk fields and beyond to serve clients better. He inspires me to do the same.

- **Inspire others**: Influence goes beyond contracts. Mentorship, encouragement, and open sharing strengthen the security profession.
- **Do your best work collaboratively**: Even solo operators hit their stride when working alongside others on a project or in a coalition. It's said that there is no competition in security. Prove it.
- **Empower partners**: Whether it's a client, contractor, or mentee, create room for them to succeed.
- **Exert influence publicly**: Social media, publications, and presentations allow you to set agendas and spread good ideas.
- **Embody your brand**: It's hard to find anyone in the security profession who is unaware of Chuck Andrews and the Friends of Chuck network. His personality is his platform, and it's helped him build a global network.

Leadership isn't confined to a department or job title. Even when you work alone, your actions echo. Intentionality, clarity, curiosity, and generosity are the hallmarks of leadership, whether you're steering a global team or consulting from a laptop at home.

Stepping Down from Leadership

After 14 years of finding last-minute goalies, securing locker room doors, and trying to parcel out equal ice time to the skaters, a few years ago I shed the captain's "C" from the jersey of my recreational (aka beer league) hockey team. Like many security professionals, I gravitate to leadership positions. But true leaders know when to step aside. And they understand that the most important thing they can do is to create a pathway for new and aspiring leaders to take their place.

With my hockey teammates, I realized I was doing them a disservice. As other life responsibilities increased, my interest waned in managing late-night ice times and questioning penalty calls by refs. One of the assistant captains had quietly stepped up to take on duties that I was too busy to handle, such as figuring out player payments and ordering new uniforms. It was both an obligation and honor to tap him as my successor. And it was my duty to clear a path for him: to serve as a human Zamboni—the machine that smooths the ice—so to speak.

Unfortunately, many leaders stick around past their expiration date. They see leadership as a status symbol or mark of accomplishment, something to be seized and held at all costs. But good leadership is about service, not self-preservation.

Remember that expression, "Old leaders never die, they just fade away"? Leaders should be like photographers: they never die, they just develop new talent.

Some security leaders consulted for this book demurred when asked how their boss handled their development. In some cases, deputies felt suppressed rather than encouraged, opting to take a CSO role elsewhere where they could shine. Those professionals may have departed eventually anyway, but a confident security executive should never stunt the growth of a direct report.

In fact, it is in the best interests of the organization for leaders to hire and refine staff with skills and talents both complementary and superior to their own. Why? For succession planning purposes, of course, but also because security executives should be focused on strategy, vision, motivation, talent management, and other 50,000-foot issues, leaving important day-to-day work to their reports.

Moreover, confident bosses seek highly gifted staff to challenge their assumptions, raise competing arguments, help decide thorny issues, and otherwise sharpen their thinking.

We've already seen examples of this elsewhere in the book, such as with Russ Cancilla, the former CSO of Baker Hughes, who consciously transitioned leadership responsibilities to his deputies, empowering them to take the reins while he moved into an advisory role. His example, along with others like him, demonstrates that true leadership includes preparing for succession, mentoring the next generation, and knowing when to get off the ice.

Leadership isn't just about knowing how to lead. It's also about knowing when to let go. Step aside with purpose, not resignation. Leave your people equipped, empowered, and inspired. And as you do, don't just exit. Make it a clean line change: time it right, alert your teammate, and skate off with purpose.

Leadership for Less-than-Stellar Practitioners: Can Charisma Beat Competence?

Here's an embarrassing admission: I'm a lifelong Jets fan. If you need proof that the organization is considered a laughingstock, a 2019 article in *Inc.* magazine is titled, "Want to Be a Great Leader? Look to the New York Jets—and Then Do the Opposite."

Since Joe Namath led the team to a Super Bowl victory in 1969, Jets fans have been looking for our next quarterback savior. Dozens of QBs have come and gone, including legends like Brett Favre and Aaron Rodgers, both of whom showed flashes of brilliance before flaming out. But few arrived with more promise, or faced more scrutiny, than Sam Darnold.

Drafted third overall in 2018, ahead of future stars Josh Allen and Lamar Jackson, Darnold had the demeanor of a leader. He handled media pressure with maturity, commanded the huddle, encouraged teammates, and showed composure in chaos. The problem? His performance didn't come close to expectations.

During his three years as the Jets' starter, Darnold went 13–35. He ranked near the bottom in passer rating and decision-making under pressure. Even his critics admitted that poor coaching, system changes, and weak supporting casts didn't fully explain the gap between his evident skills and his on-field results.

That raises the question: Can a security executive be a respected leader, even if they're not a top-tier practitioner? Can charisma and vision mask, or even compensate for, a lack of technical competence?

Mike Hurst, director of HJA Consult, believes so, but within limits. "You don't need to know how to specify a camera lens to be a chief of security," he says. "You have people who can do that." A CSO should be judged not on whether they can configure software or write policies, but on how well they align the security function with business goals.

But Jerry Brennan, CEO of Security Management Resources, offers a caution: "I've seen fine leaders who just couldn't execute. That's less of a problem when an organization has the resources to hire additional staff or outsource key functions, and when the CSO does so wisely."

British cricketer Mike Brearley may be the best sports analog for this idea. Known as a "modest batsman," he nonetheless captained England to memorable victories. His secret? Emotional intelligence. Brearley coaxed elite performances from teammates by managing anxiety, navigating conflict, and modeling steadiness. He wasn't the best player, but he made the team better.

In security, some leaders hold their roles because of strategic vision, inspiring presence, or internal capital. Others survive on relationships or external visibility: networking prowess, board affiliations, or previous government roles.

But as Hurst notes, "You could be a great person, but if the margins are bad, 'Sorry, mate.'" Eventually, KPIs—whether it's shrinkage rates, incident response times, or budget performance—catch up to you. That was Darnold's fate.

Yes, leadership can sometimes mask middling skills, but not forever. In high-stakes fields like security, results matter. If you're not technically strong, you must have the self-awareness to build a team that is.

The best leaders don't pretend to be flawless. They fill gaps, amplify others, and focus on what the organization truly needs.

Remote Teams: Commanding from the Cloud

Remember when leading remote teams was exotic? It meant that your organization had unusual reach, scale, or operations. Maybe you oversaw a team of security managers for Asian distribution centers at Amazon or globally dispersed cybersecurity architects at Microsoft.

In the hybrid work era, it's just another day (not) at the office.

We used to lead from the front: on the floor of the GSOC, at the perimeter, or in the corner office with a whiteboard full of emergency protocols. But as noted by Mike Brzozowski, who has led global teams at a past security role in Canada and a current one in Germany, the COVID-19 pandemic changed everything.

"Before the pandemic," he says, "having a dispersed team was exceptional. Then, quarantines, social distancing, and software like Teams and Zoom made remote work the norm, and with it introduced widespread responsibility for leading remote teams."

Then companies started preferring remote teams in many cases.

"Employers discovered that untethering staff from a physical workplace expanded the talent pool, reduced overhead costs, and enabled companies to tailor salaries to specific locations," among other efficiencies it generated, adds Brzozowski.

It's true. It's almost surprising today to not have geographically distant employees. I live in Washington, DC, and my team members are in New Jersey, New York, and Chicago. We see each other in person at client sites and conferences.

Pre-COVID, presence mattered. It still does, but in different ways. As remote and hybrid work reshape how organizations function, security leaders face a new reality: managing decentralized teams across time zones, functions, and cultures without daily, face-to-face engagement.

In physical security, where decision-making can't always wait for a quorum, remote leadership poses unique challenges. You can't inspire with charisma in a chat thread. You can't read fatigue through a phone line. And you can't reinforce culture with a hallway chat when your team operates in five languages across three continents.

And yet, security leadership in a dispersed world isn't just possible. It's necessary. It requires moving beyond security's beloved command-and-control model and embracing leadership built on trust, transparency, and shared mission.

Culture is easy to talk about and hard to build, especially when your team lacks a shared physical space. But culture doesn't require a campus. It requires clarity. Security leaders should codify the values that matter—integrity, discretion, and vigilance—and articulate how those show up in different roles. How does "resilience" look for a part-time security officer in Manila versus an executive protection analyst in London?

In a co-located environment, leadership can thrive on proximity. You overhear a conversation, course-correct in real time, or brainstorm over coffee. In distributed teams, that ambient awareness vanishes. You need systems to replace it.

That doesn't mean bureaucracy. It means intentionality. Establish operating rhythms: weekly standups, cross-regional hotwashes, and monthly intel shares.

Visibility tools help. Dashboards and communication platforms are useful when they align teams around common priorities. But if used punitively, they'll erode trust.

The remote environment strips away context. A terse Slack message can be read as curt. A camera-off Zoom call feels impersonal and perhaps unprofessional. Silence, in remote teams, often breeds ambiguity, and ambiguity corrodes trust.

Risk leaders must therefore overcommunicate, thoughtfully. Asynchronous channels (email, shared docs, project management apps, texts, etc.) offer clarity. Synchronous ones (calls, video chats) offer connection. Use both.

Mind your tone. Feedback that feels constructive in person can land harshly in writing. I recently emailed a colleague, telling him that a change he was pushing for would be delayed a week while I socialized it with our team. His response was unusually terse: "OK, fine." That read "angry" to me. I happened to see him a couple of days later and he wasn't upset at all.

If your role requires critique, accompany it with curiosity: "How did you arrive at this decision?" goes further than "Why did this happen?"

Remote leadership shouldn't translate into absentee management. But neither should it imply micromanagement.

We must empower regional and functional leads to own their decisions. Give them the context they need—risk appetite and exposure, threat posture, executive expectations, critical asset inventories—so they can make real-time calls without second-guessing. This is not a delegation of tasks but a delegation of trust.

Still, leaders must remain accessible, especially during incidents or escalations. Build bridges, not moats.

The most dangerous myth in remote leadership is that professionalism should eclipse personal connection.

Security is a relational business. Whether you're managing a residential patrol team or an intelligence desk, your people need to know they're seen. That starts with asking about their families, their career goals, even their frustrations.

Remote environments often create isolation, especially for frontline staff. The antidote isn't technology, at least not at first. It's empathy. If you're only checking in when something goes wrong, you're not leading, you're auditing.

"You should be connecting with, leading, guiding, inspiring and learning from your people at all times. That's leadership," says Matt Dumpert, who heads the ESRM practice for a global risk advisory firm and routinely deals with staff, partners, and issues worldwide. "You should be studying their work environment and always looking for improvements, efficiencies, tools, training and opportunities for growth. Lead from the front and demonstrate the type of behavior your team needs to be successful."

Despite the 2025 muster of the federal workforce back to the office, remote and hybrid work seem to be here to stay. Leadership is still local; local to the relationships you build, the values you model, and the consistency with which you show up.

Remote leadership is exotic no more. It's not a shift in tactics. It's a shift in mindset. For security leaders, remote is the new perimeter.

From the Lips of Gips: "I captained my beer-league team not because I was good, but because I was responsible enough to order the jerseys."

Chapter takeaways

Career Transitions and Layoffs

- Risk leadership isn't tied to a job title. True leaders maintain influence and support others even during career disruptions.
- Strategic use of professional networks, social media, volunteerism, and thought leadership platforms (e.g., professional associations, LinkedIn) helps sustain and elevate leadership visibility.
- Personal branding and purpose-driven behavior provide continuity through employment gaps.

Leadership Transitions and New Roles

- Effective transition involves cultural observation, humility, and adaptability, especially across borders or sectors.
- Risk leadership styles must evolve to meet organizational values and team dynamics.
- Risk leaders should assess both formal and informal power structures before attempting to influence change.

Job Searches and Ghosting

- Communication during the hiring process, by both employers and candidates, directly affects professional reputation.
- "Ghosting" undermines long-term credibility; timely, respectful engagement is a form of professional leadership. No one will hire an unreliable risk professional.

Startups

- Security startups require leaders to balance bold vision with cultural cohesion.
- Culture is a strategic asset: leaders must build it intentionally, often starting with the recruiting process.
- Trust, not just competence, is a critical hiring metric for high-functioning startups.

Cultural Turnarounds

- Organizational recovery demands visionary leadership, alignment across top roles, and respect for internal stakeholders.
- A clear mission, tone at the top, and investment in people catalyze cultural change.
- Rotating leadership opportunities, like changing team captains, develops bench strength and shared ownership.

Leading while Working Alone

- Risk leadership without a formal team is both possible and powerful. Influence, mentorship, and brand-building still apply.
- Solo risk and security professionals can lead by example, continuously learn, empower partners, and inspire trust across engagements.
- Like golfers or swimmers, individual risk and security professionals often perform better when part of a cause bigger than themselves.

Stepping Down from Leadership

- Knowing when to step aside is a hallmark of great risk leadership.
- Creating a succession pipeline and mentoring successors sustains team strength and institutional continuity.

- Leaders must resist clinging to authority and instead view leadership as developmental, not positional.

Leadership for Less-than-Stellar Practitioners

- Charisma and vision may enable less-proficient risk leaders to survive, but results ultimately matter.
- Some organizations tolerate or compensate for weak execution if offset by strengths like inspiration or networking.
- Sustainable risk leadership requires either technical competence or the wisdom to build a team that fills skill gaps.

Commanding from the Cloud

- In the absence of face time, risk leadership must shift from command-and-control to trust-and-context. Visibility tools and rituals help, but integrity and empowerment matter more.
- Strong remote cultures are built through clarity, not geography. Risk leaders should codify values and ensure they manifest meaningfully across diverse roles and regions.
- Casual proximity is gone, so build structure with intention. Weekly standups, cross-regional hotwashes, and shared dashboards can foster cohesion and situational awareness.

BREAKAWAY IV

Risk Leadership Lessons on the Cel-ular Level through Comics

Now for the final Breakaway: leadership in the much-maligned world of comic strips. The Sunday "funnies" were a big deal in my household as a kid, and the medium has birthed wisdom that has eluded the greatest philosophers and thinkers. Here goes:

In the 1977 animated feature *Race for Your Life, Charlie Brown*, the titular ne'er-do-well goes to summer camp looking to enhance his leadership skills. Ever the cold voice of reason, Peppermint Patty informs Charlie Brown that he "couldn't lead a dog on a leash."

In fact, the lovable loser is often a highly effective leader, and many others in the *Peanuts* gang have lessons to offer security professionals as well.

Charlie Brown

Description

Chuck, as Patty calls him, may not win much, but his friends dutifully follow him onto the baseball diamond, even when it's almost inevitable that they'll be slaughtered. Even the petulant Lucy and grandstanding

DOI: 10.1201/9781003646488-13

Snoopy look to Charlie Brown's leadership on the pitcher's mound. Though he can be gloomy and pensive, Charlie Brown is the eternal optimist. Every day is a new opportunity to finally win a baseball game or to kick the football that Lucy will probably whisk away at the last moment. And he is unfailingly kind to everyone.

Key Leadership Traits: Kindness, optimism, and perseverance.

Linus

Description

If Charlie Brown represents leadership's heart, Linus is an intriguing combination of brains and faith. He is prone to rhapsodizing and waxing philosophical, yet he is probably the best listener in the gang. The other characters admire his intelligence and perceptiveness. But he's perhaps more personally magnetic because of his faith. He's the only child who can articulate what Christmas is truly about. He steadfastly believes in the Great Pumpkin despite enormous peer pressure.

Finally, of all the *Peanuts* characters, Linus "gets" security best. Reliant on his blanket for comfort, he understands the value of totems and rituals that make us feel safe. For some people, it's a photograph of loved ones, a piece of jewelry, or a memory. For Linus, it's a blanket.

Key Leadership Traits: Listening skills, intelligence, faith, and compassion.

Lucy

Description

Beyond her bluster and captious nature, Lucy is the prototypical "girlboss." In a society that relegates females to second-class roles, Lucy shatters the glass comic-strip panel. An entrepreneur, she sets up her own plywood psychiatric office.

Ilana Levine, one of the actresses who portrayed Lucy on Broadway, described her this way: "Lucy was the first feminist character that I knew of. She wasn't afraid to be a leader. I mean, she's tremendously interested in what she looks like, but she's also tremendously interested in being powerful in the world."

Key Leadership Traits: Confidence, curiosity, and bias for action.

Snoopy

Description

Snoopy may seem like a loner living in a dreamworld atop his "Sopwith Camel," but he dutifully leads Woodstock and his friends on camping excursions. Though his imagination runs wild, Snoopy is not untethered from reality. His creative mind makes him a problem solver; he somehow engineered a sprawling living space, including a gym, a pool table, a shower, and a science lab, inside his tiny doghouse.

Key Leadership Traits: Imagination, creativity, and duty.

The *Peanuts* gang offers a full spectrum of leadership, from the brooding optimism of Charlie Brown to the bold designs of Snoopy. But leadership lessons aren't limited to Charles Schulz's world. They show up in Viking helmets and velvet smoking jackets too.

Hägar the Horrible

Description

With his horned helmet, shaggy beard, and pillaging résumé, Hägar doesn't scream "modern leadership model." But look closer. Hägar balances brute force with heart, managing both a bickering crew and a household with surprising tenderness. He's loyal, adaptable, and often wise in unexpected ways.

In one strip I've had taped to my office shelf for years, Hägar tells the king he's retiring from Viking life and would like to serve as head of castle security. The king agrees, but warns that he's a man of few words. If he beckons with a finger, Hägar will have to come like an obedient dog. Visibly provoked, Hägar replies that he, too, is a man of few words, and he'll come like a wild dog. The final panel shows him leaving the castle and telling a peasant that he's "out of retirement."

Key Leadership Traits: Personal dignity, loyalty, humor, and refusal to tolerate demeaning leadership.

Richie Rich

Description

Dubbed "the poor little rich boy," Richie Rich lives in a gilded world of robot butlers, private zoos, and cash for pillow stuffing. But Richie himself is humble, generous, and friendly to all. He treats his bodyguards, pilots, and butlers with kindness and never lords his status over classmates.

Still, one moral wrinkle always stuck with me. Richie's friends Freckles and Pee Wee live in a crumbling shack that looks like it was slapped together from discarded fence posts. Richie visits them often, but he never offers to fix up their home, not even with subtle help. As a kid, I admired Richie, but I always wished he had quietly arranged for a new roof or indoor plumbing. *I know the kids were proud, but come on.*

Key Leadership Traits: Generosity, humility, likability, and a reminder that ethical leadership means using privilege to lift others in tangible ways.

Comic strips are meant to entertain over coffee or cereal. But embedded in those four-panel worlds are profound lessons in leadership. Charlie Brown leads with vulnerability. Linus with faith. Lucy with force. Snoopy with flair. Hägar with dignity. Richie Rich with empathy.

9
Leadership Landmines

Chapter Objectives

Section objectives

- Understand the key elements that can derail leadership
- Learn how to manage these elements as they arise
- Learn how to strengthen your leadership skills by reverse engineering these pitfalls

The Ego Trap

It's the paradox of power. People in democratic societies crave public officials with minimal egos. Yet the candidates who run for the highest positions in their lands often have massive egos, and maybe they have to. It may take an enormous sense of self-regard to believe you can govern a nation and that millions of people will vote for you.

On a smaller scale, that dynamic plays out in the corporate world, including in the security and risk communities. Leadership requires confidence, which can mutate into cockiness and manifest as arrogance. So how do the most successful leaders inspire and motivate their people without gorging on power?

To get insight, I spoke to several security leaders, as well as executive coaches who work with security professionals.

In the view of Lucas de la Rosa, corporate security manager at a Buenos Aires-based gas company, ego and leadership are incompatible. "There are terms that are opposite in meaning but complementary at the same time," he says, "such as man and woman, electron and proton, oxygen and carbon dioxide." Ego and leader don't qualify. "Nothing is more counterproductive and inefficient than an egotistical leader," he says.

Still, there are so many of them.

DOI: 10.1201/9781003646488-14

"We have all seen toxic leaders," says Joe Rector, who oversees a U.S. government security forces directorate. "It is all about them. They constantly talk about themselves and consistently seek the spotlight. They take the credit of others. They abuse their authority and treat their subordinates badly. It doesn't mean they don't get the mission done, but it is usually at a cost of low organizational morale and low productivity. They are the kind of leader with whom people do not want to work and avoid if they can."

As simple as it sounds, Rector avoids this trap by focusing on the golden rule. He actively encourages his staff's wellbeing and professional development. He makes sure to credit them for their work, and he shares, or gives them exclusively, the limelight. "Also, I try to prepare them for the next leadership level in their career, making sure they have the right training and give them assignments that prepare them for the future," he says. By modeling that behavior, he avoids the ego trap and tacitly inculcates humility in his staff.

Several security executives and coaches emphasized that the ego question comes down to your "why" for being a leader. "Is it for personal glory or mission success?" asks Lori Flor, director of safety and security at the University of California San Diego (UCSD).

Executive coach Alicia Rodriguez elaborates: "First, what drives a leader to lead? Is he or she committed to something so much so that they want to participate, influence, and change it for the better from a position of authority and power? Or are they primarily driven to lead because they desire status, power, and ways to feel worthy?"

If it's for power and glory, the task to quell the ego becomes dramatically more difficult.

What about leaders who start out altruistic but become intoxicated with power as they climb the ladder? To prevent hubris from taking root, Rodriguez recommends finding something outside of work that gives you meaning, be it family, faith, or friendship. It's critical to stay grounded and reflective. "Can you wake up every morning knowing and feeling you are doing the right thing," she asks, "especially when no one is noticing, seeing, or affirming your actions?"

Periodic self-evaluation is key. "Great leaders have a high level of self-awareness: they know themselves, can take a look at themselves, but also understand their environment and dynamics at play," says JT Mendoza, senior director of global information security at a global hotel chain.

Equally important is having people who will call you out.

Mendoza says he learned a humbling lesson during his final years in the military, as he was transitioning to federal service. "I was called out for being a bad leader," he recalls. But he used it as a learning experience. Undertaking a 360-leadership assessment, he swallowed his pride and sought out colleagues who he knew would score him harshly. He used the feedback to improve his leadership skills.

I also asked these experts how far you can take your public persona before you come across as an egomaniac. There's no pat answer. Some people can keynote conferences, appear on podcasts, publish articles, and win awards (and document it all on LinkedIn) without seeming self-centered. Others come across as narcissists in a single post. It depends on what your message is and how you deliver it.

"Think about whether you want to put it on LinkedIn," advises UCSD's Flor. "It's fine if you're not overwhelming people and the information is timely and valuable."

Instead of posting about your own reward, consider using your social media clout to praise someone on your team, someone who has earned a certification, completed a course, or taken on a leadership role.

Perhaps Simon Sinek puts it best when comparing the ego-driven leader to the generous one: "A star wants to see himself rise to the top. A leader wants to see those around him rise to the top."

The best leaders, it turns out, aren't just humble, they actively elevate others, leaving no room for ego at the top.

Complacency (I'll Get around to Naming This Section Later)

The metrics look solid. Your team seems engaged. No one's complaining. So you postpone a few one-on-ones. Your coaching feels more like maintenance than momentum. Things are fine, so what's the urgency?

That's the trap. Complacency doesn't show up as failure. It disguises itself as stability.

Let's look more closely at leadership itself. We all know what complacent leadership is: it stunts innovation, basks in past performance, ignores market shifts, and yawns at new opportunities.

On the other hand, hands-off leadership may fit the moment. The question becomes, When does efficient leadership turn into complacency? When your scheduled check-ins with direct reports become routine, even if they thrive under you? When your performance reviews become performative, or as your words of encouragement get predictable, although staff performance and engagement improve or remain excellent? Or do your followers' attitude, motivation, or production have to decline before your leadership becomes complacent? In other words, can leadership still be effective when the input becomes stale or uninspired but the output still sparkles?

Complacency isn't all or nothing; it's a spectrum. It's also an easy word to throw around. Sometimes laissez-faire leadership is appropriate, especially with skilled, motivated, or experienced teams. It demonstrates trust in your people and their decision-making abilities.

I presented these issues to several accomplished security leaders to gather their insights. When does low-touch become destructive?

"Technology, remote work, geopolitics. The pace that these are changing right now is unprecedented," says a security executive who has held senior security positions in several verticals. That professional, who asked for anonymity due to the nature of his employment, draws a line between hands-off and complacent leadership. "If you're starting to feel, 'we're good,' the fact that you feel that way means you're not good." He adds, "By the time the leader suspects they may be complacent or coasting, that's a symptom of a deeper problem. It means they have fallen so far behind" that they are not keeping up with social, economic, or geopolitical developments.

He offers a couple of antidotes. For one, embrace humility. Second, he says that "Leaders should make their team members authors, not witnesses. Give people decision-power a little out of their comfort zone and your comfort zone." For example, it may be faster for you than a junior security manager to draft a policy. But encouraging them and giving them agency benefits everyone and yields growth. "The key is to always be a little bit uncomfortable," he says, to the point of willfully seeking discomfort.

Jonathan Perillo, a security executive in the insurance industry and founder of the training startup Safyst, agrees with that conclusion and offers a slightly different perspective. He stipulates that it's important to know the reason behind the hands-off approach. "Is it because of lack of bandwidth? Is it because you are comfortable with your staff's performance? Or are you checked out and not striving?"

If it's a bandwidth issue, proactivity suffers. "You can't do things like future proofing and strategy," which appear at the top of ASIS's CSO Development pyramid, he says. "You are struggling to stay compliant, you're in a reactive stance, it's creating risk gaps. But if you are cognizant enough about it, you can get your arms around it" and adjust, he says.

If you are cruising because staff are excelling, that's a happy problem and "you should take a lap around the golf course," Perillo jokes. "But if you are getting what you want all the time, you should be tasking your teams at lower levels with those assignments" to increase efficiency, build skills, and forge resilience.

Finally, if you are checked out, "find something valuable about the job again. We all struggle with it periodically. There has to be something engaging, and hopefully it's your people."

And maybe that answers the original question about what distinguishes effective laissez-faire leadership from complacent leadership: meaningful connection and engagement with your staff. In the end, complacency isn't about doing less, it's about caring less. The best leaders never stop paying attention.

Style Clashes: When Leadership Chemistry Fails

Not every failed leadership moment stems from bad decisions. Sometimes it's a matter of good leaders misfiring with their teams.

One believes in blunt honesty, the other in careful consensus. One wants fast action, the other values methodical process. Neither approach is inherently wrong, but when they collide, productivity stalls and morale frays. These aren't failures of character or competence. They're style clashes.

As a leader, I try to accommodate different personalities and approaches, but I'm far from immune to style clashes. I like to engage and inspire my direct reports, but that falls flat with different personalities. In one case, one of my newer reports was proposing an idea for revenue generation in a meeting where many of the attendees were either indifferent to the idea or downright skeptical. When he faced the first hint of resistance from his peers, he shut down. I threw him a lifeline but he didn't take it. He was used to his boss riding to the rescue and imposing ideas by fiat. My approach was to have him fight for buy-in for his idea, which didn't happen. That's a style clash that could have been ameliorated by improved communication.

Melissa Agnes, founder of the Crisis Ready Institute, worked with a communications leader in a large urban school district through her leadership certification program whose experience also demonstrates this type of style clash. When immigration policy changes created widespread fear in her community, affecting over half of their student population, she advocated for direct, compassionate communication to address families' concerns about their children's safety at school.

Her instinctive leadership style was heart-centered and community-focused: it acknowledged the fear, validated the emotions, provided clear information about safety protocols, and demonstrated care for the families they served. But the board and superintendent operated from a completely different paradigm: risk-averse and politically cautious. They viewed her approach as "wading into politically charged waters" and dismissed her concerns entirely.

For months, she had pushed her human-centered messaging approach and got nowhere. The clash wasn't about competence or intent; both sides wanted what was best for students. But their fundamental approaches to crisis leadership were incompatible: she led with emotional intelligence and connection, while they defaulted to avoidance and control.

Leadership style shapes everything: how direction is given, how feedback is received, how decisions are made. Daniel Goleman's work on emotional intelligence and leadership styles outlines six major modes (visionary, coaching, affiliative, democratic, pacesetting, and commanding) each useful in the right context. Problems arise when leaders default to one style, fail to read the room, or assume that their way is universally effective.

These clashes can show up anywhere: between executives, between manager and team, even between peer leaders in different departments. In the security and risk world, where stakes are high and coordination is critical, style friction doesn't just cause awkward meetings. It can delay decisions, create turf battles, and discourage escalation.

Style differences are often misinterpreted as generational divides. A Gen Z analyst might expect inclusive brainstorming and near-instant feedback, while their Gen X boss leans toward autonomous work and formality. But these aren't just generational issues; they're cultural expectations shaped by upbringing, education, and work environment. Pew Research and Jean Twenge's *iGen*, document younger professionals more openly questioning hierarchy and craving feedback loops, while older professionals may view this as immaturity or entitlement. That gap can harden into misunderstanding.

As someone born between Boomers and Gen X, I've worked with every generation currently in the workforce, and one of the most persistent, frustrating challenges I face is communication. Not the message itself, but the method: text, email (which one?), phone call, LinkedIn DM, Slack, WhatsApp, Microsoft Teams, association and professional platforms. The options feel endless. One colleague will only communicate with me through Snapchat. If I get a mobile message and don't check it immediately, I have to scroll through 11 pages of apps to figure out where it came from. Layer on the six active email accounts I juggle—for my full-time job, personal life, consultancy, industry association, advisory board role, and a partner company—and it's easy to feel like communication isn't about clarity but about decoding preferences. Generational norms explain part of this, but so do personality, context, and role.

Even trying to match tone, pace, and platform can become a minefield. I also carry two phones, one personal and one from my employer, which I keep separate, adding another layer of complication. And if the two phones get too close to each other, they start humming in an Apple mating ritual. Navigating this complexity is an everyday example of how style clashes don't have to be dramatic to be disruptive.

To be fair, I've heard younger colleagues voice their own frustrations. To them, my generation's love for long emails, scheduled calls, or formality can feel inefficient or dilatory. Why write a five-paragraph email with impeccable grammar and punctuation when a dashed-off voice note could say it faster?

Adds Executive Coach Kat Fariss, who navigates her share of intergenerational fault lines: "Why wait three days for a calendar slot when a DM gets an instant reply? For many younger professionals, platforms *are* the language, not a distraction from it." They're not trying to be difficult; they're operating from a different set of assumptions about time, access, and what respect looks like.

Fariss advises creating clarity rather than coping with chaos. "One of the most helpful practices I've adopted is setting *communication agreements* with my teams: simple, shared norms around how we connect, when we expect responses, and which platforms we'll use for what," she says. It sounds basic, but she insists that it builds trust fast. "Instead of assuming, we align. We can't eliminate every misfire or missed message, but we *can* name our preferences, stay curious about others', and co-create a rhythm that works across generations, not against them."

At the end of the day, leadership isn't about mastering every app or communication style. It's about modeling clarity, empathy, and flexibility, and staying humble enough to keep learning.

In *Tribal Leadership*, Dave Logan and his co-authors describe five stages of organizational culture, ranging from alienation to world-class cooperation. Most style clashes emerge between Stage 3 leaders ("I'm great") and Stage 4 teams ("We're great"). If a team values collective achievement and collaboration, but its leader seeks personal wins and spotlight, trust erodes. The problem isn't malice but misalignment.

The first fix isn't change, but recognition. Leaders must first understand their default style, and how it lands with others. Tools like 360 reviews, team charters, and facilitated discussions can illuminate these differences.

But feedback alone isn't enough. Leaders must cultivate behavioral agility, the ability to shift tone, approach, and communication style without losing authenticity. Deborah Ancona's "sensegiving" framework highlights how leaders influence meaning and momentum by adjusting their narrative to the audience.

When leaders learn to recognize style mismatches early, and adjust intentionally, they prevent friction from calcifying into dysfunction.

That's what happened in the case of the school district communications officer. As Melissa Agnes relates, through training, "the same school district leader began to understand that behavioral agility didn't mean abandoning her values. It meant learning to communicate them in ways that different stakeholders could receive. As part of her leadership development, she committed to stretching beyond her comfort zone by approaching this same challenge from an entirely different angle."

The officer adapted her approach for the board and superintendent. "Instead of leading with emotional appeals," Agnes recalls, "she led with financial data: approximately 1500 students represented nearly $10 million in lost revenue. She connected community fear directly to enrollment decline and budget deficits, then showed how compassionate communication was actually a retention strategy. Suddenly, her 'politically charged' approach became sound business practice."

Agnes says the transformation was remarkable: "Within one week of reframing her approach, she secured board approval for comprehensive family communications, district-wide principal training, and direct community engagement. Her heart-centered values remained unchanged, but she had learned to translate them into language that created connection rather than resistance."

Leadership chemistry doesn't require sameness. But it does require awareness. What often feels like insubordination, aloofness, or fragility may just be a style out of sync. The best leaders don't just drive results; they tune in, match tone, and bridge the gap between how they lead and how others hear them.

The Isolation Spiral: When Leaders Lose the Thread

Leadership failures aren't always explosive. Sometimes, they unfold quietly. A once-effective leader begins to feel off, and no one knows quite why. Decisions still get made, emails still go out, but something's missing. Over time, the leader becomes more distant, more reactive, and less attuned. They haven't failed in a dramatic sense. But they've entered the isolation spiral: a slow drift away from context, connection, and consequence.

Leaders in isolation often don't even realize it. They think they're staying out of the weeds or empowering others. But over time, they stop asking questions. They start talking more than listening. Their meetings become status updates rather than strategic dialogues.

In security and risk leadership, the consequences are acute. Isolation dulls the senses. Threat signals are missed. Frontline concerns don't surface. Cultural fractures widen. The risk isn't just operational. It's reputational, cultural, and systemic.

Melissa Agnes recently worked with a senior executive who exemplified this isolation spiral. As the CEO of a government organization she had led for over a decade, she had built her reputation on authentic, grounded practices, such as starting meetings with breathing exercises, leading with emotional intelligence, and prioritizing genuine connection over rigid hierarchy. But over time, resistance from stakeholders began chipping away at her confidence. The feedback was never direct criticism, just subtle signals: eye rolls during her centering practices, preference for more "traditional" approaches, quiet suggestions that her methods weren't "particularly received well."

Agnes picks up the thread: "Gradually, she began suppressing her instincts. She stopped the grounding exercises. Her meetings became more conventional, more transactional. She started leading from what others expected rather than from what she knew to be effective. The shift wasn't dramatic. It was a slow erosion of authenticity. Her team noticed the change before she did: less connection, more distance, communications that felt more corporate and less human. What they had valued most about her leadership—her presence, her ability to create safety—began disappearing."

Sometimes success is the culprit. As leaders rise, they leave behind the informal channels and peer networks that kept them grounded. The higher you go, the thinner the feedback. Add in hybrid work, packed calendars, and professional fatigue, and disconnection becomes the default.

Isolation can also come from overexertion: leaders stretched so thin they stop reaching out. Or it stems from fear; fear of seeming uncertain, outdated, or out of step. So they say less, listen less, and slowly vanish from the everyday pulse of their teams.

How to Spot the Spiral

Ask the uncomfortable questions:

- When was the last time someone challenged you?
- When were you last surprised by your team's feedback?
- Are you relying on proxies rather than people?

Leaders deep in the spiral often don't know what their teams are working on or worrying about. The calendar fills up, but alignment thins out.

For the CEO coached by Agnes, the turning point came when she began to recognize that the discomfort she felt wasn't about her leadership being wrong. Rather, it was about her abandoning what made her effective. Through their work together, Agnes says, she began to see that "the resistance she encountered wasn't evidence of failure; it was often evidence that she was challenging outdated models that needed challenging."

Her recovery wasn't about changing her leadership style. It was about reclaiming it. She made a commitment to herself: I can reassert myself in those spaces because it's not wrong. Agnes continues: "She returned to starting meetings with breathing exercises, despite knowing some people wouldn't immediately embrace it. She led from emotional intelligence rather than pure analytics. Most importantly, she stopped letting others' discomfort with her authentic leadership undermine her confidence in what she knew worked."

There's no single fix, but there is a mindset shift. The goal isn't more meetings. It's more meaning. Here are a few ways to reverse the drift:

- Conduct skip-level conversations (between an employee and their manager's manager—thus "skipping a level") or anonymous team surveys.
- Revisit team rituals: regular roundtables, informal check-ins, walk-and-talks.
- Assign a trusted colleague to "red team" your blind spots.
- Say: "What am I missing?" and mean it.

The hardest part? Willingly inviting discomfort. Leaders who recover from isolation are those who make intentional reconnection a habit.

The transformation for Agnes's leader was remarkable. Within weeks of recommitting to her authentic approach, something shifted in the organizational culture. As she returned to her grounded leadership style with renewed confidence, people began responding differently, not because they suddenly embraced every practice, but because they felt her conviction and presence. Her team started engaging more openly, sharing concerns they had previously kept to themselves. Decision-making became more collaborative because people felt safer to contribute authentically.

What struck her most was realizing that when she had tried to lead according to others' expectations, she had actually become less effective, not more. "The very qualities that made her an exceptional leader—her emotional intelligence, her ability to create psychological safety, her authentic presence—were what her organization needed most, especially during challenging moments," Agnes says.

The longer you lead, the easier it is to drift and fallout of touch. The best leaders don't wait for a wake-up call. They build systems that keep them grounded, humble, and in rhythm with the people they serve.

From the Lips of Gips: "This chapter would have included more leadership pitfalls, but I was getting self-conscious."

Chapter Takeaways: Leadership Hazards and Pitfalls

- Confidence becomes a liability when it blinds leaders to others. The best leaders guard against ego not by denying it, but by redirecting it toward service, humility, and shared growth.
- Style clashes aren't failures of competence, they're failures of fit. Understanding your own leadership style, and how it lands with others, is key to avoiding unnecessary friction.
- Complacency isn't always visible. When performance is "good enough," leaders may coast without realizing it. But momentum decays silently, and trust erodes before metrics catch up.
- Leadership isn't static, and neither are followers. What worked six months ago may not work today. Leaders must continually recalibrate their tone, approach, and presence.
- Isolation is leadership's quietest hazard. Drift happens gradually: fewer questions, fewer challenges, fewer signals from the ground. Connection is not a luxury.
- Recovery is possible, but it requires intentional discomfort. Whether it's inviting criticism, changing routines, or rediscovering your "why," resilient leaders make reconnection a habit, not a one-time fix.

10 Risk Leadership into the Future

Chapter Objectives

- Identify emerging inflection points in security leadership and understand how to anticipate transformative shifts.
- Explore the dynamic evolution of leadership theory and prepare for future paradigms shaped by technology, complexity, and culture.
- Recognize and respond to converging risks that blur traditional boundaries between physical, cyber, and organizational security functions.
- Understand how adaptive frameworks like Cynefin and Presilience® help leaders navigate increasingly chaotic and interdependent threat environments.
- Promote wellness as a foundational leadership competency in high-pressure, high-responsibility roles.

Monitoring Trends and Developments

Monitoring trends isn't just about staying current. It's about sensing inflection points, which are those rare moments when a field, a profession, or a generation stands at the edge of transformation.

Is the security field nearing one of those moments? What does it take to recognize a shift while it's happening?

To explore that, it's worth turning to Malcolm Gladwell's *Outliers*, where he dismisses the notion of the self-made individual and instead focuses on the power of context and timing.

Gladwell writes, "It makes a difference where and when we grew up. The culture we belong to and the legacies passed down by our forebears shape the patterns of our achievements in ways we cannot begin to imagine."

DOI: 10.1201/9781003646488-15

Would the Beatles have been the Beatles if not for a chance encounter that got them playing live 1200 times, mostly in Hamburg, often for eight hours at a go, enabling them to improve dramatically? And what about Bill Gates, who Gladwell says benefitted from going to an elite school in 1968 with a computer connected to a mainframe? Starting from eighth grade, he was able to get free computer time to do programming, an extraordinary rarity, eight hours a day, seven days a week, for seven years.

Gladwell's thesis transcends individuals to cultures and periods of time: 14 American industrialists who constitute 20% of the richest people in history were all born between 1831 and 1840; at least nine Silicon Valley pioneers born between 1953 and 1956 created the tech boom; Jewish immigrants to the United States in the early 20th century, who had skills in the clothing trade at a time New York was becoming the fashion center of the world, rose to prominence in that industry.

Is security having its "outlier" moment? In other words, has the industry or profession hit an inflection point in which it has recently or is about to take off, with security professionals gaining commensurate status?

The argument can be made that we are getting close. The September 11 attacks kicked off a new era in public recognition of the importance of security. Security has professionalized significantly over the last few decades, paced by the introduction of standards, guidelines, research, maturity models, frameworks, and certifications.

Many security executives now have business backgrounds and sit either in the C-suite or just below. Security is being increasingly accepted into the fold of risk management. The proliferation and pervasiveness of cyber threats have caught the attention of corporate boards, and cybersecurity has become a booming startup market.

Still, you would be hard-pressed to identify a security superstar that has either singlehandedly remade the profession or is well-known to the public besides, say, the head of the U.S. Federal Bureau of Investigation (FBI) or the Department of Homeland Security (DHS). People like Bruce Schneier, Cathy Lanier, Brian Tuskan, and Kevin Mandia turn heads in our world, but they are far from household names.

As disinformation, climate change, social divisions, and other underlying troubles continue to grow, security will only become more critical. So perhaps today's generation of early to mid-careerists will be the outliers. Or maybe the next generation after that.

If the lessons of the Beatles, Bill Gates and other success stories are any indication, it will take the perfect combination of cultural factors, opportunities, timing, hard work, and luck to get there.

Security professionals of the world: Is it time to seize the moment?

Whether this is security's breakout era or merely its dress rehearsal, leaders in this field must learn to spot the patterns behind the momentum, to watch the cultural currents, not just the compliance updates. Monitoring trends, after all, isn't just a skill. It's a form of leadership.

This Leadership Theory, Too, Shall Pass

Leadership, like every other domain shaped by human knowledge, is subject to revision. What seems immutable today (emotional intelligence, servant leadership, agile organizations) may seem quaint or limited in a few decades. This chapter considers why that's inevitable, and what the next transformation might look like. Something will displace the current leadership orthodoxy.

In the next few decades, if not years, a new theory is bound to upend our current notions of what makes a great leader and how one is developed.

What makes me so sure? Continuing research and reevaluation of every aspect of the universe, including the physical and social sciences.

Reading Bill Bryson's *The Body: A Guide for Occupants* drives home how little we know about the bundle of bones, muscles, tendons, organs, systems, hormones, processes, and electrical impulses that make us who we are. Here are a few theories that carried the day in the past:

- Bloodletting cures illness
- Ulcers are caused by stress (as opposed to bacteria)
- The body has 10 times more bacteria cells than human cells (we now say it's 1:1)

Some of today's theories that are already wobbling:

- Intelligence resides mostly in the brain's processing power
- Saturated fat is per se bad for the heart
- Junk DNA has no function

Others that seem likely to fall:

- The appendix has no function
- Consciousness is confined to a single individual
- Aging can be slowed but not regulated

And I'm not even halfway through the book.

Let's move to other fields. Isaac Newton discovered and described the laws that govern everything we know, the laws of motion and universal gravitation, until Einstein and others showed that those rules didn't apply at the microscopic level. Now we live in a combo world of quantum and classical mechanics.

Every few years an archaeologist finds a fossil that rewrites what we thought about the development of humans and animals, pushing timelines forward or backward thousands or millions of years. Since 2000 alone, new experiments, discoveries, and theories have exploded what we knew about our hunter-gatherer past, the expansion of the universe, human consciousness, genetics and evolution, infant learning, life in the depths of the ocean, interbreeding among humans and Neanderthals, plant biology, cancer metabolism, and dark matter. The James Webb Space Telescope has observed galaxies forming just 300 million years after the Big Bang, far earlier and more massive than previously thought possible, prompting scientists to reconsider the timeline and mechanisms of cosmic evolution.

Leadership theory, including security leadership, doesn't stand a chance of resisting a theoretical overhaul. Security professionals, accustomed to rapidly evolving threats and technologies, may be among the first to feel the pull of new leadership paradigms and the tensions they create.

Such a prediction isn't, excuse me, a quantum leap. An earlier chapter traced the evolution of leadership theory from the 1840s to today, spotlighting many different approaches that emerged and evolved over the years. Each approach lives on today in some way.

So what's tomorrow's new approach to leadership?

Since we are talking quantum, a philosophy called quantum leadership exists, and it can be traced all the way back to the late 1990s. According to the 2019 book *Quantum Leadership: New Consciousness in Business*, by Frederick Chavalit Tsao, that style involves changing someone's consciousness to unlock "his or her leadership potential to create wealth and serve humankind."

Rob Balmer's 2020 *Quantum Leadership: Igniting the Limitless Power of People in Disruptive Times* (yes, there are multiple books on the subject) defines its subject matter as "supercharg[ing] many established approaches to organizational leadership and enabl[ing] leaders to excite a quantum leap in performance to match the seismic shifts confronting their organizations."

Or will tomorrow's dominant leadership style be AI-driven leadership, which was described back in 2018 in the *MIT Sloan Management Review*? The authors of that piece identified seven attributes of the AI-driven leader, including understanding the technologies, establishing clear business objectives, and looking beyond pilots and proofs of concept. While AI-driven leadership seems more operational than philosophical, in a world of dominant AI, perhaps this style rises to the top.

Metaverse leadership could be another contender. Lessons in leading in the metaverse may evolve into a general approach to leadership. That style may, for instance, involve juggling leadership approaches between the real and virtual worlds.

Most likely, these contenders for the mantle of Next Great Leadership Paradigm are mere buzzword-specific pretenders: epiphenomenal offshoots of or blends of other leadership theories. The heir to the throne's fate rests on the vicissitudes of business, academia, human resources, and cultural shifts. Personally, I'm eager for Shared-Consciousness Leadership, but I'm afraid I won't be around to experience it. Whether we lead through quantum principles, artificial intelligence, or shared consciousness, the best leaders will adapt not by clinging to doctrine, but by staying receptive to the next shift in human understanding.

Converged Leadership: Speaking Risk in Every Language

Security threats have never respected silos. And yet for decades, security leadership did: physical on one side, cyber on another, with business continuity, fraud, safety, and crisis management slotting into one or the other or traveling in their own orbits. That world is fading fast.

Ron Worman, who created "The Great Conversation" to connect professionals across the risk spectrum, has explained the pre-9/11 security-scape, much of which remains disturbingly intact to this day.

"'Silos of excellence' were operating in the risk, resilience, and security ecosystem," he recalls. It was a market sector composed of transfers from law enforcement, the military, and intelligence agencies who knew little about their employers' business. Other major components of the sector, he says, included security executives' (primarily operational) staff, trusted consultants to conduct risk audits, integrators favoring specific vendors or competing on cost, and technology vendors trying to get their products in the hands of integrators and consultants.

"And every one of them was desperately asking this question: Why don't I have a seat at the table?"

Today's risk landscape is converged by default. Threat actors blend social engineering with access control exploits. Cyberattacks trigger physical consequences. Workplace violence threats play out over social media. Facilities and IT must coordinate as systems and buildings grow smarter and more connected.

Yet the siloed pre-9/11 security world described by Worman tenaciously persists.

In a world where ransomware can shut down pipelines and rogue insiders can weaponize social media, leadership that treats risks as separate domains is not just outdated, it's dangerous. The age of siloed security is over. The future belongs to leaders who think and speak in convergence.

As roles converge, so must leadership. The future belongs to security professionals who are multilingual in risk: fluent across domains, trusted across departments, and comfortable leading beyond legacy swim lanes.

Insights from a 2024 report by SIA underscore this shift. An earlier signal came in 2019, when ASIS International published a report I co-authored with David Beck and Beth McFarland on the convergence of physical security, cybersecurity, and business continuity. That paper emphasized that leadership would be the linchpin of successful integration across domains. SIA's 2024 *Security Convergence* report highlights how convergence is maturing beyond initial expectations, emphasizing the need for leadership that can navigate the complexities of integrated security functions.

The road to convergence is anything but smooth. Leaders navigating it must be part translator, part diplomat, and part strategist.

Convergence promises a more efficient, aligned, and resilient enterprise: fewer blind spots, better resource allocation, streamlined decision-making. It's not a plug-and-play proposition.

Converged organizations face new tensions: skill gaps, turf battles, incompatible systems, and an identity crisis among professionals who fear losing their expertise or autonomy. The solution isn't a single reorg chart but a leadership mindset shift.

Conferences such as CTG Intelligence's Managed Security Services Forum, held globally and online, have played a vital role in shaping the dialogue around convergence, risk, and modernization. As an organizer and frequent moderator, Phelim Rowe has helped surface evolving leadership challenges and opportunities in this space.

Other platforms, initiatives, and tools are also shaping converged leadership. The SANS Cyber Security Summit and Gartner's Security & Risk Management Summit, for example, unite physical, cyber, and OT professionals to address integrated risks. Don Taussig, a senior security executive who has held top roles in organizations including the U.S. Bureau of Reclamation and Land O'Lakes, notes that tools like the Nozomi Networks-Skybox Security alliance or Dataminr Pulse for Cyber Risk also enable cross-disciplinary collaboration with real-time insights. These tools aren't silver bullets, but they signal a growing recognition: that no one function owns risk anymore, and no one leader can afford to operate in a vacuum.

Most organizations still struggle to find leaders who can span domains credibly. That's not surprising: the skill sets, cultures, and terminologies of physical and cyber security are distinct. Physical security has historically spoken the language of "gates, guards, and guns" Cyber has communicated via code, compliance, and controls. Bridging that divide takes more than technical knowledge; it takes cultural fluency. Leading in this space requires translation, empathy, and an ability to build coalitions from formerly disconnected units.

Though the trend towards convergence may seem inevitable, many professionals throughout the world of security—physical, cyber, intelligence, resilience, etc.—still dismiss it as a bad idea, at least in their operating environments.

Yet, as James Willison, an indefatigable advocate for convergence, has long emphasized, "Converged security demands converged leadership." It's not enough to understand the technologies; leaders must grasp the workflows, incentives, and languages that shape each domain.

Traits of a Converged Risk Leader

The SIA report also points out that successful convergence requires leaders who are not only technically proficient but also adept at fostering collaboration across traditionally siloed departments. This aligns with such traits including systems thinking and adaptive communication.

- Systems Thinking: Seeing risk as an interconnected ecosystem, not a checklist of domains.
- Relational Intelligence: Building bridges between stakeholders with conflicting priorities.
- Adaptive Communication: Knowing when to speak IT, when to speak facilities, and when to speak executive.
- Strategic Credibility: Translating risk into language the board and C-suite understand.
- Resilient Decision-Making: Acting decisively in uncertainty, adapting strategies as cyber, physical, and operational risks evolve rapidly.

Converged leaders don't need to be technical experts in every area, but they must know enough to connect dots, ask the right questions, and broker alignment.

Leading convergence is about shifting mindsets, reshaping incentives, and realigning teams around a shared understanding of risk. It's cultural. Leaders must:

- Align incentives across departments
- Build interdisciplinary teams
- Clarify roles while encouraging cross-training
- Develop shared metrics that reflect collective risk posture

Convergence doesn't erase legacy expertise. It reframes it, as essential components of a broader, integrated strategy. The converged leader respects those histories while shaping a more unified future.

In addition, "future security leaders must also cultivate a culture of continuous learning, encouraging teams to stay ahead of emerging threats by embracing cross-disciplinary knowledge sharing," emphasizes Taussig.

Security leadership is no longer about running a department, it's about uniting a fragmented risk landscape into a cohesive strategy. The most effective leaders of the next decade will be translators, connectors, and visionaries: communicating across functions, guiding diverse teams, and leading at the intersections where risk is most complex.

Managing Complexity: Leading in a Polycrisis World

The term "polycrisis" may sound like an entry on a buzzword bingo board, but it reflects a real and intensifying condition of modern leadership. Coined by the historian Adam Tooze and adopted by the World Economic Forum, polycrisis describes the reality of multiple, overlapping, and mutually reinforcing crises. Climate disruption, geopolitical volatility, pandemics, cyberattacks, social unrest, and misinformation don't arrive one at a time anymore; they collide, compound, and cascade.

For security and risk leaders, this isn't just complexity. It's a whole new operating environment.

Traditional crisis leadership assumes a beginning, middle, and end. It prizes clarity, control, and coordination. But in a polycrisis world, problems don't resolve neatly. A data breach may provoke reputational harm, financial instability, regulatory scrutiny, and internal distrust, all while a parallel crisis (say, a supply chain breakdown or workplace violence threat) unfolds.

As the architect of Presilience, Dr. Gavriel Schneider, puts it like this: "The challenge really is that most of our modern systems were designed or conceived based on Industrial Age thinking, so we have a weird intersection of approaches in the modern operating environment. Simple systems mix with complex and chaotic ones, which means that when things go wrong, it's not just one basic fix but a polycrisis across intersecting and interdependent systems." For academically inclined readers, Schneider recommends reading about complex adaptive systems theory and chaos theory.

The challenge isn't just scale. It's simultaneity and interdependence.

That requires a different kind of risk leadership: one that's adaptive, systemic, and humble. Leaders must learn to act without full visibility, communicate amidst uncertainty, and resist the false comfort of oversimplification.

The Cynefin (pronounced "kin-evan") framework, developed by Dave Snowden, is particularly helpful here. It divides problems into domains: *obvious*, *complicated*, *complex*, *chaotic*, and *disorder*. Most polycrisis scenarios land squarely in the complex or chaotic space, where cause and effect are only clear in retrospect, and experimentation, not command-and-control, is the path forward.

Cynefin is invaluable for teaching adaptive thinking in dynamic environments. It's a powerful tool for helping leaders interpret the nature of the system they're in and match their actions to the type of challenge they face. It's indispensable for understanding complex adaptive systems.

But while Cynefin improves response selection, Presilience broadens the landscape entirely.

Presilience is not simply a proactive form of resilience It's a comprehensive mindset, methodology, and culture-building approach. It enables individuals and organizations to turn risk into opportunity, to thrive in both business-as-usual and disruptive contexts, and to achieve sustained high performance over time.

Where resilience asks how to bounce back, Presilience asks how to *bounce forward.*

Presilience entails:

- Mindset: Recognizing disruption as a source of advantage, not just danger
- Tools & Frameworks—Drawing from foresight, agility, psychology, and operational readiness
- Culture: Creating systems and rituals that normalize adaptation and strategic learning
- Scope: Addressing the self, team, organization, and society as interconnected domains

I hold a Graduate Certificate in Organisational Resilience, Risk, and High Reliability from Schneider's Institute of Presilience, where systems thinking and fields of study such as chaos theory are foundational and, I'll admit, still a work in progress to fully internalize. But what Presilience taught me is that enduring leadership isn't just about planning for disruption; it's about cultivating the conditions in which organizations can *transform through* disruption.

In that sense, Presilience is the architecture and framework to develop the right mindset and culture to thrive. Systems thinking and approaches such as Cynefin are among the essential tools inside it.

Used together, they provide a dual lens:

- Cynefin: Understand the environment and select the right response.
- Presilience: Build the mindset and leadership system that thrive in business as usual as well as amid and beyond disruption.

Leadership Traits for the Polycrisis Era

- Pattern Recognition: Seeing weak signals and connecting dots across domains
- Emotional Agility: Staying grounded while others panic or disengage
- Collaborative Reflexes: Leading through influence, not just authority
- Decision Tolerance: Acting amid ambiguity without false certainty
- Narrative Discipline: Framing evolving challenges without spinning or sugarcoating

---

The polycrisis leader is less of a commander and more of a sensemaker, interpreting complexity, creating clarity, and guiding action through shared understanding.

We used to talk about crisis response as a muscle. In the polycrisis age, it's a whole central nervous system. The leaders who thrive won't be those who predict every problem but those who learn how to lead in the spaces where problems overlap, mutate, and multiply.

Not everyone is comfortable with retaining the "crisis" mindset, however, be it crisis, multicrisis, polycrisis, or maybe the eventual "infinicrisis." Switzerland-based security risk management expert Luca Tenzi considers the crisis perspective to be outdated. For example, I talked to Tenzi in 2025 as Israel had just attacked Iran's nuclear and military infrastructure and Iran had responded with volleys of rockets at Israeli population centers.

"What's happening in Iran and Israel is not a crisis," Tenzi says, "but another step" in an evolving situation between two countries (and a whole region) in conflict. "What's changed is that it's wave after wave" of conflict, not discrete crises, Tenzi explains. Navigating complexity means managing climate effects and sustainability efforts, LGBTQ issues, social fragmentation, cultural differences, technological disruption, and so on.

"In the past, everything was decided at the crisis management level," Tenzi continues, noting that the military's command and control structure has migrated to mission control. "You need to allow more space to maneuver and make decisions, to adapt to complexity. Now the platoon commander has the freedom to make decisions" as long as it contributes to the mission's goals.

Tenzi uses skiing as a metaphor for adaptation in the business world. Experts on the slopes often have many different types of skis, depending on the type of skiing, snow conditions, weather, and other factors. But like business executives, they often have to do with the tools they have on hand. When a skier hits an icy patch, they can't switch skis or poles. Instead, they adjust their speed, stance, weight distribution, direction, and turns. Similarly, management at a distribution facility facing a truck shortage can adjust staffing, communication, transportation routes, and logistics operations.

Wellness and the Will to Lead

Growing up with three brothers (and a sister who was smart enough to avoid us), we spent our time playing tackle football, hacking at each other with street hockey sticks, jumping 15 stairs onto a wooden floor, skiing down said stairs with oblong blocks on our feet, staging our own boxing matches, and having iceball or acorn fights against kids down the street. And that was when we weren't fighting—hurling sharp glass ashtrays at each other's heads, siccing the family dog on each other, preying on each other's greatest emotional weaknesses.

But you complained at your own peril, lest you be called a quitter, snitch, or crybaby. I once gashed my hand so badly that I had to put it in a vise to stop the bleeding. Going to the hospital was a concession to weakness. Three of us ganged up on our baby brother, stuck him in a baby carriage, and set him off down a hill. He never said a word to our parents.

That upbringing taught me, and many others in this profession, that toughness meant silence. Vulnerability was a liability. Those lessons followed us into adulthood and into leadership.

After law school, I worked for the New Jersey Supreme Court reviewing death penalty cases. Being responsible for advising the seven justices on life and death matters and critical precedents, I gave the cases the attention they deserved, often working 10 hours a day, seven days a week. Because the high court had identified so many instances of error in the lower courts in previous cases, the attorneys for every defendant larded every possible argument into their briefs, from the constitutionality of the selection of the jury pool to the weighing of aggravating and mitigating factors in the sentencing phase.

But the torrent of procedural arguments never numbed me to why the case got to the court in the first place. The pictures always reminded me. Invariably, the prosecution would enter crime-scene photographs into evidence and the defense would claim that their prejudicial effect outweighed their probative value. I had to dutifully review them. To me, their disturbing effect outweighed my ability to rationally process them.

Exhibit A-Z: Dozens of pictures of a wife and child hammered into mush by a mallet. Pictures of a wife with the icy stare of a stabbing victim. Pictures of women (the deceased were almost always women or girls, killed by jealous, savage, or cheating men) mutilated in horrific ways, including one woman who had been cut into pieces, her parts stashed in suitcases.

One night, my co-clerk and I went to get hamburgers at a chain called Fuddruckers. As we entered the vestibule, we saw that the restaurant had hung photographs of dead cattle hanging on hooks, presumably to suggest that their meat was fresh. It looked so similar to the chopped-up murder victim that I couldn't go inside. My coworker was surprised, but to his credit he didn't challenge me. That's when I realized that mental health had to be part of the job.

For generations, wellness was a taboo subject in the security and law enforcement worlds, especially among men. Leadership meant stoicism. Stress was just part of the job. Burnout, trauma, exhaustion? Keep it quiet, keep going. That mindset is finally changing.

Today, wellness isn't just permissible, it's becoming foundational. The shift is partly generational: younger professionals expect work-life balance, mental health resources, and emotionally intelligent leaders. But the shift is also philosophical. Wellness is no longer about indulgence or weakness; it's about longevity, clarity, and performance. Vulnerability is increasingly viewed not as a liability, but as credibility.

To comment, I sought experts who best occupy the intersection of crisis management, security, leadership, wellness, and empathy.

Like me, Executive Coach Kat Fariss grew up with a suck-it-up mindset. "Achievement was valued over authenticity," she recalls. "The message was 'do, don't feel.' I internalized early on that worth was earned through output, not presence. Emotions were inconvenient. Vulnerability was weakness." And trauma was suppressed.

She's been gratified to witness a growing cultural shift in recent years. "More and more strong, courageous leaders are saying out loud, 'I'm not okay,' and reaching out for help, not as a last resort, but as a first act of strength."

Jon Harris, a security professional/performance coach/podcaster, has had a traumatic background as well. When he was in the military, his father committed suicide. Harris buried his feelings and plowed ahead. That repression likely contributed to his ensuing depression, alcoholism, and suicidal thoughts.

Confronting his emotions enabled Harris to blossom as a leader. "When I finally unpacked the damage of not dealing with my issues, it not only got me better but it also unlocked a level of personal and professional performance unlike anything I could have ever imagined," Harris says. That's astounding insight and testimony.

Melissa Agnes agrees that the "transformation from stoicism to emotional intelligence isn't just cultural. It's strategic. "In my work with crisis leaders," she says, "I've observed a fundamental truth: the moments that require the greatest leadership strength are precisely the moments when vulnerability becomes your greatest asset."

How so?

She explains: "Traditional crisis leadership teaches us to suppress emotion and project unwavering certainty. But here's what actually happens when leaders try to 'logic' people out of their emotional reactions during challenging moments: resistance increases, trust erodes, and teams become more anxious, not less."

I asked her how leaders can draw upon emotion without being performative, maudlin, or insincere.

"The leaders who create real stability during uncertainty understand that leaning into emotion—acknowledging fear, validating concerns, speaking to what people are actually experiencing—requires enormous courage," she says. "It takes far more strength to remain present with discomfort than to push it away with false reassurance or rigid control."

Denying emotions can have a psychological, spiritual, and physical toll.

"When we suppress our own emotions, we disconnect from our bodies and lose access to the deeper resonance that people desperately need during crisis moments," Agnes continues. "A leader who's burnt out, emotionally depleted, or operating from chronic suppression simply cannot lead effectively. They can manage tasks, deliver information, even make decisions, but they cannot create the kind of trust and connection that transforms challenging situations into opportunities for deeper alignment."

Harris's experience bears out Agnes's words. "When we let go of baggage and talk about it, it opens up other people to their admit their issues." Since he revealed his struggles in a podcast and other platforms, people have been opening up to him, creating bonds of trust.

Who better to deal with crises than someone who has successfully confronted and managed their own? "In a field where we are always racing to the next crisis, people who have come to terms with their own issues are often at their finest when things are the most challenging," Harris says.

The first step is admitting vulnerability. I admit that I am lousy at it.

In fact, despite the two words being synonyms in general, vulnerability isn't weakness. "True vulnerability entails showing up fully present when others cannot," says Agnes. That presence, that capacity to remain grounded while honoring the emotional reality of the moment, is what separates leaders who merely survive crises from those who guide meaningful transformation through them."

Agnes weighs in again: "What many leaders don't realize is that their emotional state is contagious. Neuroscience shows us that our nervous systems co-regulate with those around us. A leader operating from chronic stress or emotional depletion doesn't just make poorer decisions; they unconsciously invite their entire team and stakeholders into that same dysregulated state."

I've seen this play out repeatedly. Teams mirror their leader's energy, whether that's calm presence or anxious reactivity. The leaders who understand this don't treat wellness as self-care but as stakeholder care. When you prioritize your own emotional regulation and coherence, you're creating the conditions for your team to think more clearly, communicate more openly, and respond rather than react during critical moments.

This isn't about meditation retreats or wellness perks. It's about recognizing that your presence, your ability to remain grounded when others are destabilized, is your most valuable leadership tool when you need to lead through change, crisis, and resistance.

For many long-serving professionals, though, embracing that mindset is a real challenge. After decades of reward systems that favored self-sacrifice and endurance, it's hard to unlearn the reflex to suppress and grind.

Security and risk professionals often absorb moral injury, vicarious trauma, and performance fatigue. Yet because the wounds are invisible, they're often minimized. The culture of hyper-resilience, if left unchecked, breeds isolation, emotional shutdown, and eventual burnout.

Tanya Spencer's story, shared earlier in this book in Chapter 5, captures this vividly. A seasoned professional with deep experience in global security and crisis response, Tanya faced profound personal and emotional challenges yet chose to speak openly about them. Her courage to describe the toll and to model recovery has helped destigmatize wellness for others in the field. Her example is a beacon for a profession still catching up to its emotional realities.

Fariss can empathize. Her mother passed away suddenly in 2004, forcing her to confront layers of unprocessed trauma: her mother's and her own. Her mother had lived with undiagnosed PTSD after losing a child at six weeks old. "And in our home, shaped by military culture, emotional expression was off-limits," Fariss says. "I was raised to suppress pain, to function over feel. Stress, grief, and conflict were pushed down and numbed with food, alcohol, and performance. That legacy became mine until it nearly cost me everything."

She shared a time when she avoided freeway overpasses because she didn't trust herself to drive over them: "I was depleted, disconnected, and dangerously close to collapse. But one day, in a moment of quiet desperation, I cried. Then I called my stepmother. That phone call was the first crack in the armor I had worn for decades."

Healing didn't come quickly or easily. It took five months of therapy, spiritual direction, coaching, and walking away from toxic leaders who treated her like a machine rather than a person. "By 2017, I left it all behind," she says. "I sat in the mess of vulnerability and began to reframe my story. I was no longer a human 'doing.' I was reclaiming my place as a human 'being.'"

In that space, she found the light again. "It wasn't outside of me. It was me. My healing gave me permission to stop carrying generational trauma and begin inviting others to do the same."

Wellness isn't a soft benefit It's a strategic lever. Leaders who protect their physical and emotional health:

- Make better decisions under stress
- Communicate with more clarity and empathy
- Set sustainable norms for their teams
- Model boundaries that others are empowered to adopt

Your presence is your most valuable asset as a leader. Treating wellness as a necessity rather than a reward is a way of preserving that asset.

"Wellness isn't a break from leadership," says Fariss. It *is* leadership. When we care for our whole selves, we lead with clarity, empathy, and integrity. We stop running on fumes and start showing others what it means to lead fully human."

According to the American Psychological Association's 2023 Workplace Survey, more than 70% of Millennials and Gen Z employees rank mental health support as a "non-negotiable" when evaluating employers. Harvard Business Review reports that organizations investing in employee well-being see a 5:1 return in productivity, engagement, and retention.

As discussed in Chapter 5's description of The Kindness Games, a quiet revolution may already be underway. Leaders who once viewed kindness as a sign of weakness now see it as central to trust, morale, and influence. That same evolution is happening with wellness.

Sasha Larkin, the former Assistant Sheriff for the Las Vegas Metropolitan Police Department, exemplifies this new posture. After leading parts of the response to the 2017 mass shooting at the Route 91 Harvest Festival, where a gunman opened fire from a tower at the Mandalay Bay Hotel, she became a vocal advocate for wellness in policing. She's spoken about the toll the experience took on her and her team, and the steps she's taken since: trauma counseling, alternative therapies, nutrition, and mentoring.

"It is incumbent on leadership to normalize wellness and therapy to help officers shed layers of trauma and process it," she's said. "It has to start at the top."

Her words apply far beyond law enforcement and security. The cultural shift starts with leaders who are willing to acknowledge reality, and to treat wellness not as a retreat from leadership, but as a condition of it.

Leadership requires endurance, but not martyrdom. The work is hard enough. Carrying it alone, silently, makes it unsustainable. The leaders who last are those who learn to recover, reframe, and rest.

From the Lips of Gips: "I heard quantum leadership comes with a super-position."

Chapter Takeaways

- Trendspotting Is Leadership: The ability to detect cultural, technological, and operational shifts before they crystallize is a critical form of modern leadership.
- Leadership Theory Will Evolve—Again: Just as past paradigms faded, new ones will rise, potentially driven by quantum models, AI integration, or cross-dimensional (e.g., metaverse) considerations.
- Risk Is Converging and So Must Leadership: The future belongs to leaders who can bridge silos, integrate perspectives, and translate across domains of risk.

- Polycrisis Leadership Benefits from Fluency With Frameworks: For example, Cynefin provides a lens for understanding complexity, while Presilience builds the mindset, methods, and culture to thrive through it.
- Wellness Is Strategic: Emotional regulation, mental health, and recovery are not luxuries but strategic assets that sustain effective leadership.

Bibliography

This is a not a typical reference section for a leadership book. Or even a risk book. There are thousands of leadership and risk books, the vast majority of which I haven't read. Or even heard of. That doesn't mean they aren't worthwhile. Everyone knows the major works in the field. They are cited in every leadership or risk book. Not here. There are exceptions, such as Doris Kearns Goodwin, whose storytelling is spellbinding.

The references and bibliography here represent works that I have cited in the text or that have influenced my thinking on or practice of leadership, even obliquely. Some of the best writing on leadership comes from books that putatively don't involve leadership at all, such as *How to Live: The Life of Montaigne.*

These works were directly cited or clearly influenced the book's core content:

Allen, Brian, and Loyear, Rachelle. *Enterprise Security Risk Management: Concepts and Applications.* Rothstein Associates, 2018.

American Psychological Association. *Work in America: Survey of Workplace Mental Health.* 2023.

Andrews, Chuck. *Yes, S.I.R.* Friends of Chuck Publishing, 2022.

Asker, Jennifer, and Badonas, Naomi. *Humor, Seriously: Why Humor Is a Secret Weapon in Business and Life (And How Anyone Can Harness It. Even You.).* Crown Currency, 2021.

Balmer, Rob. *Quantum Leadership: Igniting the Limitless Power of People in Disruptive Times*. Myidentifiers.com.au, 2020.

Bazerman, Max H. *The Power of Noticing: What the Best Leaders See*. Simon & Schuster, 2014.

Beard, Alison. "Leading With Humor," *Harvard Business Review*, Volume 92, pp. 130–131, May 2014.

Beck, David, Gips, Michael, and McFarland, Beth. *Convergence of Physical and Cybersecurity: 2019 Report*. ASIS International, 2019.

Bernstein, Peter L. *Against the Gods: The Remarkable Story of Risk*. Wiley, 1996.

Biswas, Debanjana Deb, "Balancing Employee Well-being and Organizational Resilience: Redefining HR Practices for a Dynamic Business Environment," *International Journal of Humanities Social Science and Management*, Volume 4, Issue 6, pp 735–744, 2024.

Brooks, Beth. *The New CEO's Guide: Advice for the First-Time, Aspiring, or Current Association Executive*. ASAE Management Press, 2015.

Burns, James MacGregor. *Leadership*. HarperCollins, 1978.

Brubaker, John. *The Lasso Way: Leadership Lessons from the World's Favorite Football Coach*. Coach Bru, 2021.

Bryson, Bill. *The Body: An Occupant's Guide*. Doubleday, 2019.

Carnegie, Dale. *How to Win Friends and Influence People*. Simon & Schuster, 1936.

Caro, Robert A. *The Power Broker: Robert Moses and the Fall of New York*. Vintage, 1975.

Caro, Robert A. *The Years of Lyndon Johnson Series*. Vintage, 1982.

Cathcart, Thomas, and Klein, Daniel. *Plato and a Platypus Walk Into a Bar: Understanding Philosophy Through Jokes*. Penguin Books, 2007.

Chamorro-Premuzic, Tomas. "How to Strengthen Your Curiosity Muscle," *Harvard Business Review*, November 3, 2023. https://hbr.org/2023/11/how-to-strengthen-your-curiosity-muscle

Collins, Jim. *Good to Great: Why Some Companies Make the Leap… and Others Don't*. HarperBusiness, 2001.

Doyle, Shawn. "Critical Thinking Is the Skill Many Leaders Lack," *Entrepreneur*, August 7, 2019. https://www.entrepreneur.com/leadership/critical-thinking-is-the-skill-many-leaders-lack/337563

Duke, Annie. *Thinking in Bets: Making Smarter Decisions When You Don't Have All the Facts*. Portfolio, 2018.

Gips, Michael. "The Spy in My Basement." *Washingtonian*, Volume 57, Number 9, pp. 46–52, 171–172, June 2022.

Gladwell, Malcolm. *David and Goliath: Underdogs, Misfits, and the Art of Battling Giants*. Little, Brown and Company, 2013.

Gladwell, Malcolm. *Outliers: The Story of Success*. Little, Brown and Company, 2008.

Gladwell, Malcolm. *The Tipping Point: How Little Things Can Make a Big Difference*. Little, Brown and Company, 2000.

Goleman, Daniel. *Emotional Intelligence: Why It Can Matter More Than IQ*. Bantam Books, 1995.

Goodwin, Doris Kearns. *Leadership in Turbulent Times*. Simon & Schuster, 2018.

Goodwin, Doris Kearns. *No Ordinary Time: Franklin and Eleanor Roosevelt: The Home Front in World War II*. Simon & Schuster, 1994.

Goodwin, Doris Kearns. *Team of Rivals: The Political Genius of Abraham Lincoln*. Simon & Schuster, 2005.

House, Robert, and Howell, Jane. "Personality and Charismatic Leadership," *The Leadership Quarterly*, Volume 3, Issue 2, pp. 81–108, 1992.

Kahneman, Daniel. *Thinking, Fast and Slow*. Farrar, Straus and Giroux, 2011.

MIT Sloan Management Review. "The Seven Attributes of the AI-Driven Leader." 2018.

Moxness, Kirsten, and Paul. *Spin the Bottle Service: Hospitality in the Age of AI*. How2Conquer, 2021.

Oatman, Robert L. *The Art of Executive Protection*. Noble House, 2006.

Oughton, Lee, and Wenzel, Tim. *The Kindness Games: How Kindness Saved Our Lives*. Independent, 2023.

Schneider, Gavriel. *Can I See Your Hands: A Guide to Situational Awareness, Personal Risk Management, Resilience and Security*. Universal Publishers, 2017.

Schneider, Gavriel. *Presilience: How to Navigate Risk, Embrace Opportunity, and Build Resilience*. Amplify Publishing Group, 2025.

Security Industry Association (SIA). *Security Convergence 2024*. February 2024.

Stitt, Christopher. *Scaling Pyramids: Lessons from a Mid-Level Bureaucrat*. Routledge Press, 2025.

Tsao, Frederick Chavalit. *Quantum Leadership: New Consciousness in Business*. World Scientific, 2019.

Useem, Michael. *The Leader's Checklist: 15 Mission-Critical Principles*. Wharton Digital Press, 2011.

Useem, Michael. *The Leadership Moment: Nine True Stories of Triumph and Disaster and Their Lessons for Us All*. Crown Business, 1998.

Wells, Rachel. "3 Reasons Curiosity Is An In-Demand Leadership Skill," *Forbes*, December 17, 2023. https://www.forbes.com/sites/rachelwells/2023/12/17/3-reasons-curiosity-is-an-in-demand-leadership-skill-how-to-build-it/

Recommended Reading

These works shaped my mindset, style, or writing approach:

Aurelius, Marcus. *The Meditations of Marcus Aurelius*. Translated by Gregory Hays, Modern Library, 2003.
Bakewell, Sarah. *How to Live: A Life of Montaigne in One Question and Twenty Attempts at an Answer*. Other Press, 2010.
Bryson, Bill. *A Walk in the Woods: Rediscovering America on the Appalachian Trail*. Broadway Books, 1998.
Burg, Bob, and Mann, John David. *The Go-Giver: A Little Story About a Powerful Business Idea*. Portfolio, 2007.
Falcones, Ildefonso. *Cathedral of the Sea*. Penguin Books, 2008.
Feynman, Richard P. *Surely You're Joking, Mr. Feynman!: Adventures of a Curious Character*. W. W. Norton & Company, 1985.
Golding, William. *Lord of the Flies*. Faber and Faber, 1954.
Gostick, Adrian, and Elton, Chester. *What Motivates Me: Put Your Passions to Work*. The Culture Works Press, 2014.
Hesse, Hermann. *Siddhartha*. New Directions Publishing, 1951.
Isaacson, Walter. *The Innovators: How a Group of Hackers, Geniuses, and Geeks Created the Digital Revolution*. Simon & Schuster, 2014.
Kahn, Erik. *Canned Goods*. 2024 (play script provided by author).
Kriegel, Mark. *Namath: A Biography*. Viking, 2004.
McCullough, David. *The Path Between the Seas: The Creation of the Panama Canal 1870-1914*. Simon & Schuster, 1977.
McPhee, John. *A Sense of Where You Are*. Farrar, Straus and Giroux, 1965.
McPhee, John. *Draft No. 4: On the Writing Process. Farrar*, Straus and Giroux, 2017.
McPhee, John. *Heirs of General Practice*. Farrar, Straus and Giroux, 1986.

Menand, Louis. *The Metaphysical Club: A Story of Ideas in America*. Farrar, Straus and Giroux, 2001.
Messier, Mark. *No One Wins Alone*. Gallery Books, 2021.
Modly, Thomas B. *Vectors: Heroes, Villains, and Heartbreak on the Bridge of the U.S. Navy*. Knox Press, 2023.
Morris, Edmund. *Theodore Rex*. Random House, 2001.
Nozari, Mohammad. *Team Intelligence: A New Method Using Swarm Intelligence for Building Successful Teams*. CRC Press, 2025.
Orwell, George. *Animal Farm*. Harcourt, Brace, 1945.
Orwell, George. *Shooting an Elephant*. Penguin Classics, 2021.
Pink, Daniel H. *A Whole New Mind: Why Right-Brainers Will Rule the Future*. Riverhead Books, 2006.
Roth, Philip. *The Ghost Writer*. Farrar, Straus and Giroux, 1979.
Sample, Steven B. *The Contrarian's Guide to Leadership*. Jossey-Bass, 2001.
Schrager, Allison. *An Economist Walks into a Brothel: And Other Unexpected Places to Understand Risk*. Portfolio, 2019.
Sacks, Oliver. *The Man Who Mistook His Wife for a Hat*. Touchstone, 1998.
Stone, Irving. *The Agony and the Ecstasy*. Doubleday, 1961.
Taleb, Nassim Nicholas. *The Black Swan: The Impact of the Highly Improbable*. Random House, 2007.
Venable, Stephen Blair. *The Commencement Odyssey: Why We All Have a Stake in Transforming the American Workplace*, 2nd ed. Surgo Books, 2015.
Wakefield, Alison. *Crime and Security: Converging Perspectives on a Complex World*. SAGE Publications, 2021.
Warren, Robert Penn. *All the King's Men*. Harcourt, Brace, 1946.
Wohleben, Peter. *The Hidden Life of Trees: What They Feel, How They Communicate*. Greystone Books, 2016.
Womack Jr., John. *Zapata and the Mexican Revolution*. Vintage Books, 1969.

Index

D

E